AMERICA'S STAGE:

TIMES SQUARE

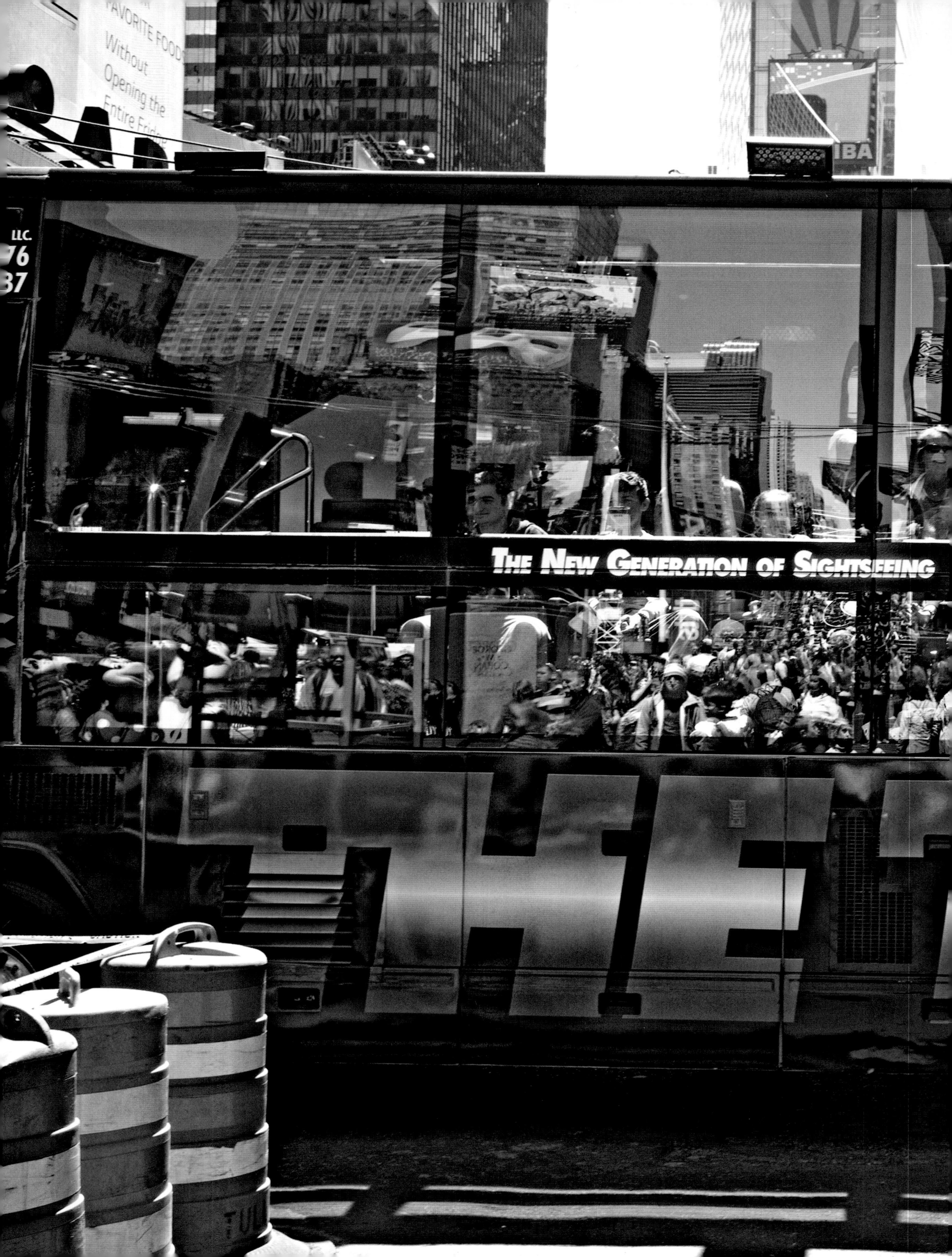

FAVORITE FOOD
Without
Opening the
Entire Fridge
LLC.
76
37
THE NEW GENERATION OF SIGHTSEEING

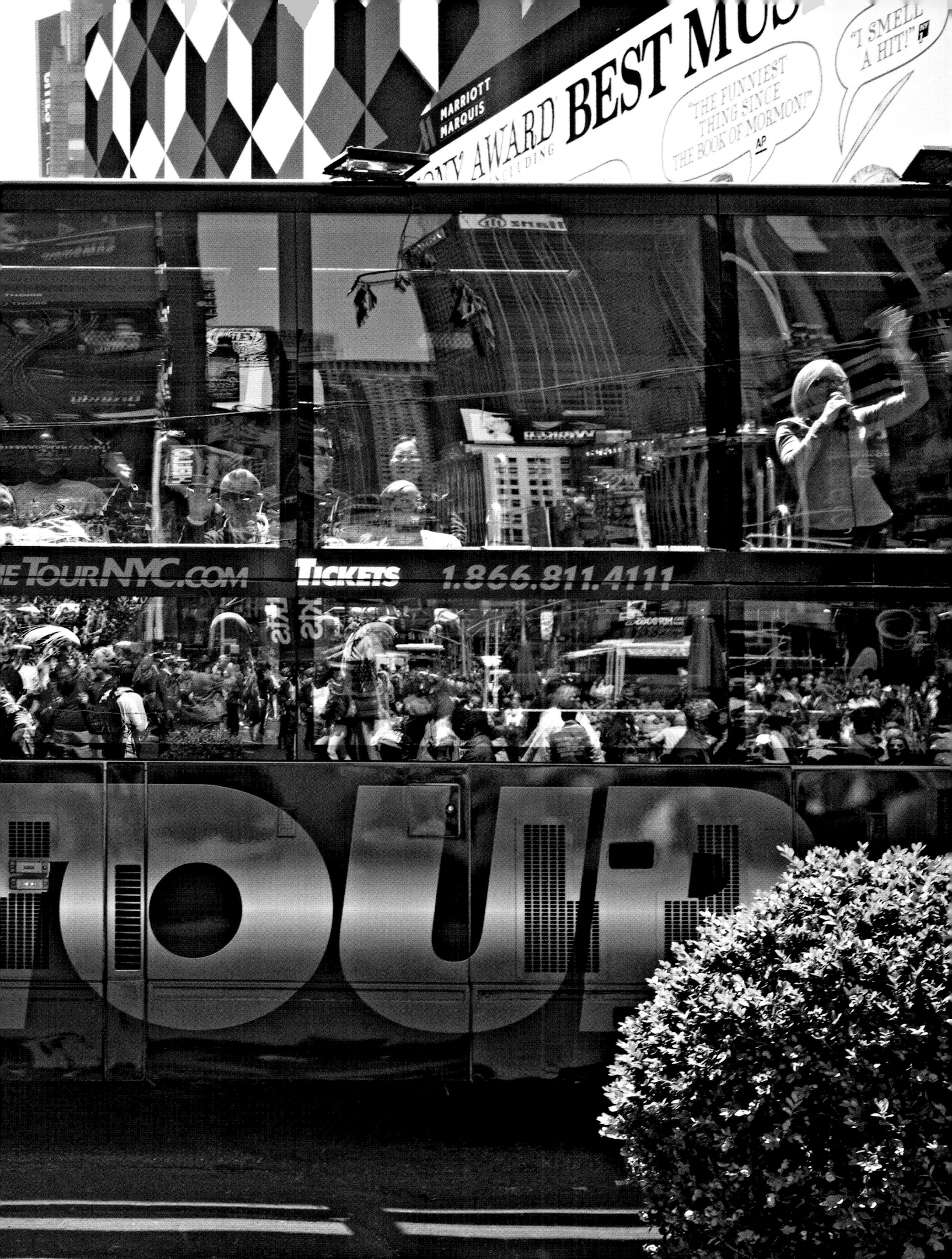

MARRIOTT MARQUIS
...NY AWARD BEST MUS...
INCLUDING
"THE FUNNIEST THING SINCE THE BOOK OF MORMON!"
AP
"I SMELL A HIT!"
...e TourNYC.com   TICKETS   1.866.811.4111
TOUR

AMERICA'S STAGE:

TIMES SQUARE

BETSY KAREL

STEIDL

"On a busy street one quickly becomes a voyeur. An air of danger, eroticism, and crushing solitude play hide-and-seek in the crowd. The indeterminate, the unforeseeable, the ethereal, and the fleeting rule there. The city is the place where the most unlikely opposites come together, the place where our separate intuitions momentarily link up. The myth of Theseus, the Minotaur, Ariadne, and her thread continue here. The city is labyrinth of analogies, the Symbolist forest of correspondences.

Like a comic-book Spider-Man, the solitary voyeur rides the web of occult forces."

"The disorder of the city is sacred. All things are interrelated. As above, so below. We are fragments of an unutterable whole. Meaning is always in search of itself. Unexpected revelations await us around the next corner."

Excerpted from *Dime-Store Alchemy: The Art of Joseph Cornell* by Charles Simic, 1993

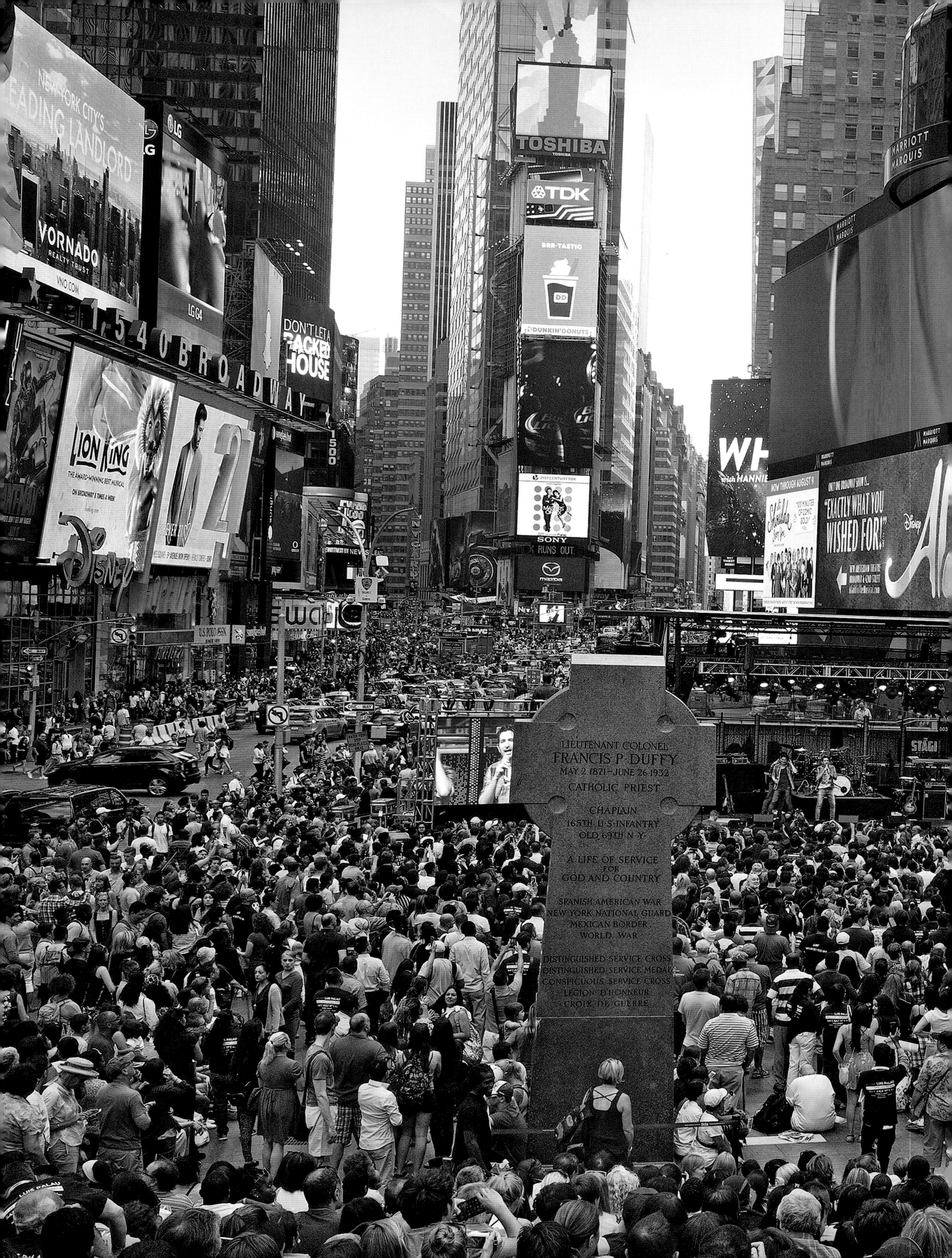

LIEUTENANT COLONEL
FRANCIS P. DUFFY
MAY 2 1871 – JUNE 26 1932
CATHOLIC PRIEST

CHAPLAIN
165TH. U·S·INFANTRY
OLD 69TH N·Y·

A LIFE OF SERVICE
FOR
GOD AND COUNTRY

SPANISH AMERICAN WAR
NEW YORK NATIONAL GUARD
MEXICAN BORDER
WORLD WAR

DISTINGUISHED SERVICE CROSS
DISTINGUISHED SERVICE MEDAL
CONSPICUOUS SERVICE CROSS
LÉGION D'HONNEUR
CROIX DE GUERRE

NEW YORK CITY'S
LEADING LANDLORD
VORNADO
REALTY TRUST
VNO.COM
LG
LG G4
1540 BROADWAY
DON'T LET A
PACKED
HOUSE
LION KING
THE AWARD-WINNING BEST MUSICAL
ON BROADWAY 8 TIMES A WEEK
Disney
U.S. POLO ASSN.
TOSHIBA
TDK
BRR-TASTIC
DD
DUNKIN' DONUTS
SONY
RUNS OUT
Mazda
21ST CENTURY FOR
MASTERS OF
MARRIOTT
MARQUIS
WH
with HANNI
NOW THROUGH AUGUST 9
ON LY ONE BROADWAY SHOW IS...
"EXACTLY WHAT YOU
WISHED FOR!"
Disney
NEW AMSTERDAM THEATRE
BROADWAY & 42ND STREET
ONE WAY

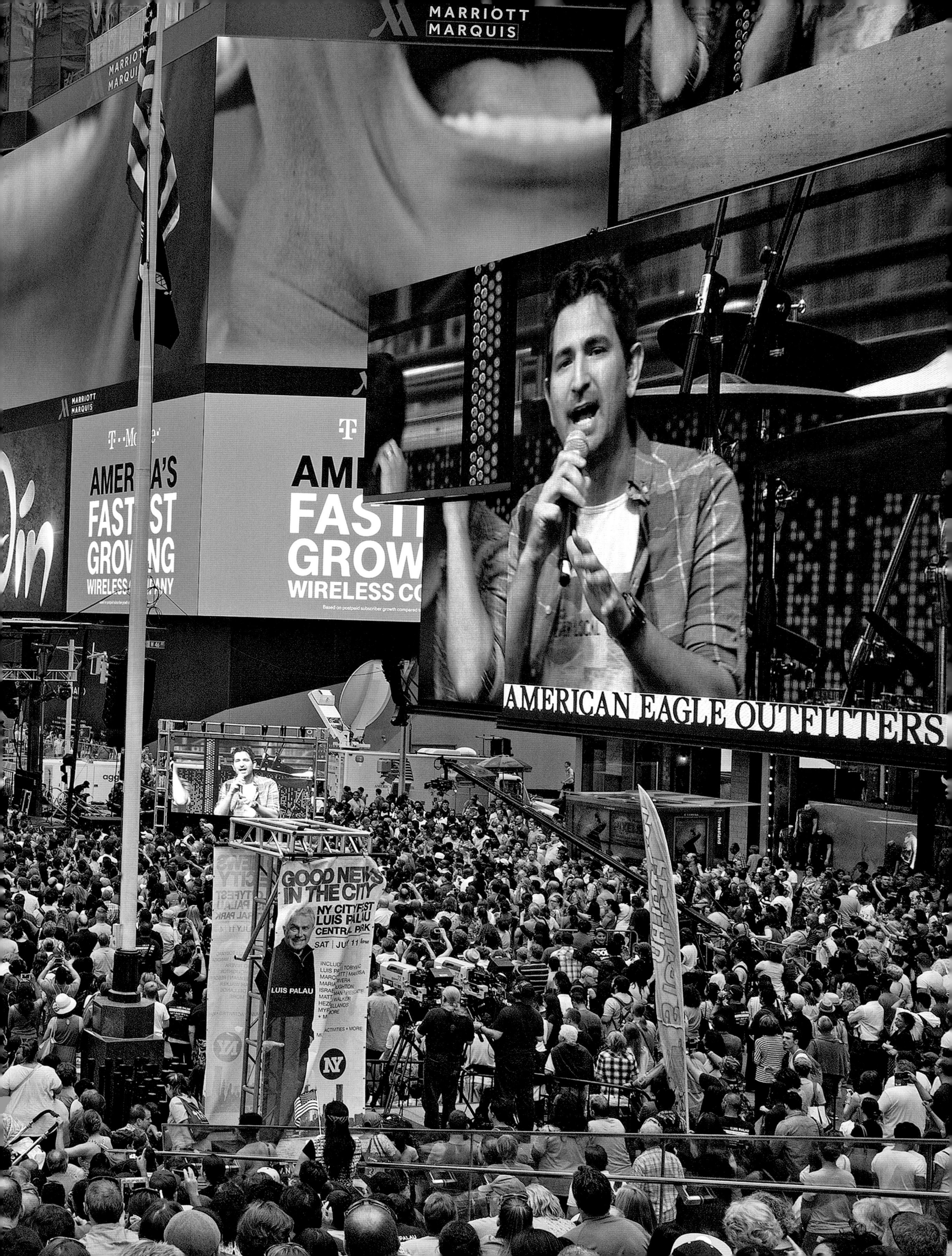

MARRIOTT MARQUIS
MARRIOTT MARQUIS
T Mobile
AMERICA'S
FASTEST
GROWING
WIRELESS COMPANY
AM
FASTEST
GROW
WIRELESS CO
AMERICAN EAGLE OUTFITTERS
GOOD NEWS
IN THE CITY
NY CITYFEST
LUIS PALAU
CENTRAL PARK
SAT | JUL 11 4pm
LUIS PALAU

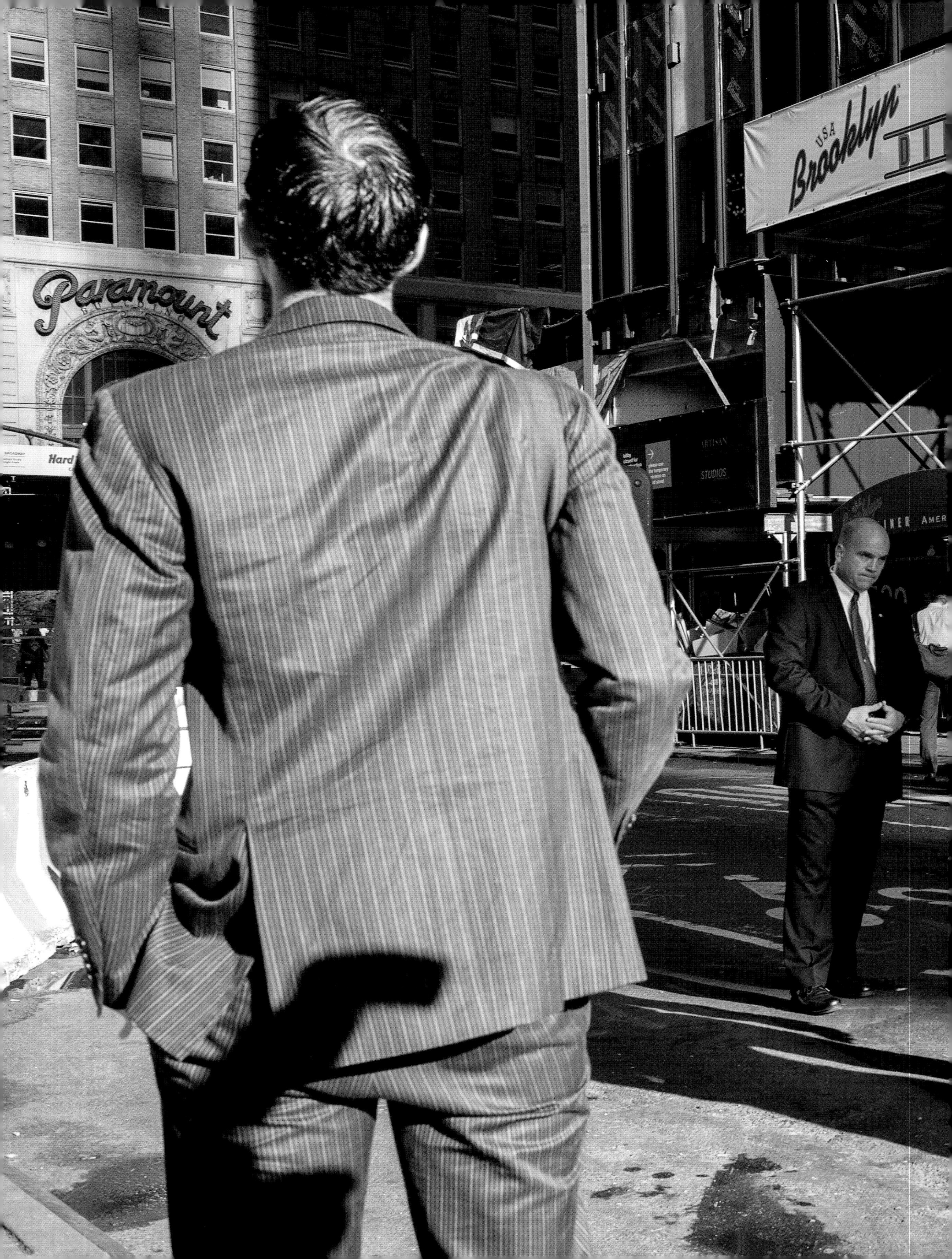
Paramount
USA
Brooklyn
Hard
ARTISAN
STUDIOS
DINER AMER

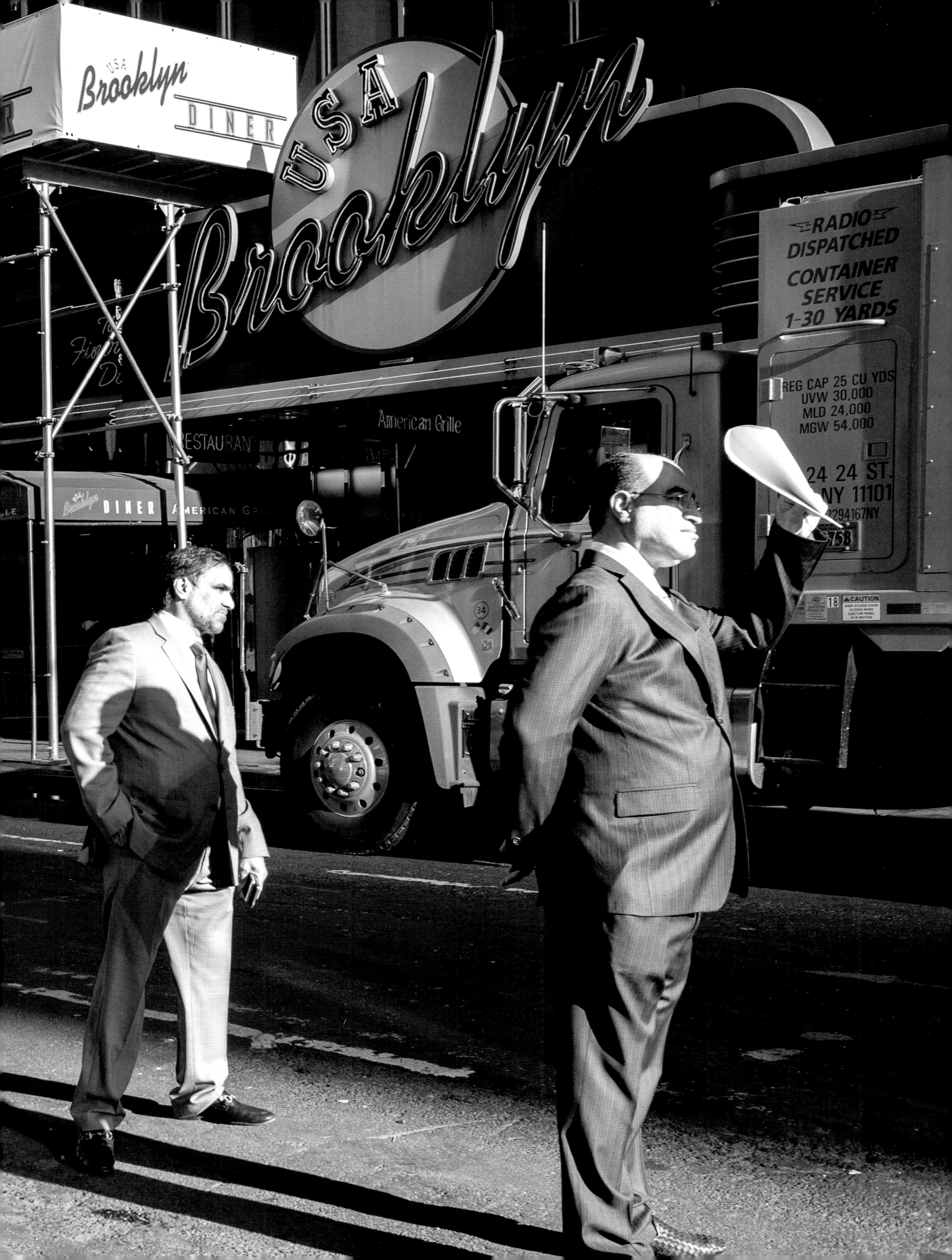

USA
Brooklyn
DINER
USA
Brooklyn
The Finest
Diner
RESTAURANT
DINER AMERICAN GRILLE
American Grille
RADIO DISPATCHED
CONTAINER SERVICE
1-30 YARDS
REG CAP 25 CU YDS
UVW 30,000
MLD 24,000
MGW 54,000
24 24 ST.
NY 11101
0294167NY
758
18 CAUTION
34

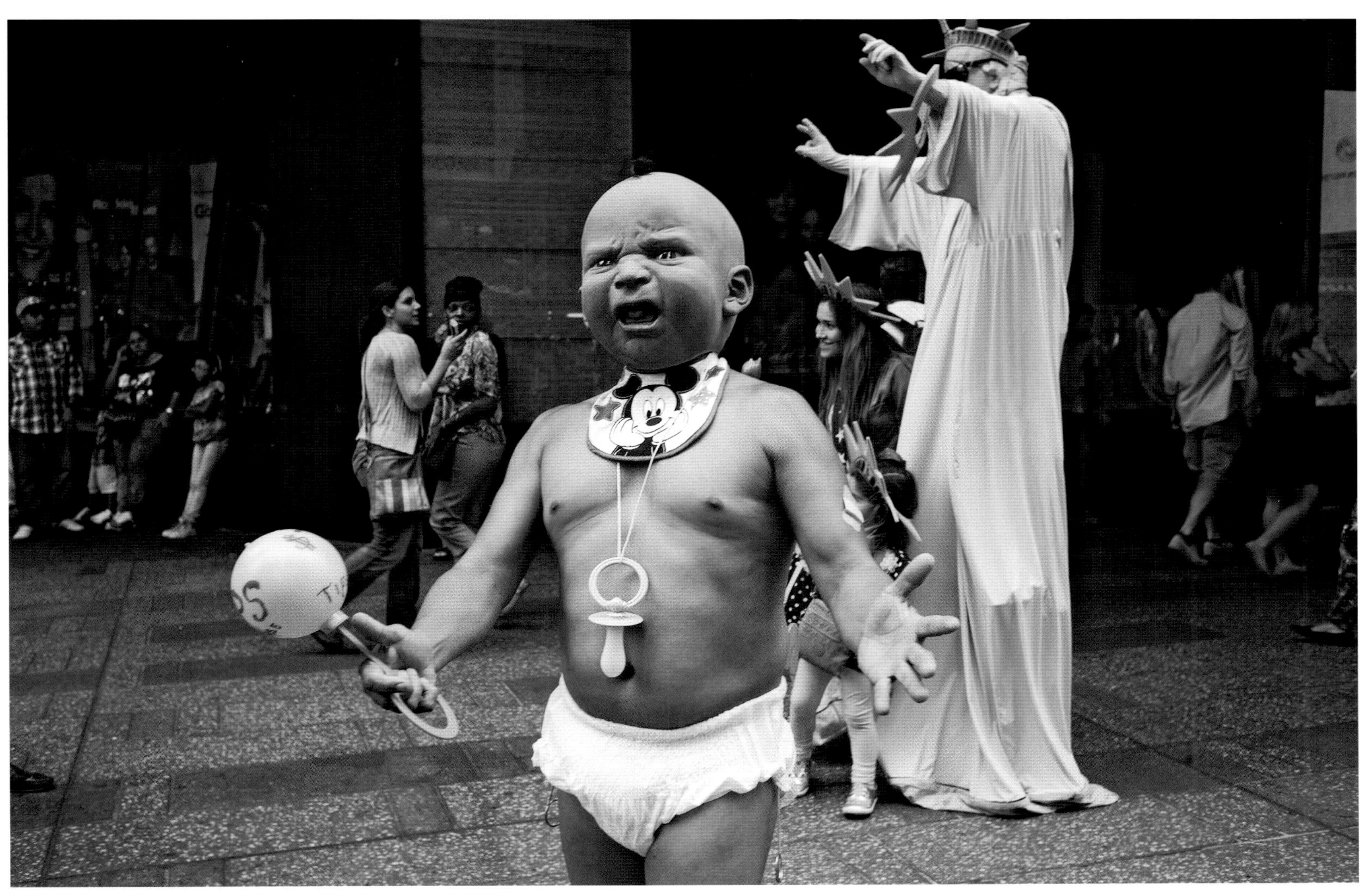

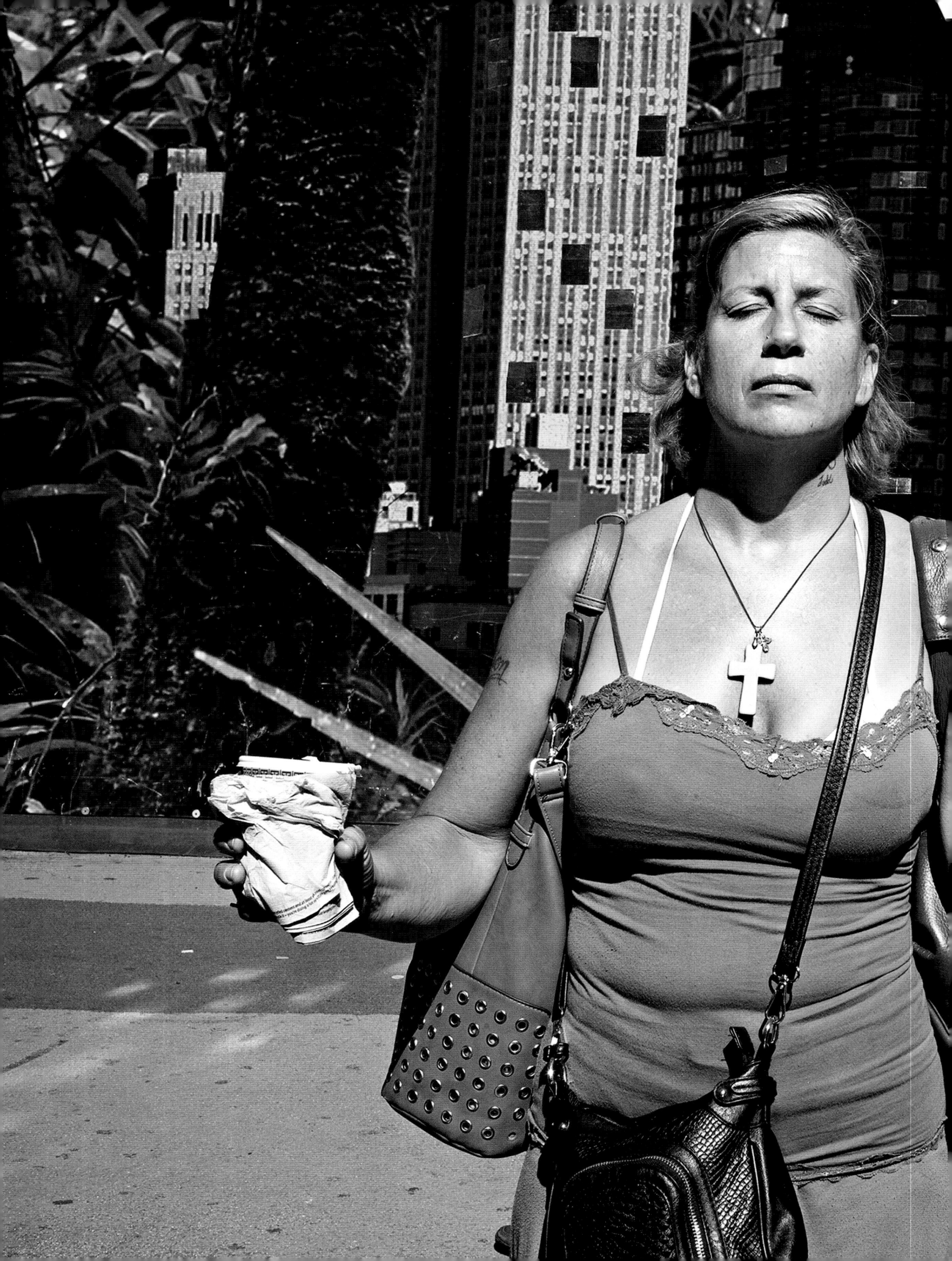

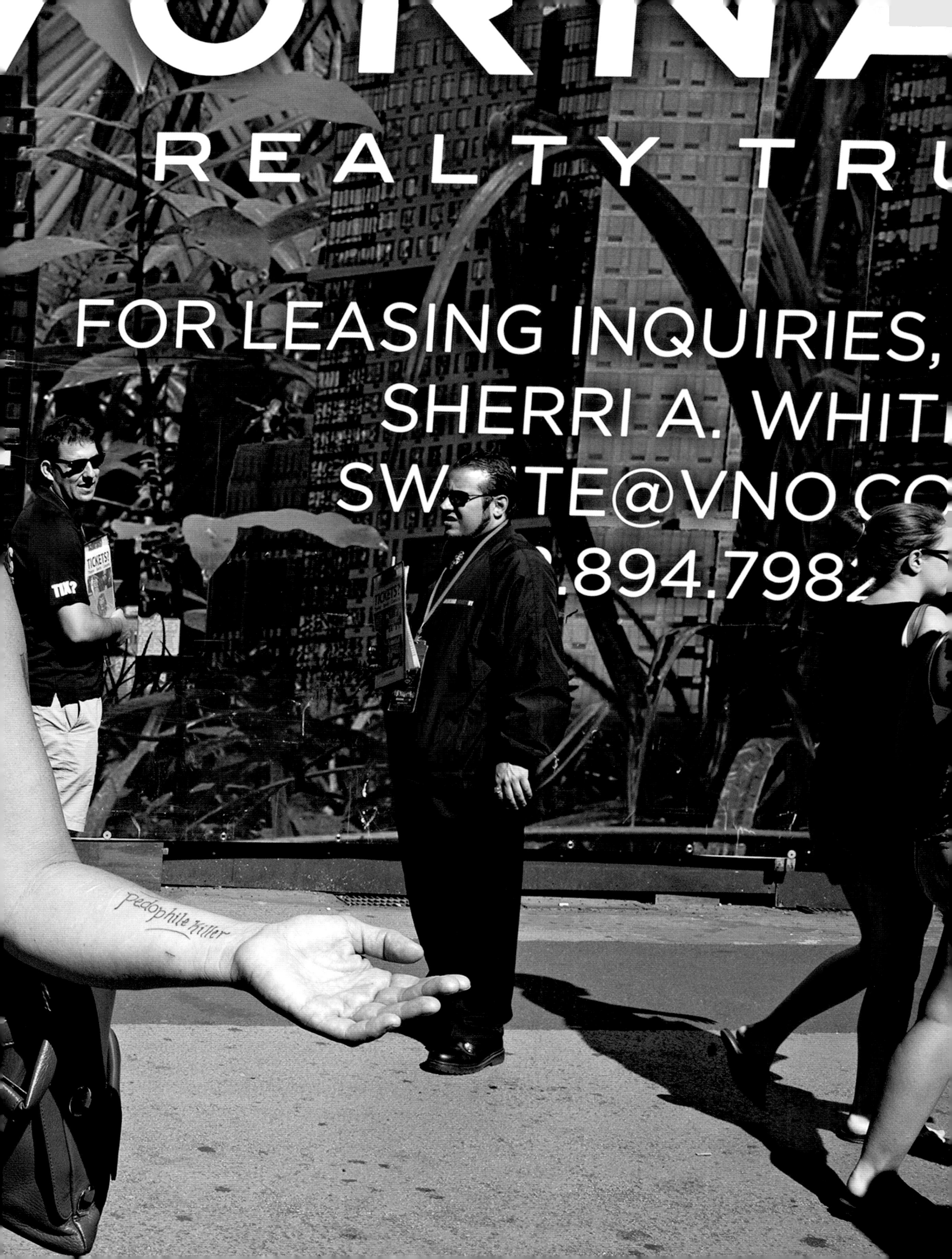
ORNA
REALTY TRU
FOR LEASING INQUIRIES,
SHERRI A. WHIT
SW ITE@VNO CO
.894.7982
TICKETS?
Pedophile Killer

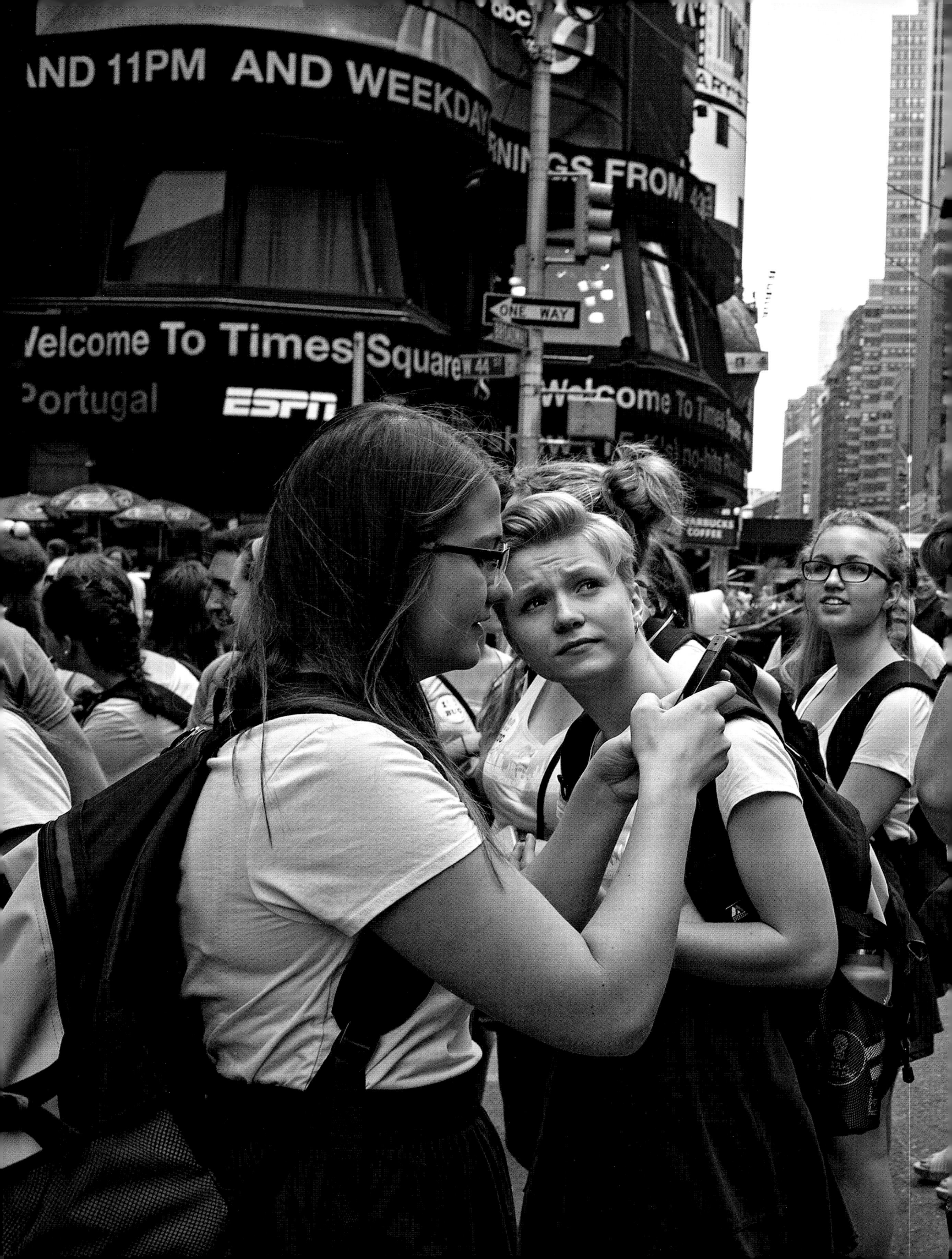

AND 11PM   AND WEEKDAY
Welcome To Times Square
Portugal
ESPN
ONE WAY
W 44 ST
Welcome To Times
STARBUCKS
COFFEE

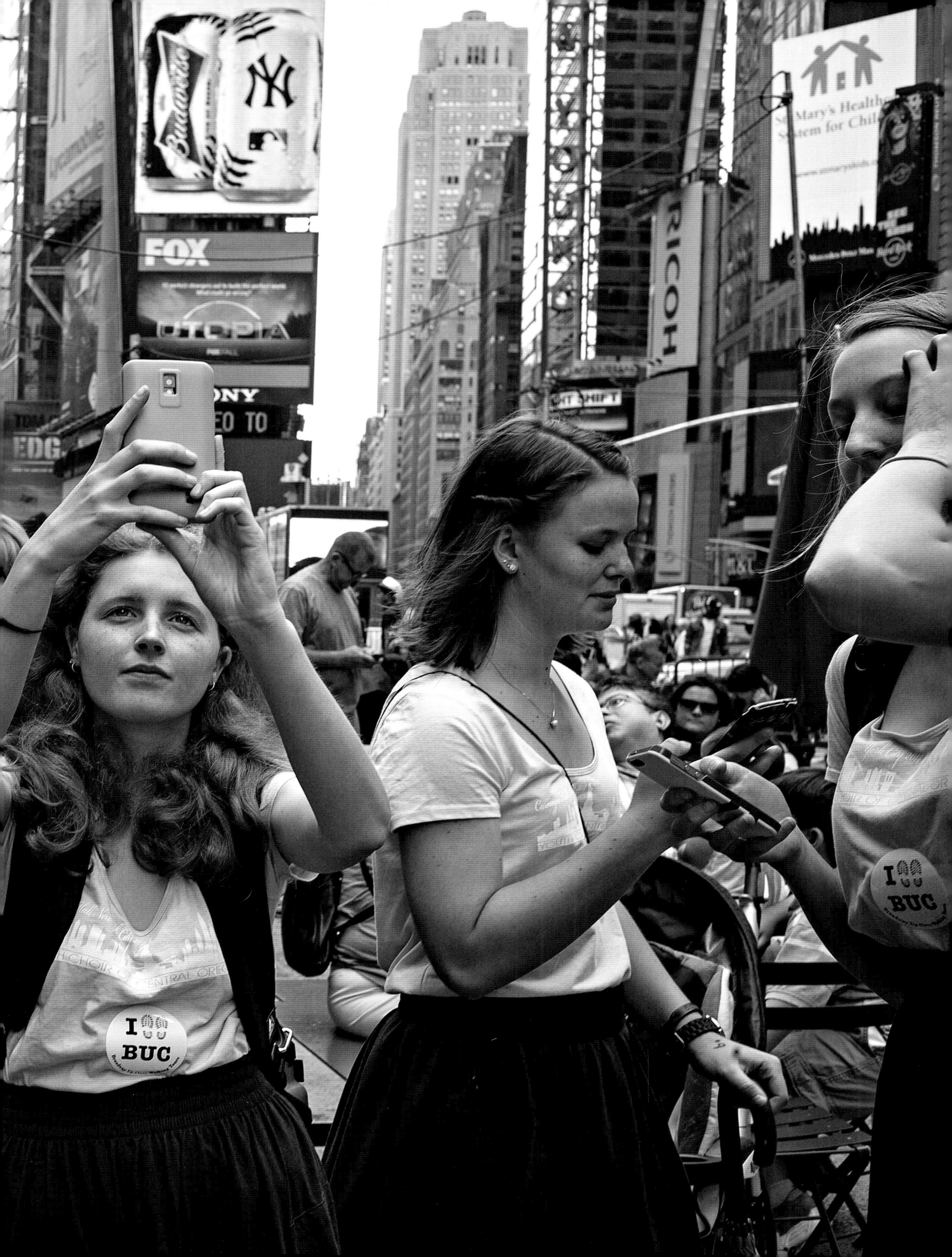

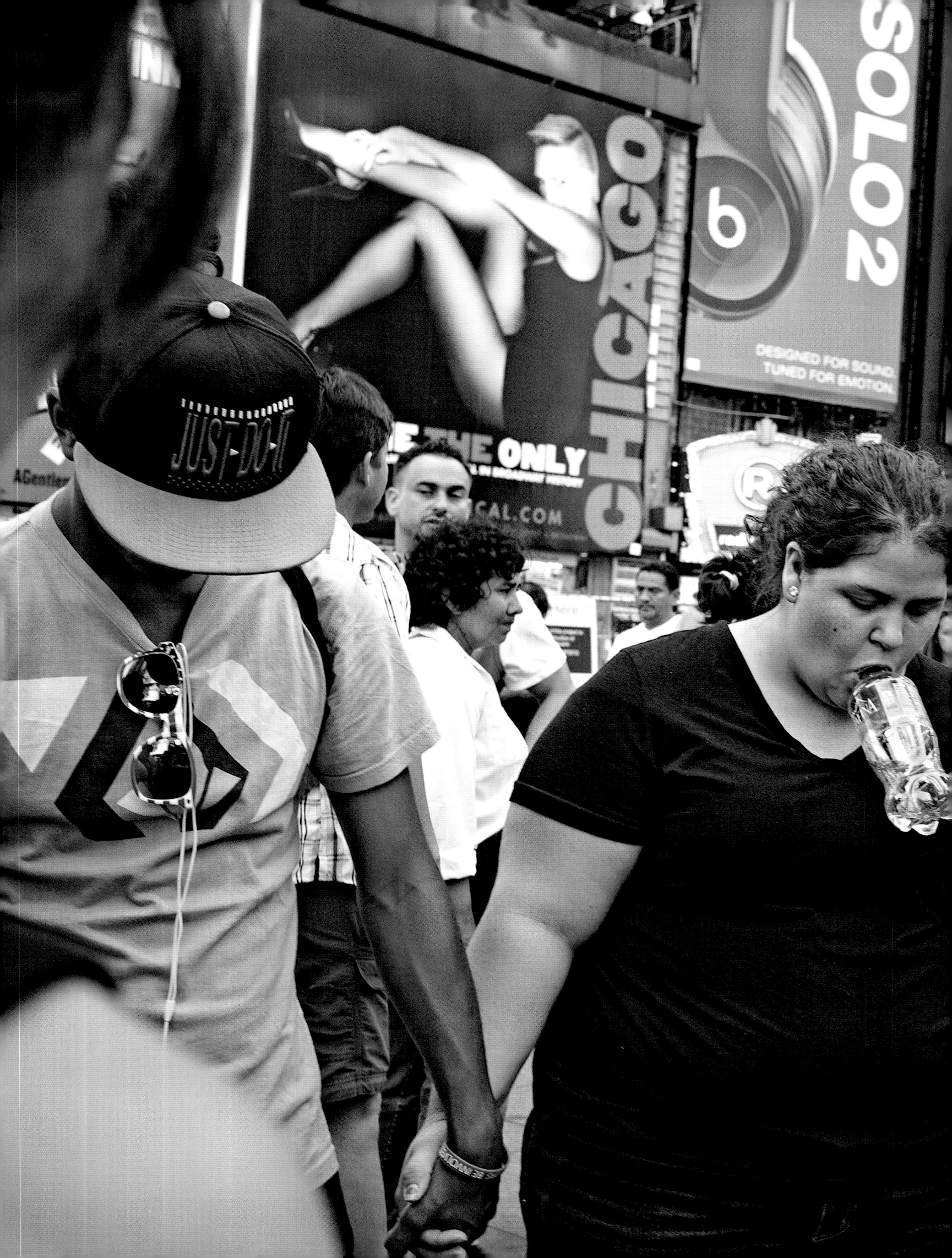
JUST DO IT
SOLO 2
b
CHICAGO
DESIGNED FOR SOUND
TUNED FOR EMOTION
THE ONLY
...CAL.COM

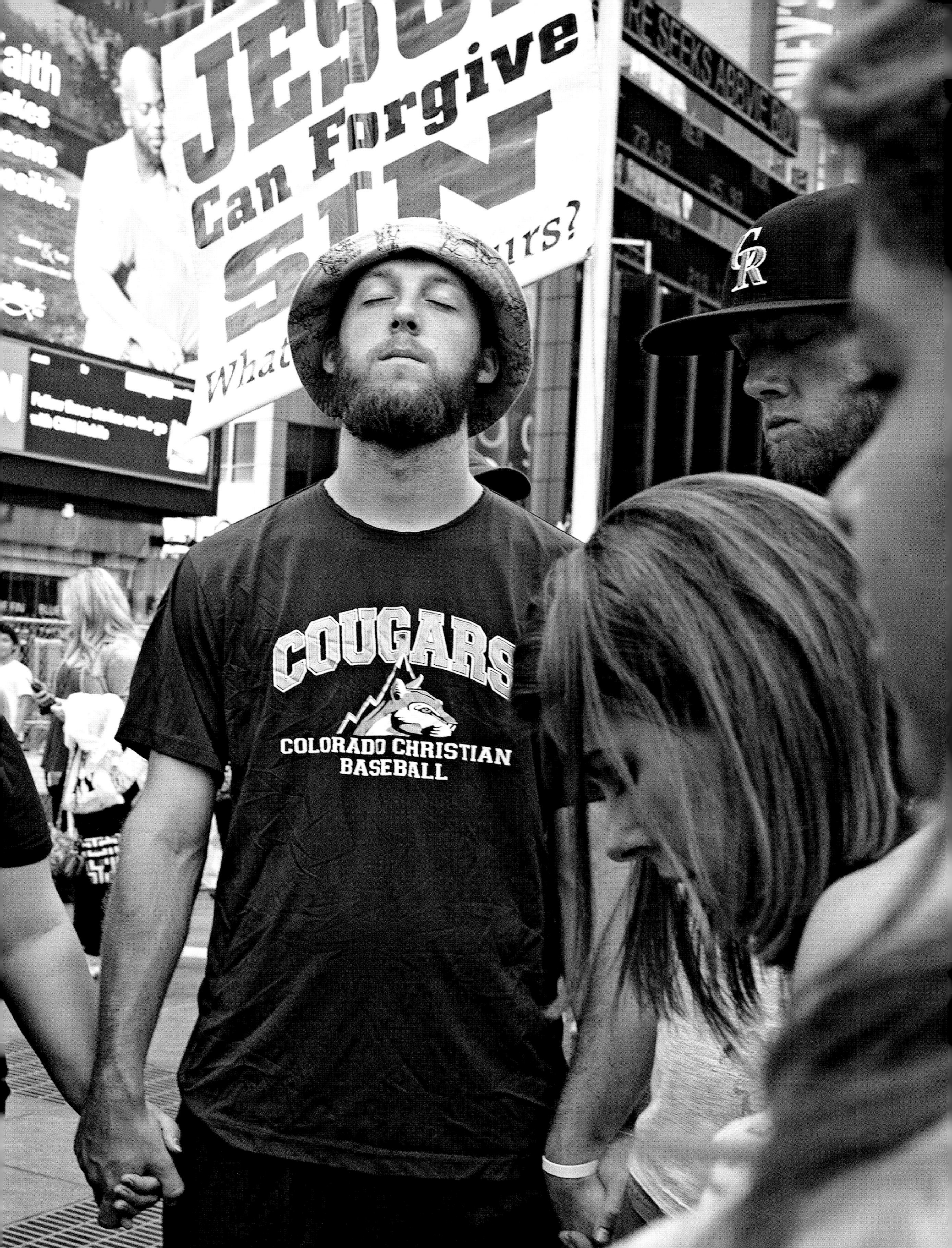

aith
JESUS
Can Forgive
SIN
What
urs?
SEEKS ABOVE
COUGARS
COLORADO CHRISTIAN
BASEBALL
CR

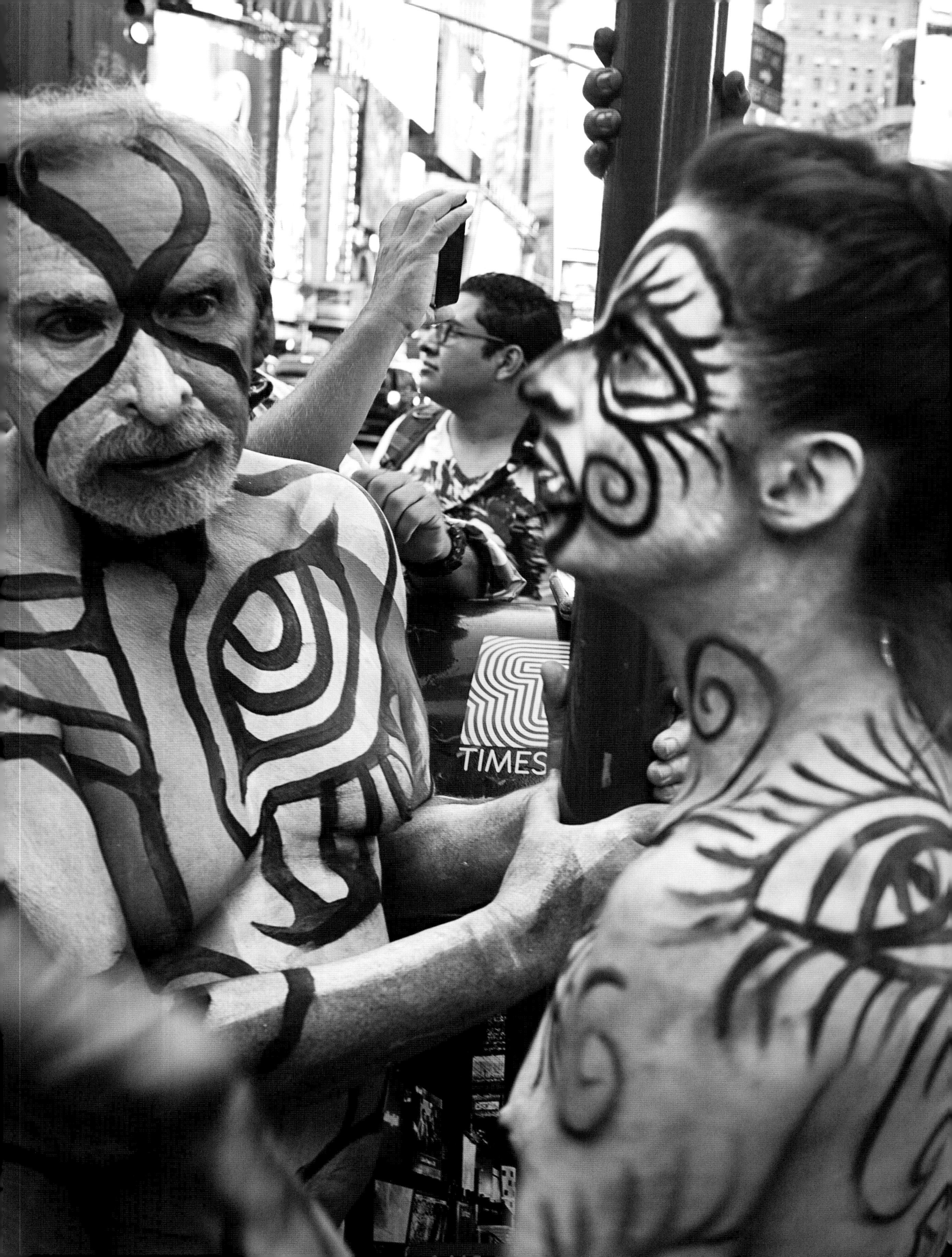

TIMES

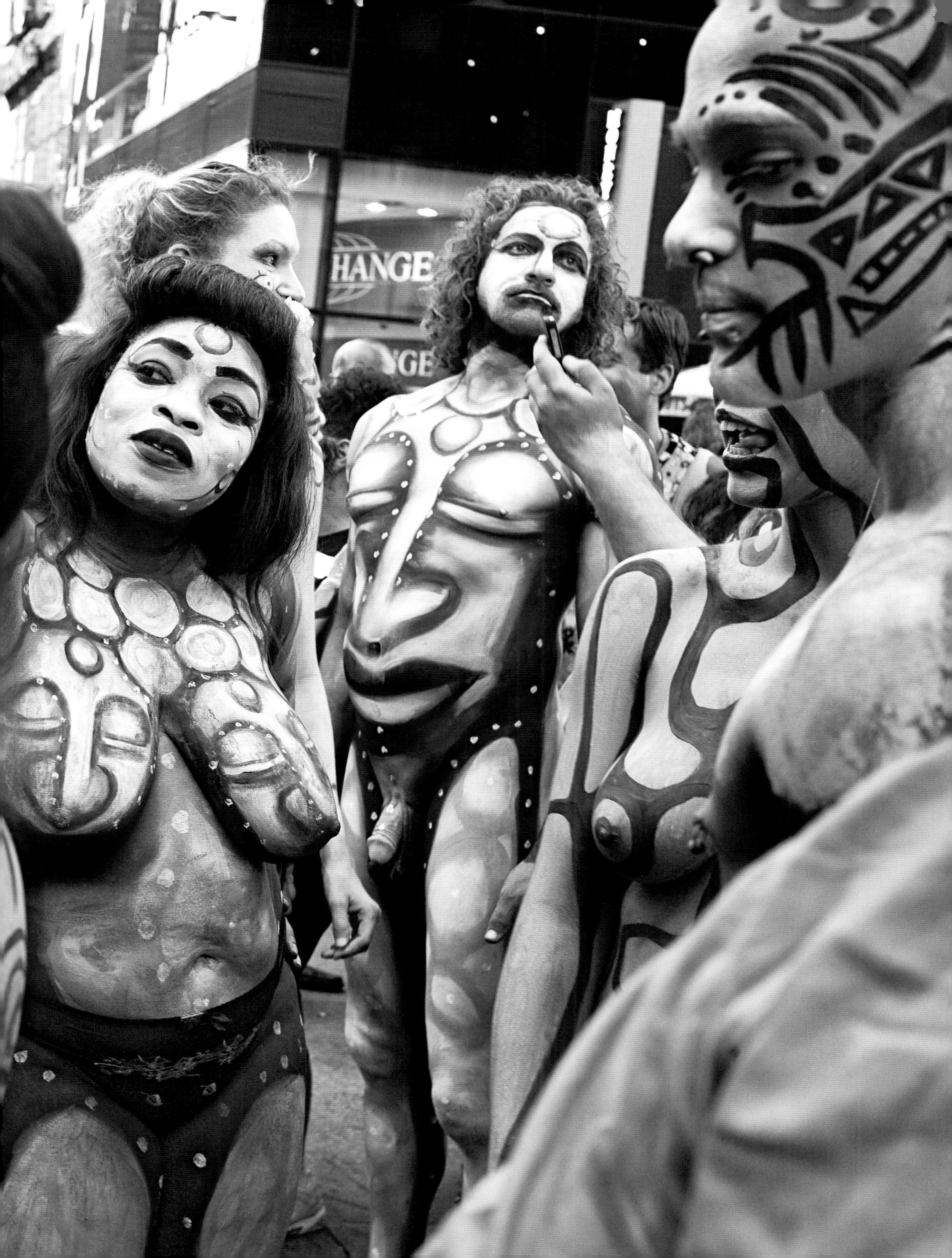

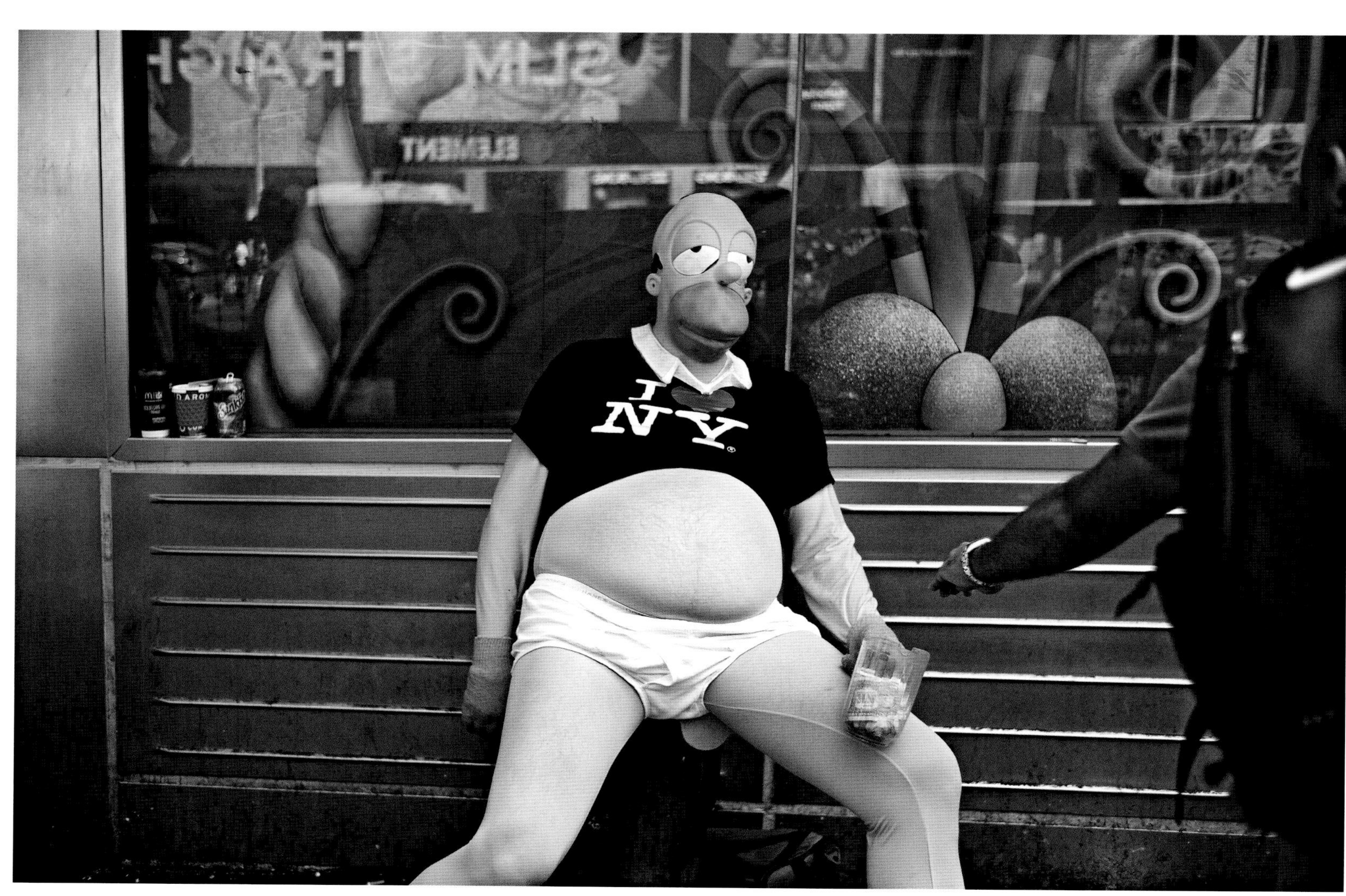

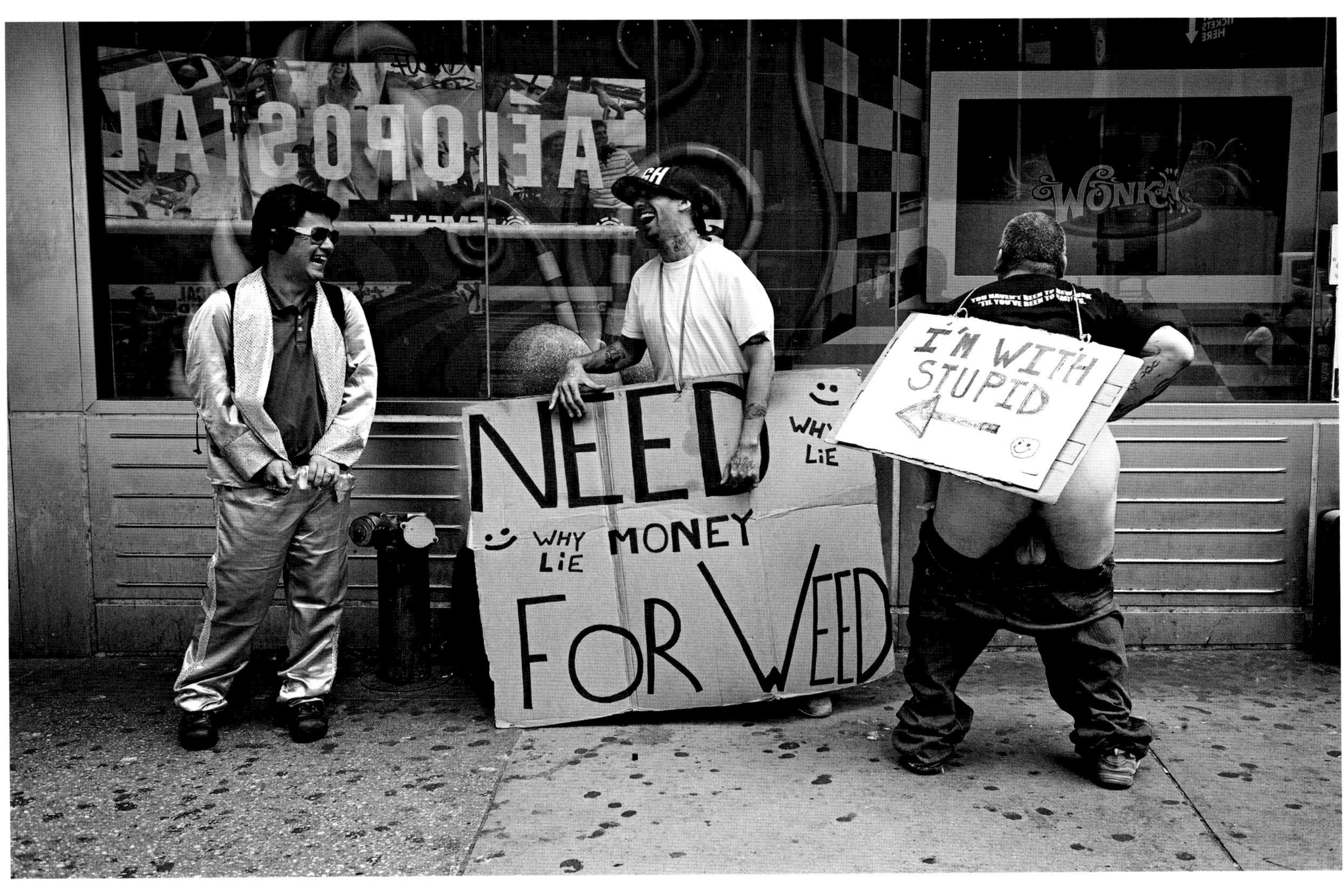
AEROPOSTAL
WONKA
NEED
WHY
LiE
WHY MONEY
LiE
FOR WEED
I'M WITH
STUPID

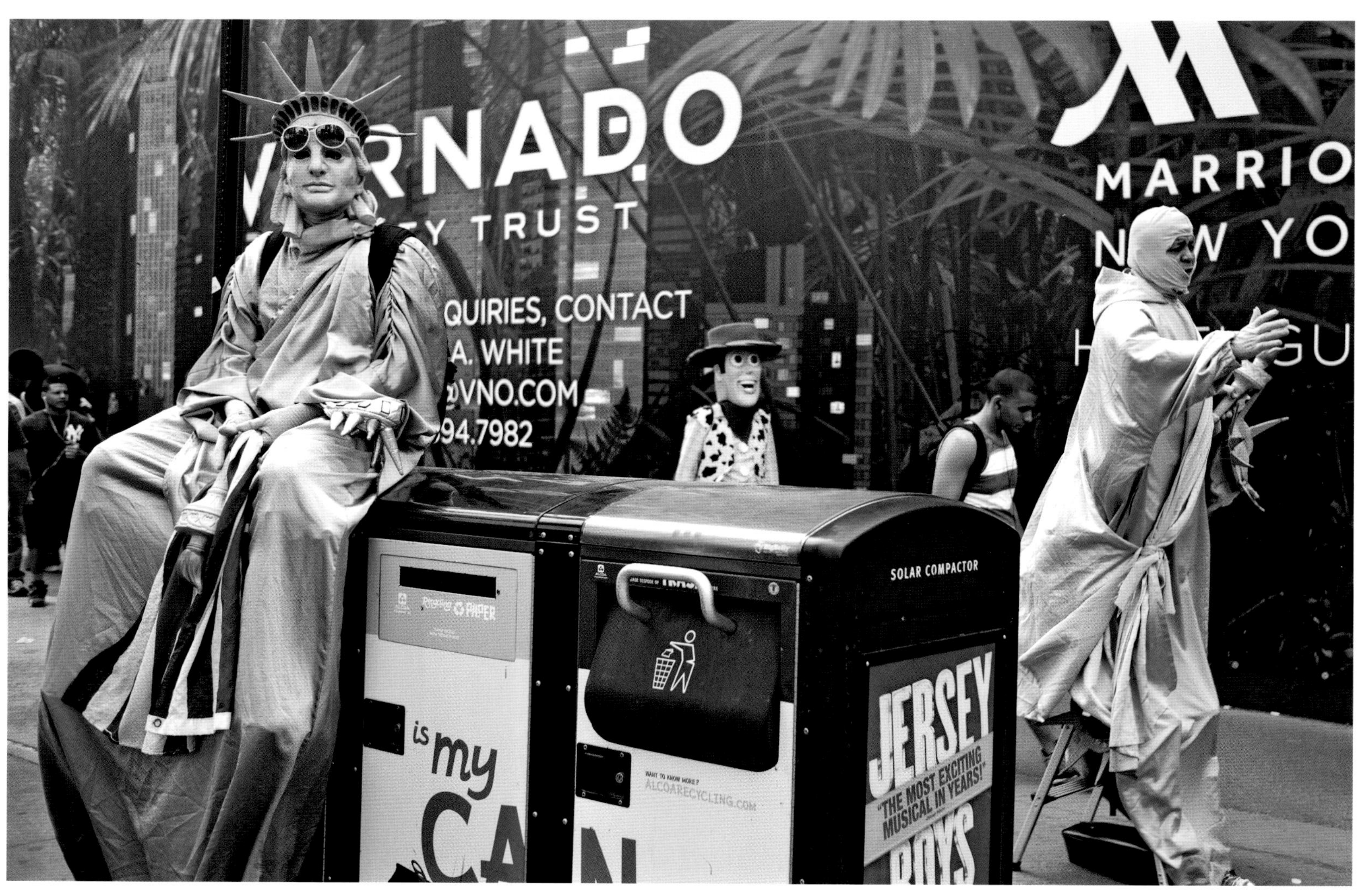
RNADO
TRUST
QUIRIES, CONTACT
A. WHITE
VNO.COM
94.7982
MARRIO
NEW YO
SOLAR COMPACTOR
PAPER
is my
CAN
ALCOARECYCLING.COM
JERSEY
"THE MOST EXCITING
MUSICAL IN YEARS!"
BOYS

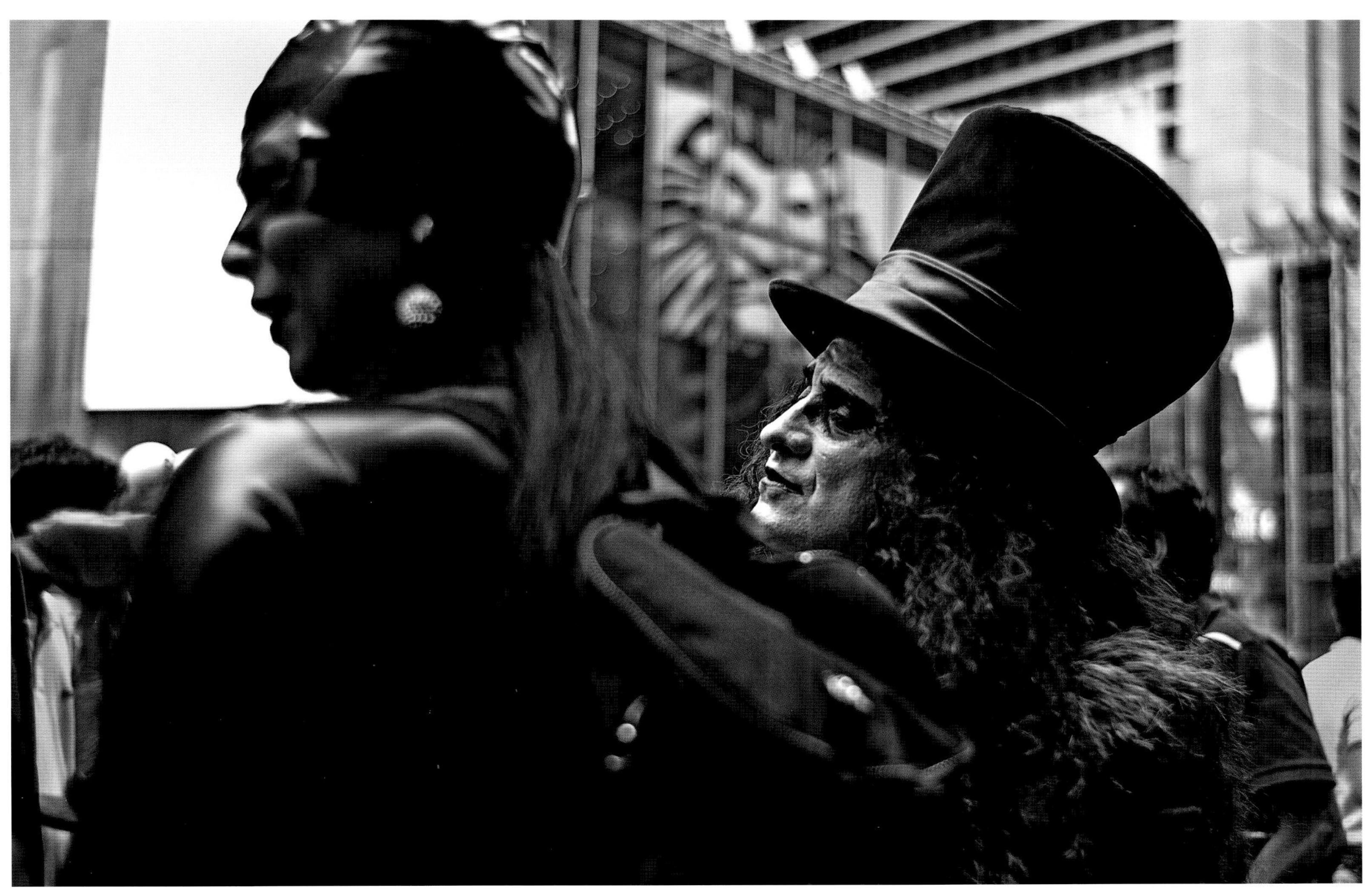

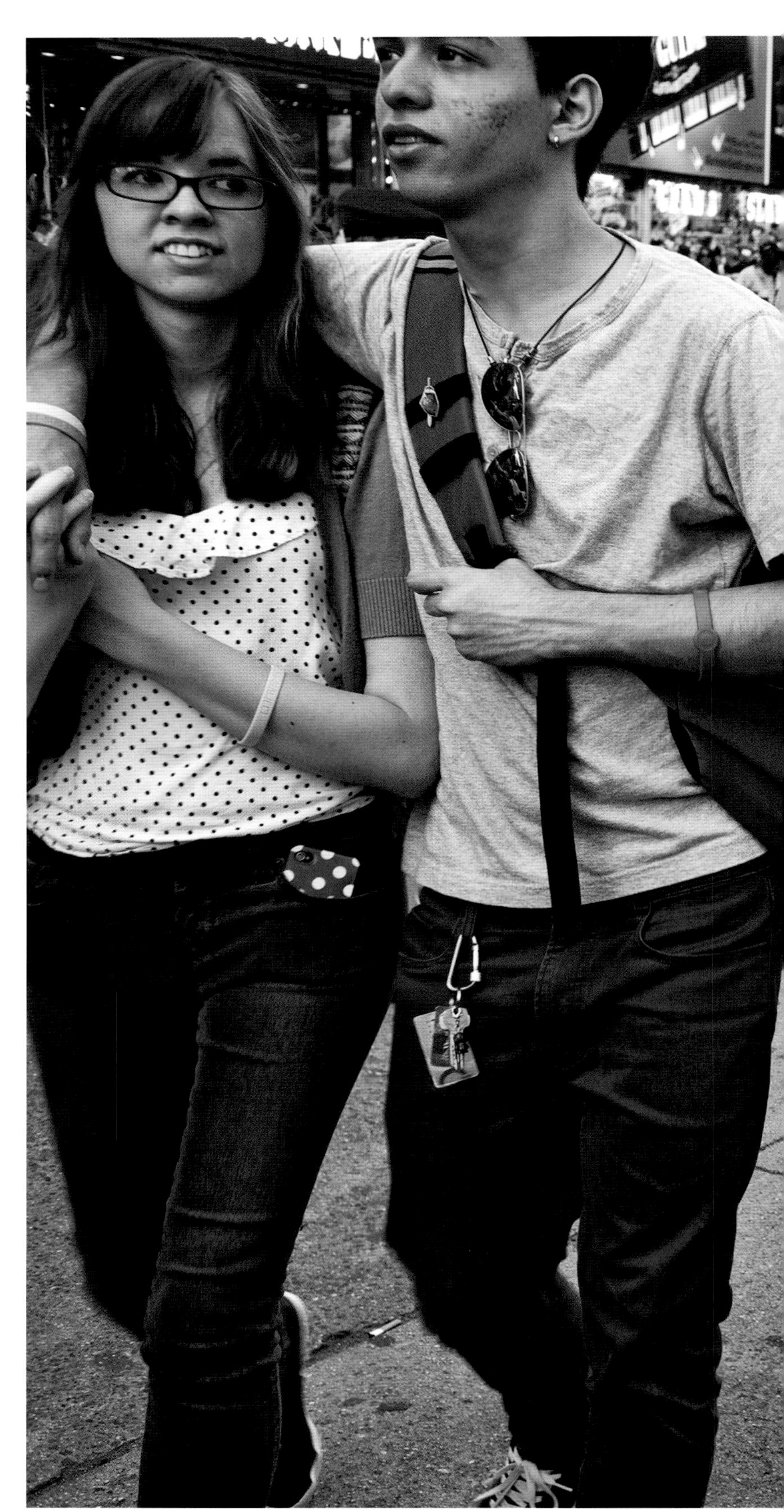

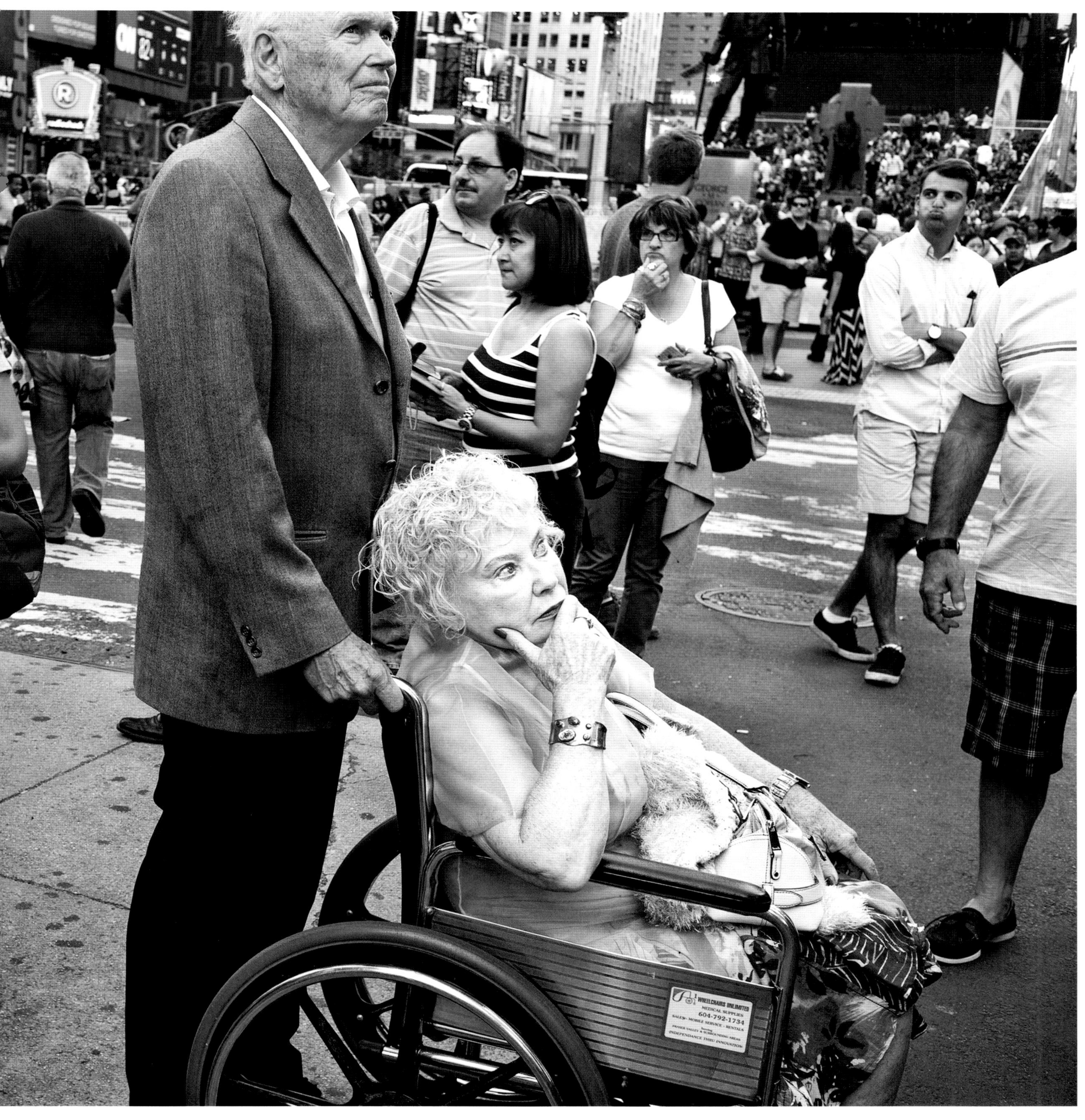
A-1 WHEELCHAIRS UNLIMITED
MEDICAL SUPPLIES
604-792-1734
SALES · MOBILE SERVICE · RENTALS
Serving
FRASER VALLEY & SURROUNDING AREAS
INDEPENDANCE THRU INNOVATION

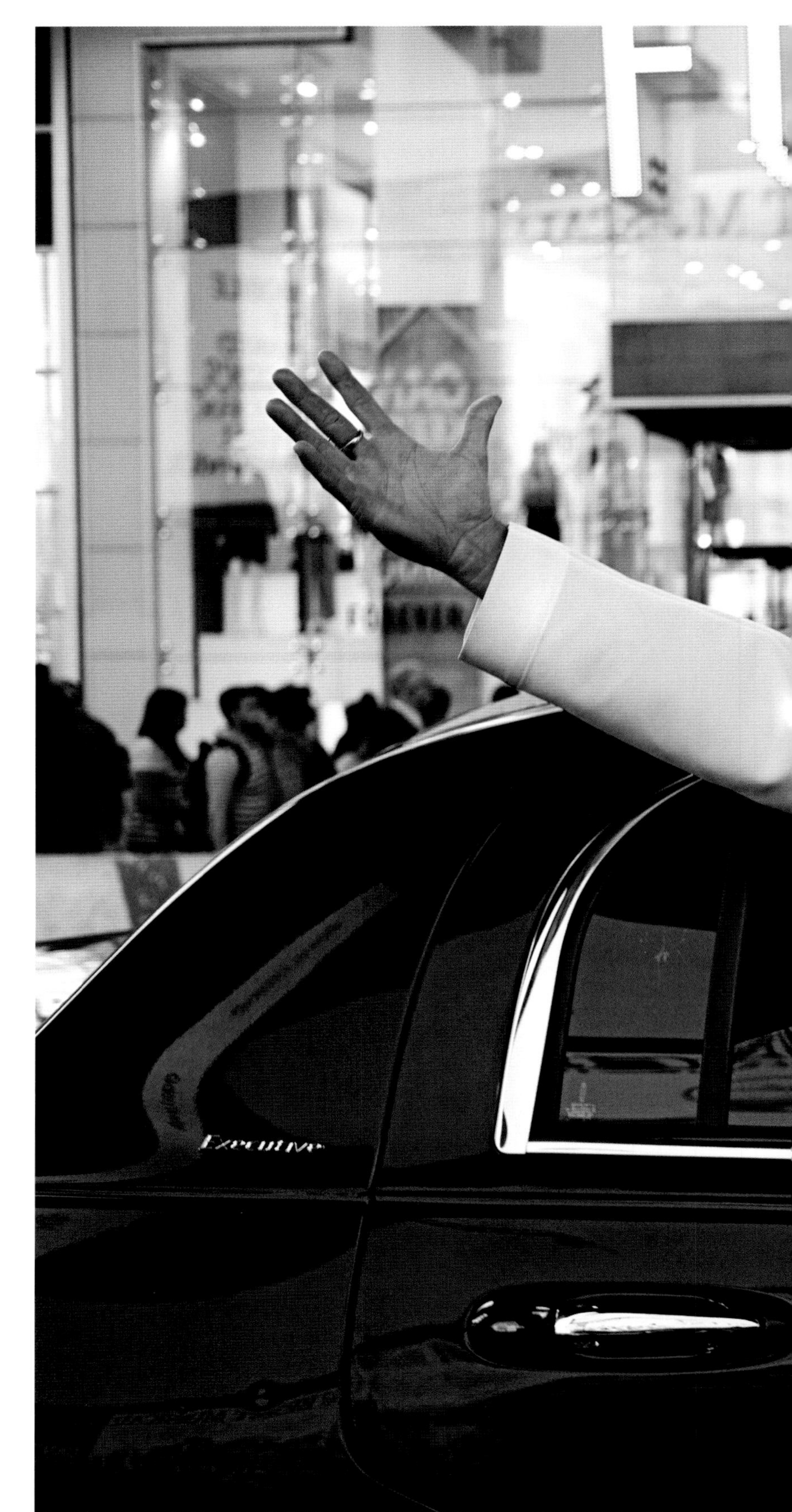

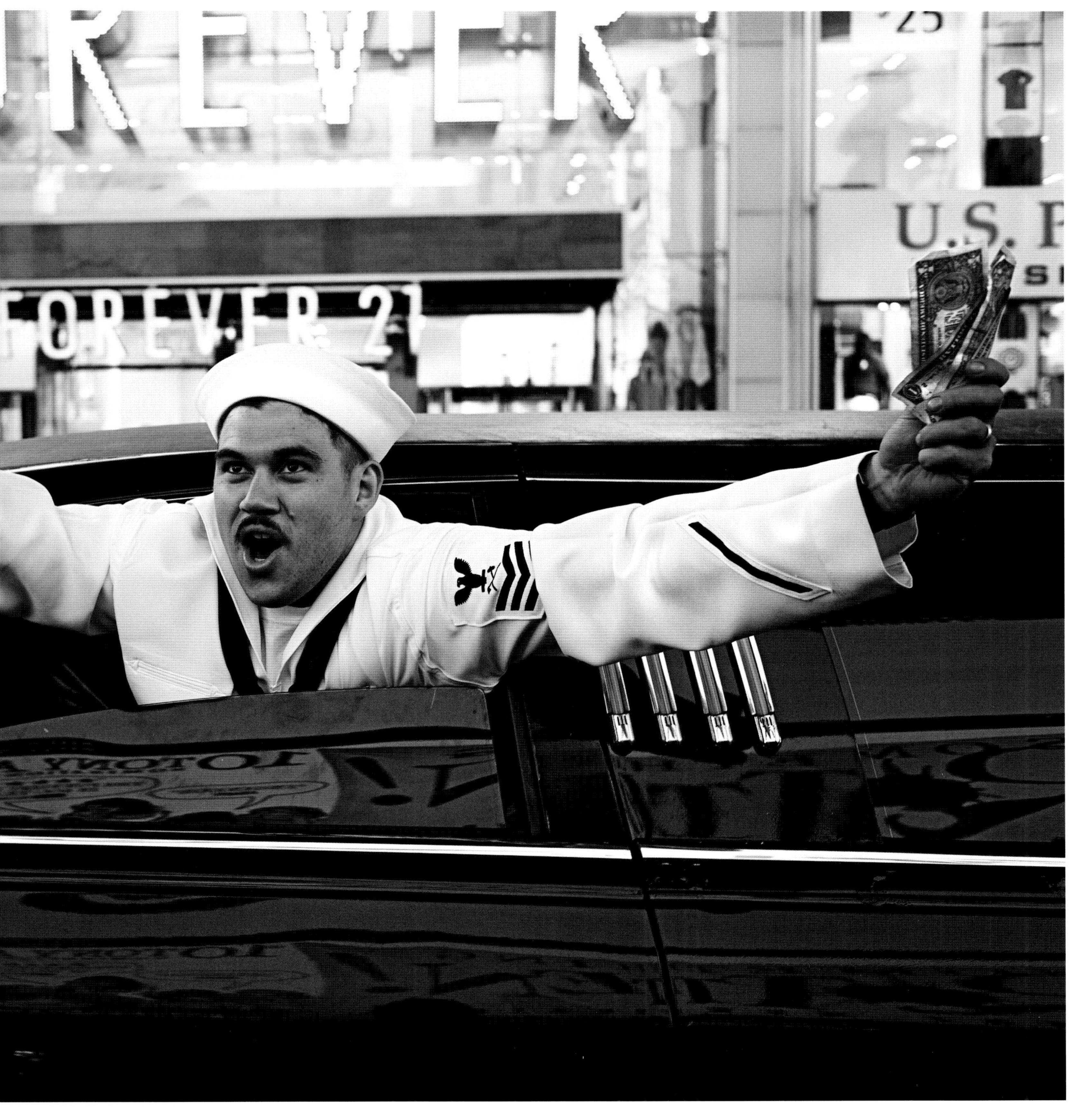
REVER
FOREVER 2
FOREVER 21
U.S. P
'25

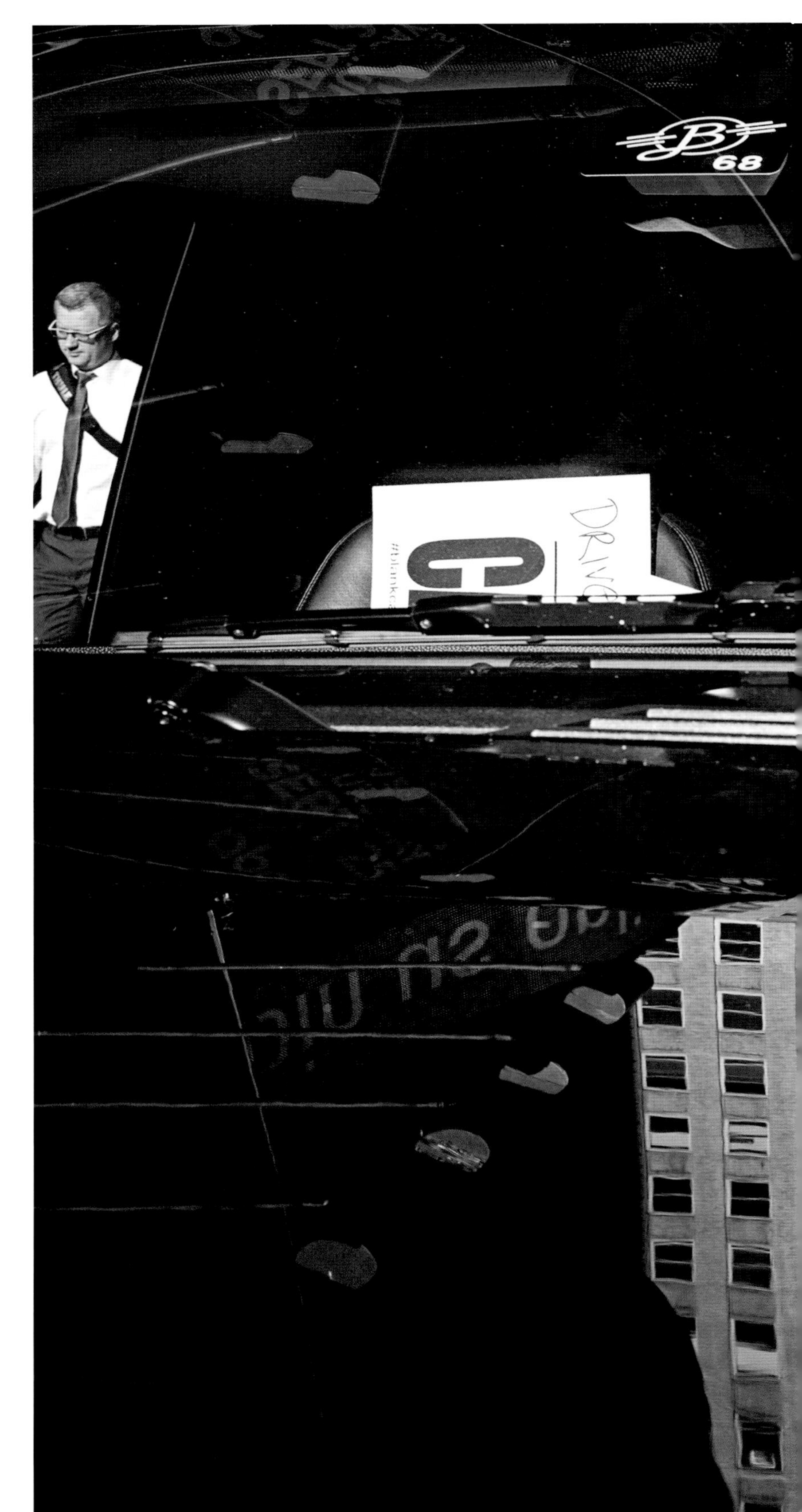

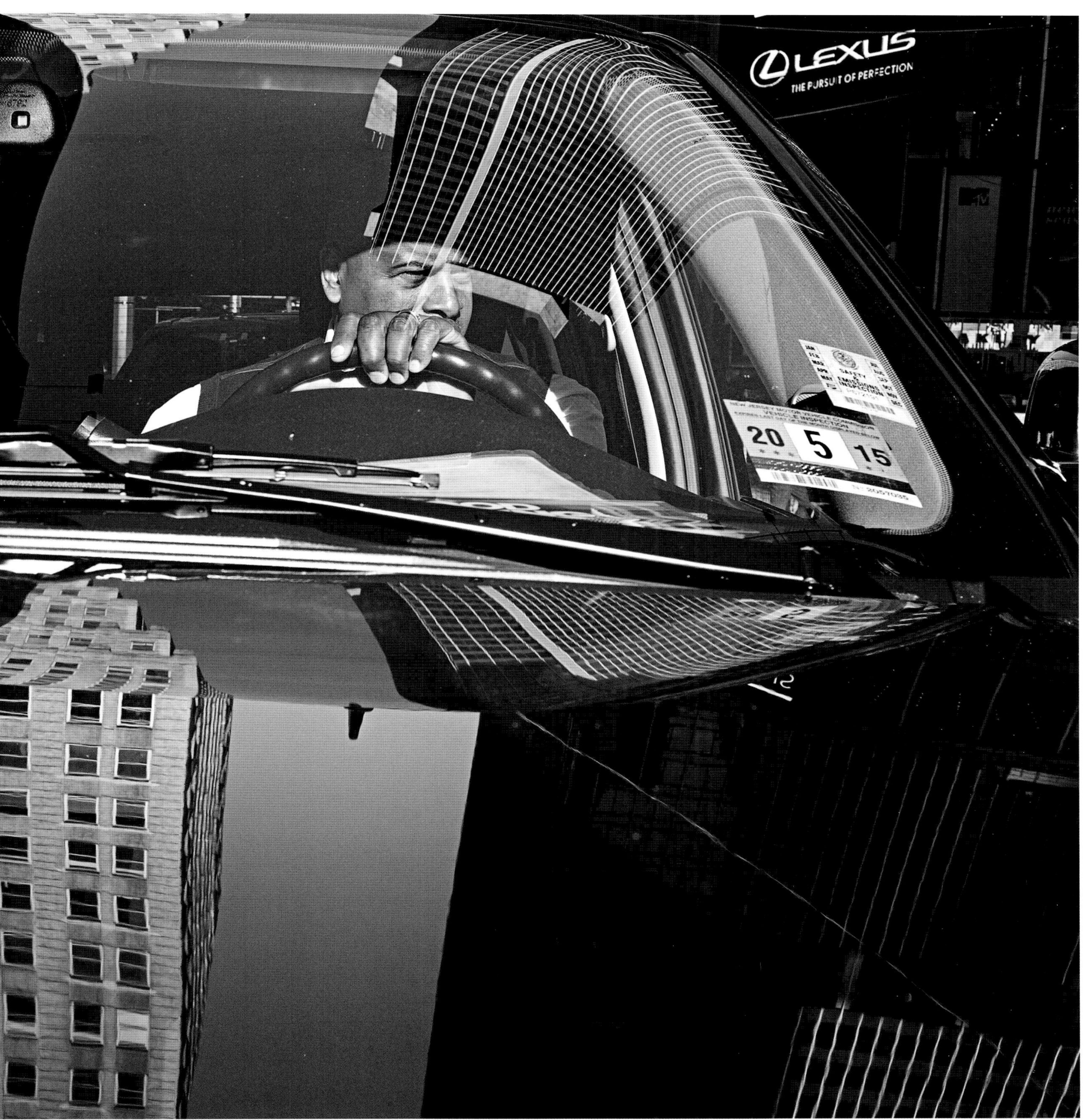
LEXUS
THE PURSUIT OF PERFECTION

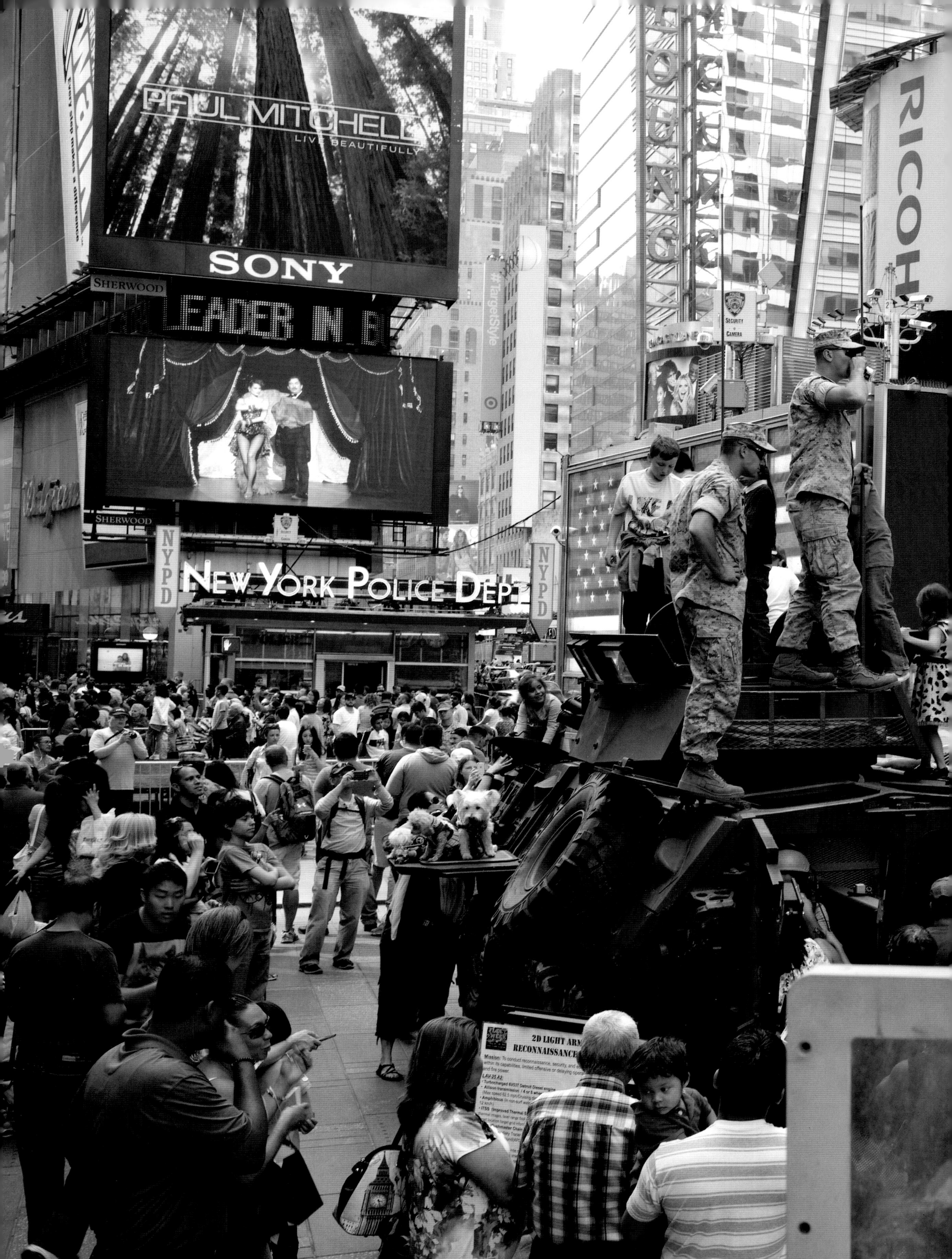

PAUL MITCHELL
LIVE BEAUTIFULLY
SONY
LEADER IN B
SHERWOOD
SHERWOOD
NYPD
NEW YORK POLICE DEPT
NYPD
RICOH
SECURITY
CAMERA
#TargetStyle
2D LIGHT ARMORED
RECONNAISSANCE
Mission: To conduct reconnaissance, security, and
within its capabilities, limited offensive or delaying oper
and fire power.
LAV-25 A2

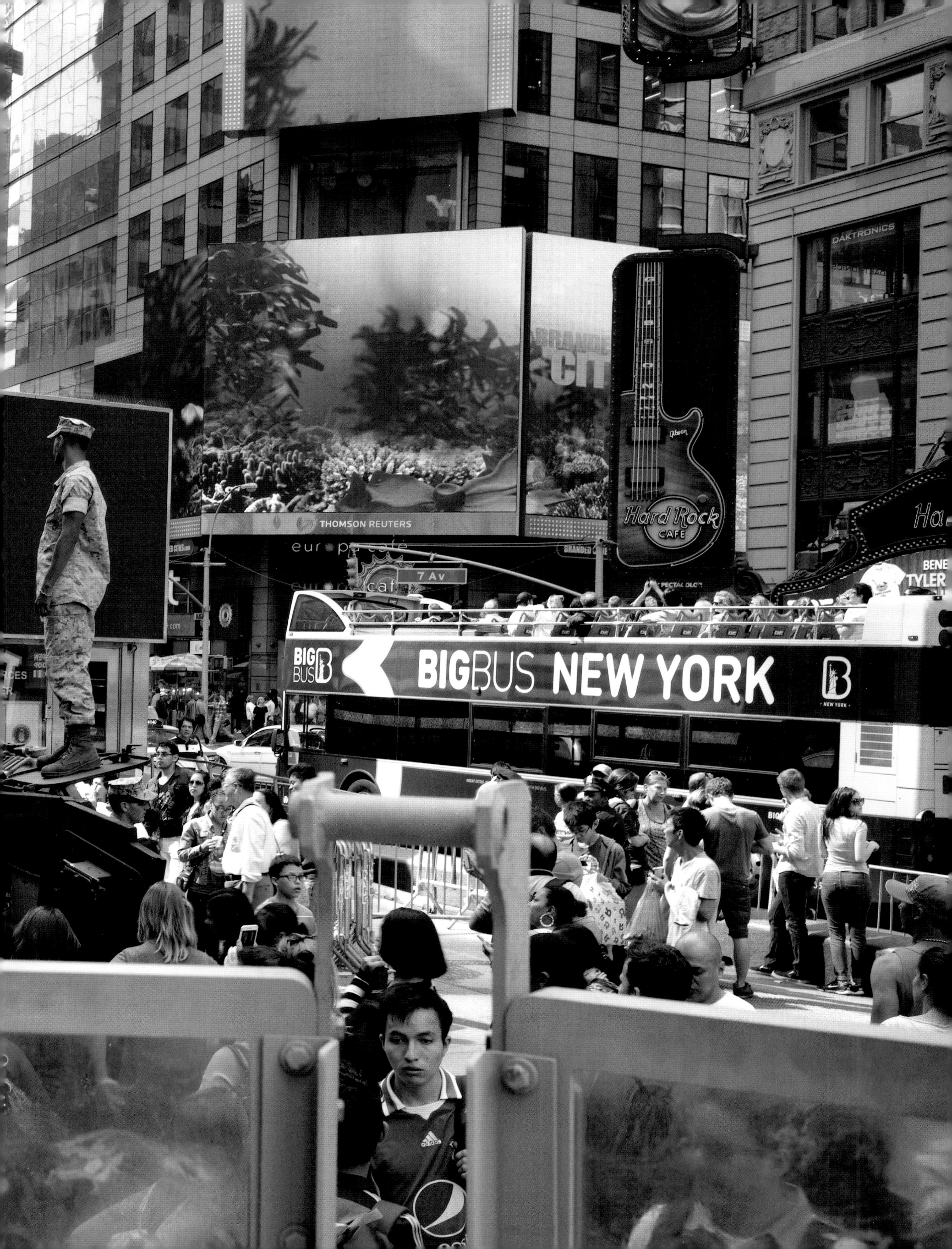
THOMSON REUTERS
BRANDED CITY
DAKTRONICS
Hard Rock CAFE
Gibson
7 Av
BIGBUS NEW YORK
BIG BUS
NEW YORK

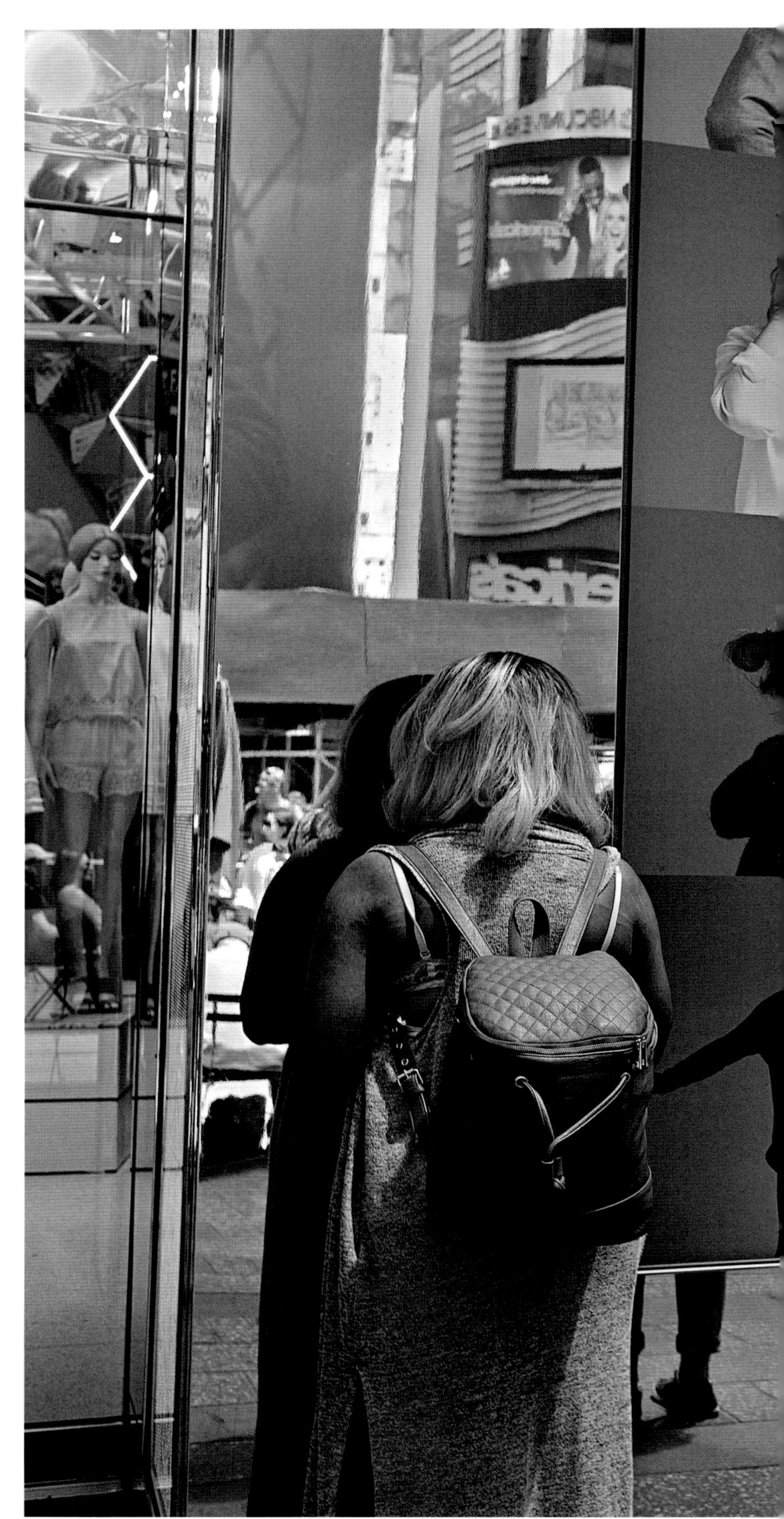

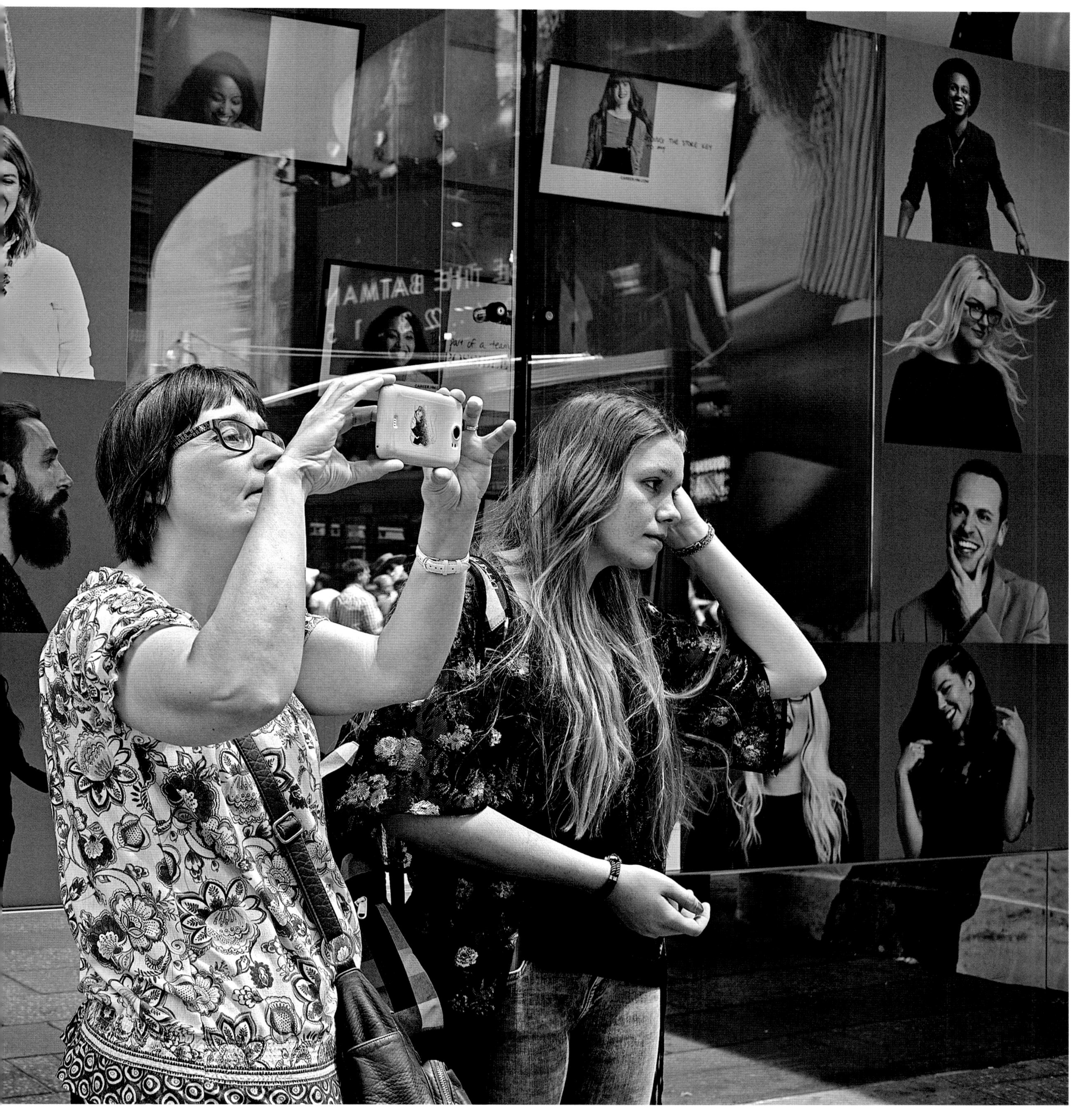

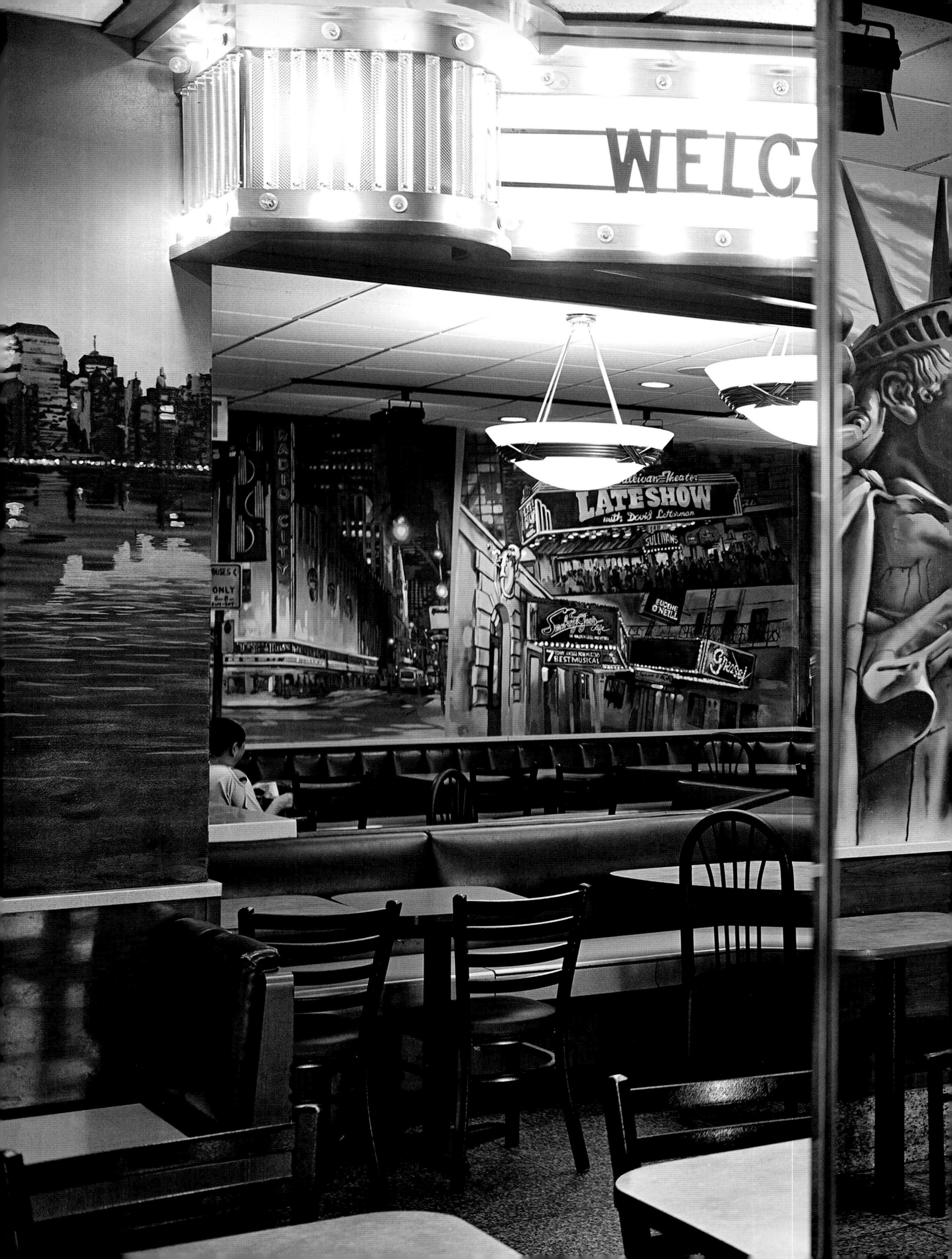

WELCO
RADIO CITY
LATE SHOW
with David Letterman
Sullivan Theater
SULLIVANS
EUGENE O'NEILL
7 BEST MUSICAL
Grease
ONLY

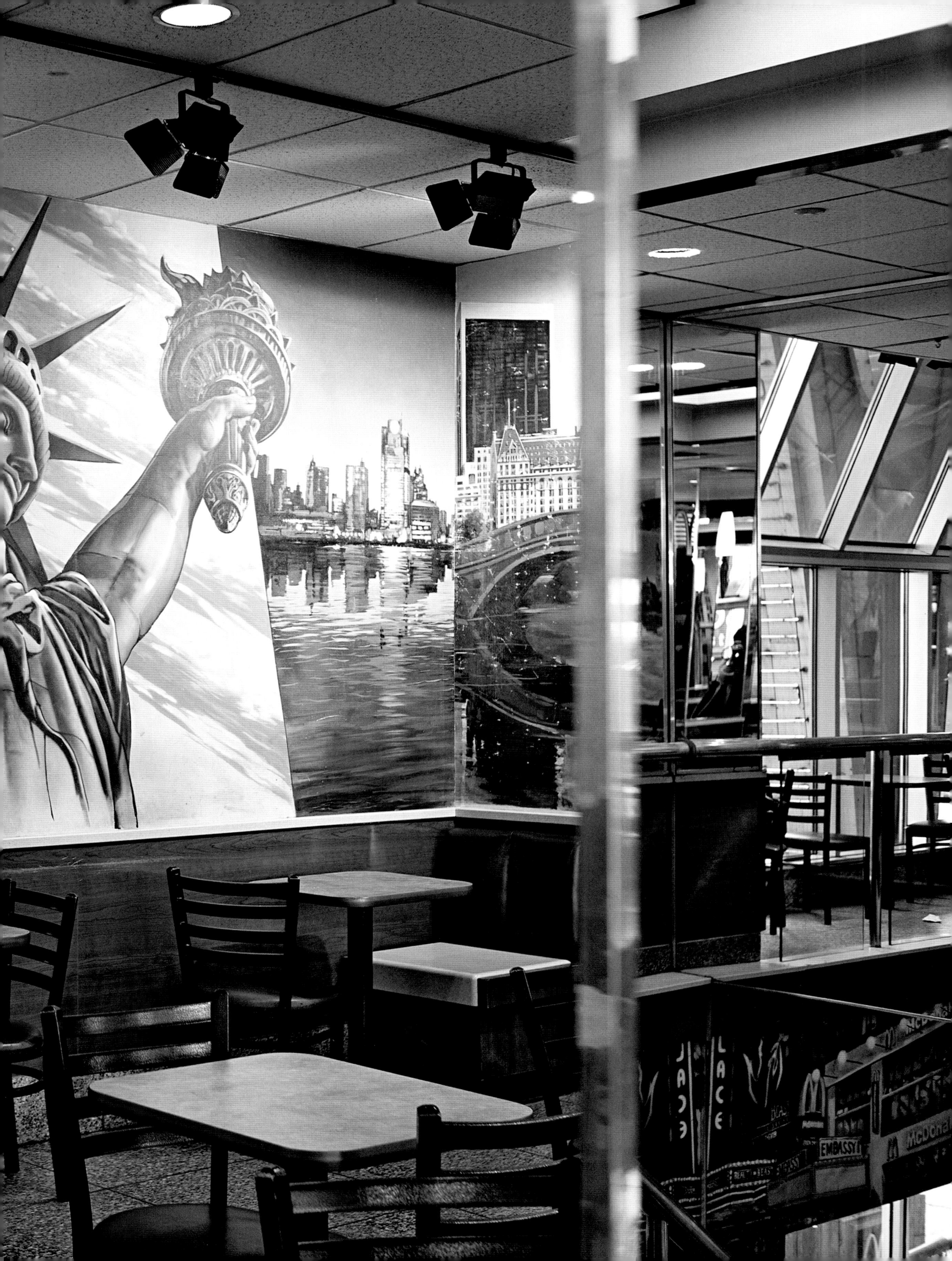

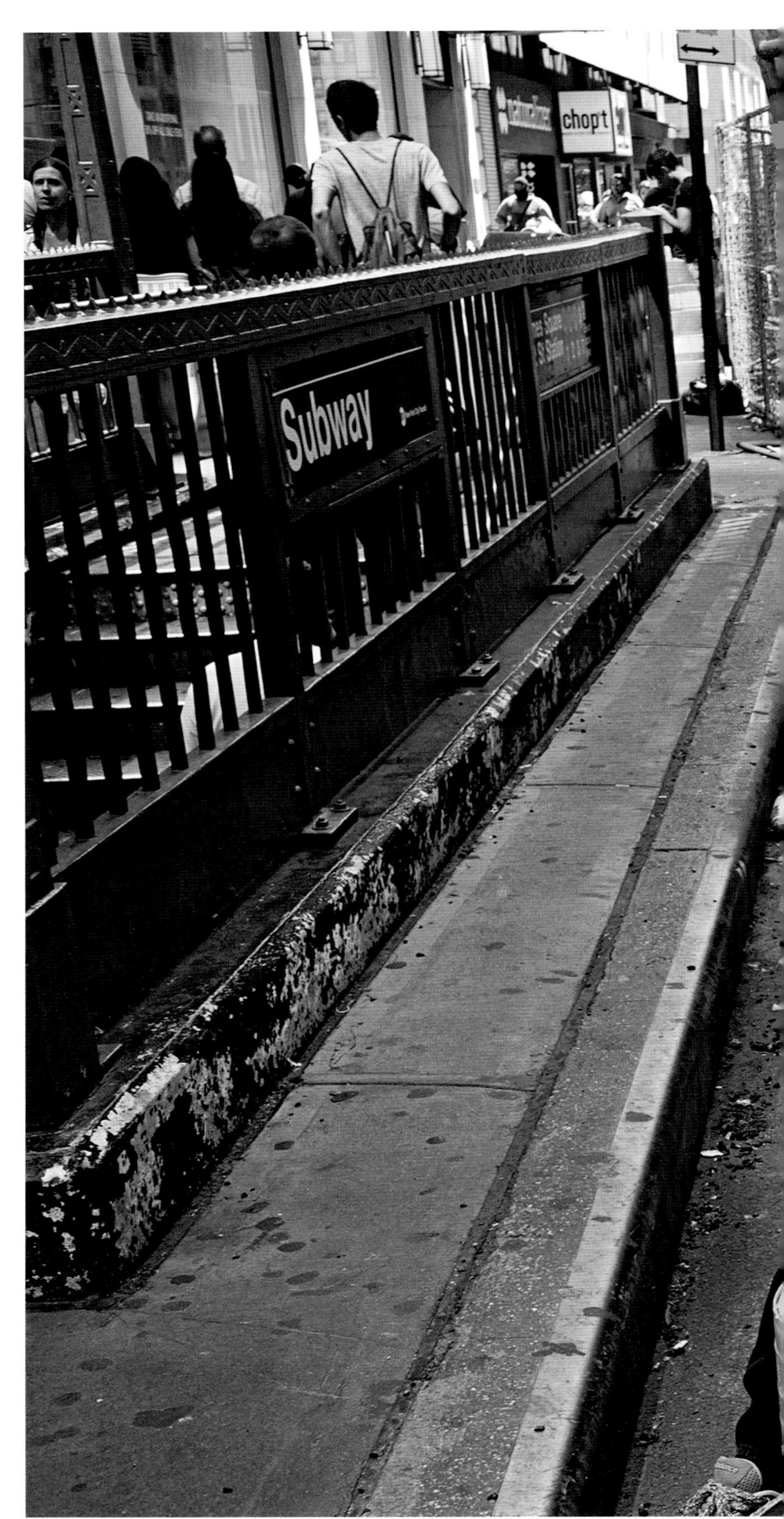

chopt
Subway

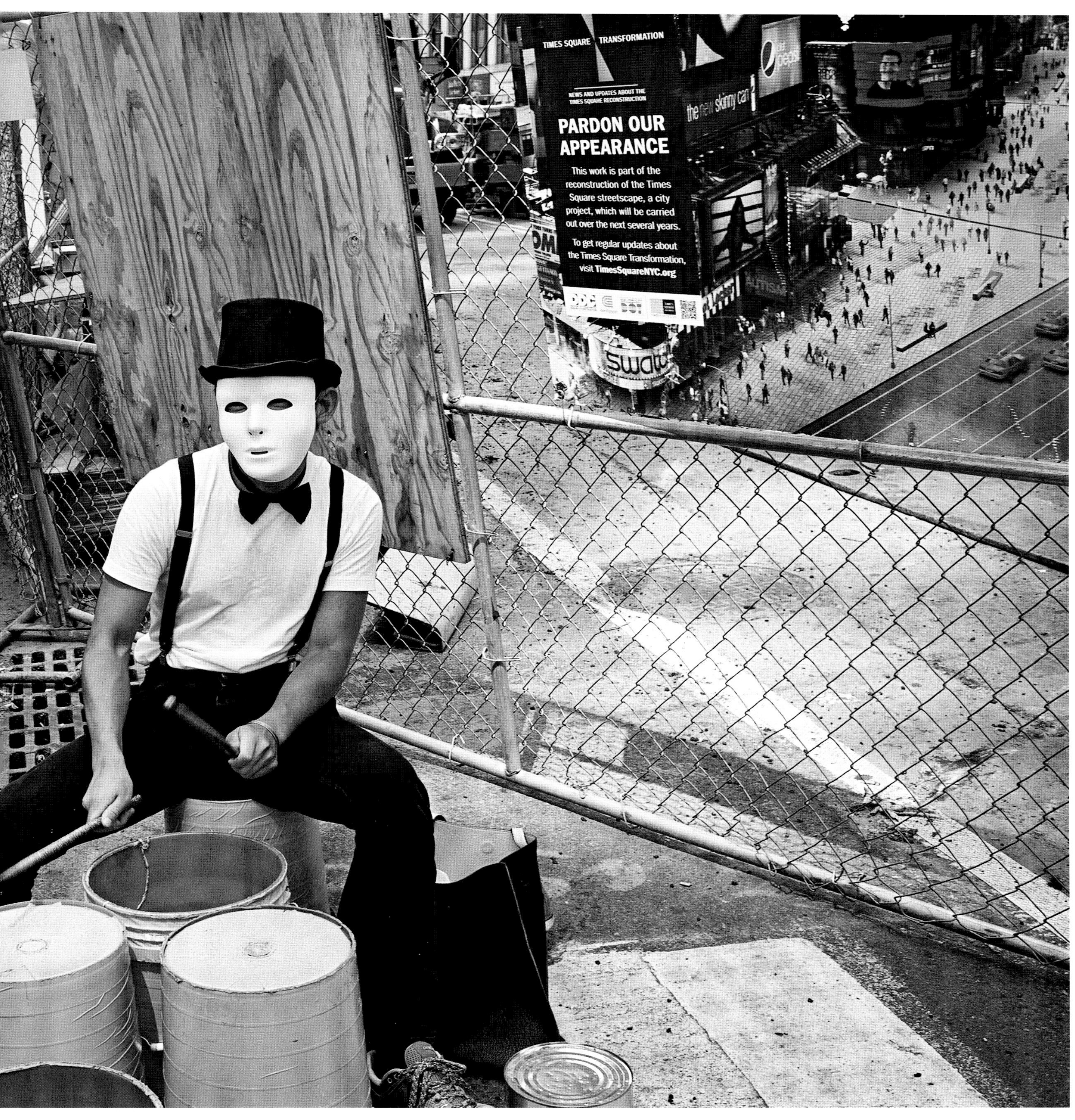

TIMES SQUARE   TRANSFORMATION

NEWS AND UPDATES ABOUT THE
TIMES SQUARE RECONSTRUCTION

PARDON OUR
APPEARANCE

This work is part of the
reconstruction of the Times
Square streetscape, a city
project, which will be carried
out over the next several years.

To get regular updates about
the Times Square Transformation,
visit TimesSquareNYC.org

the new skinny can

pepsi

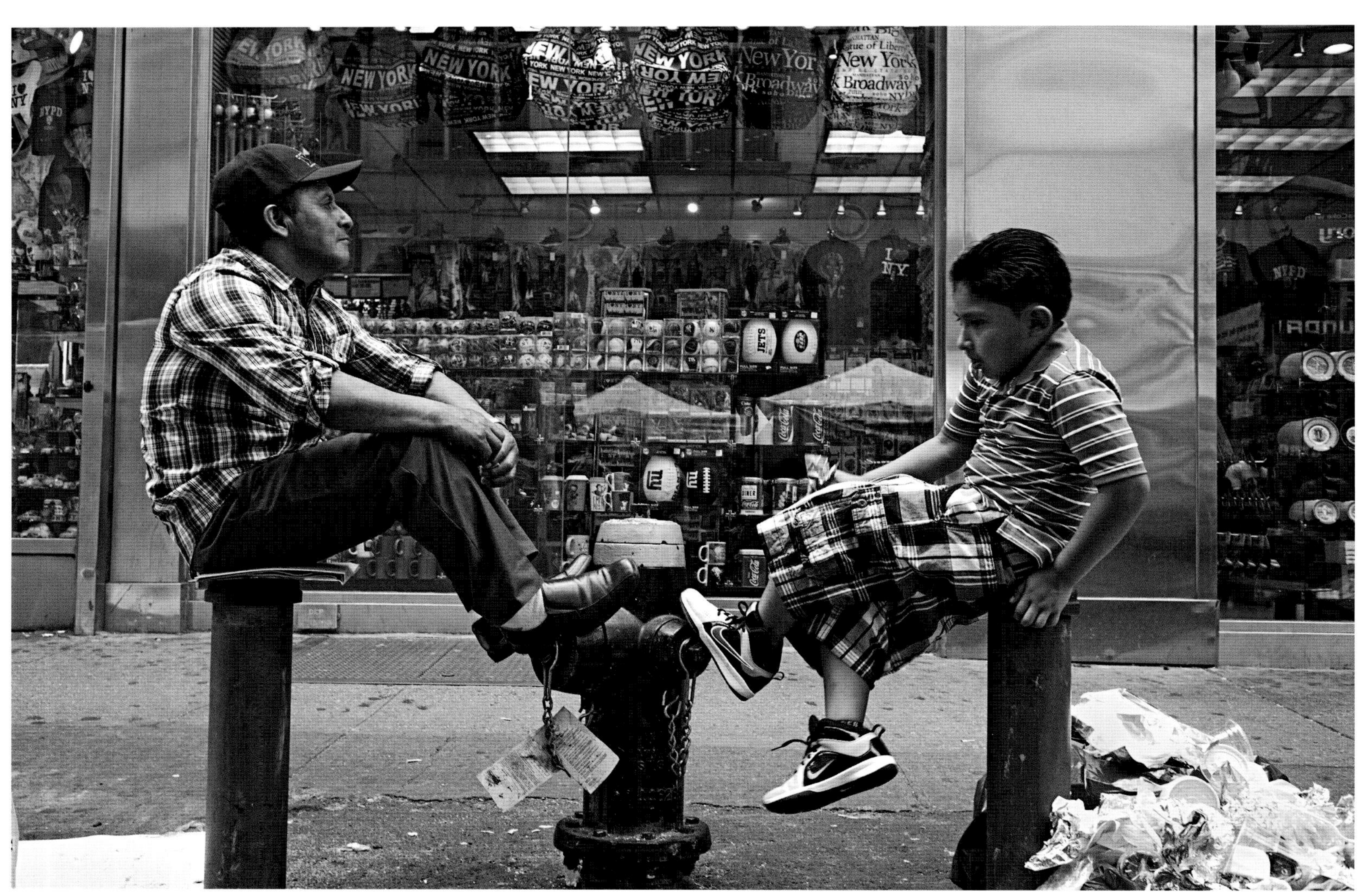

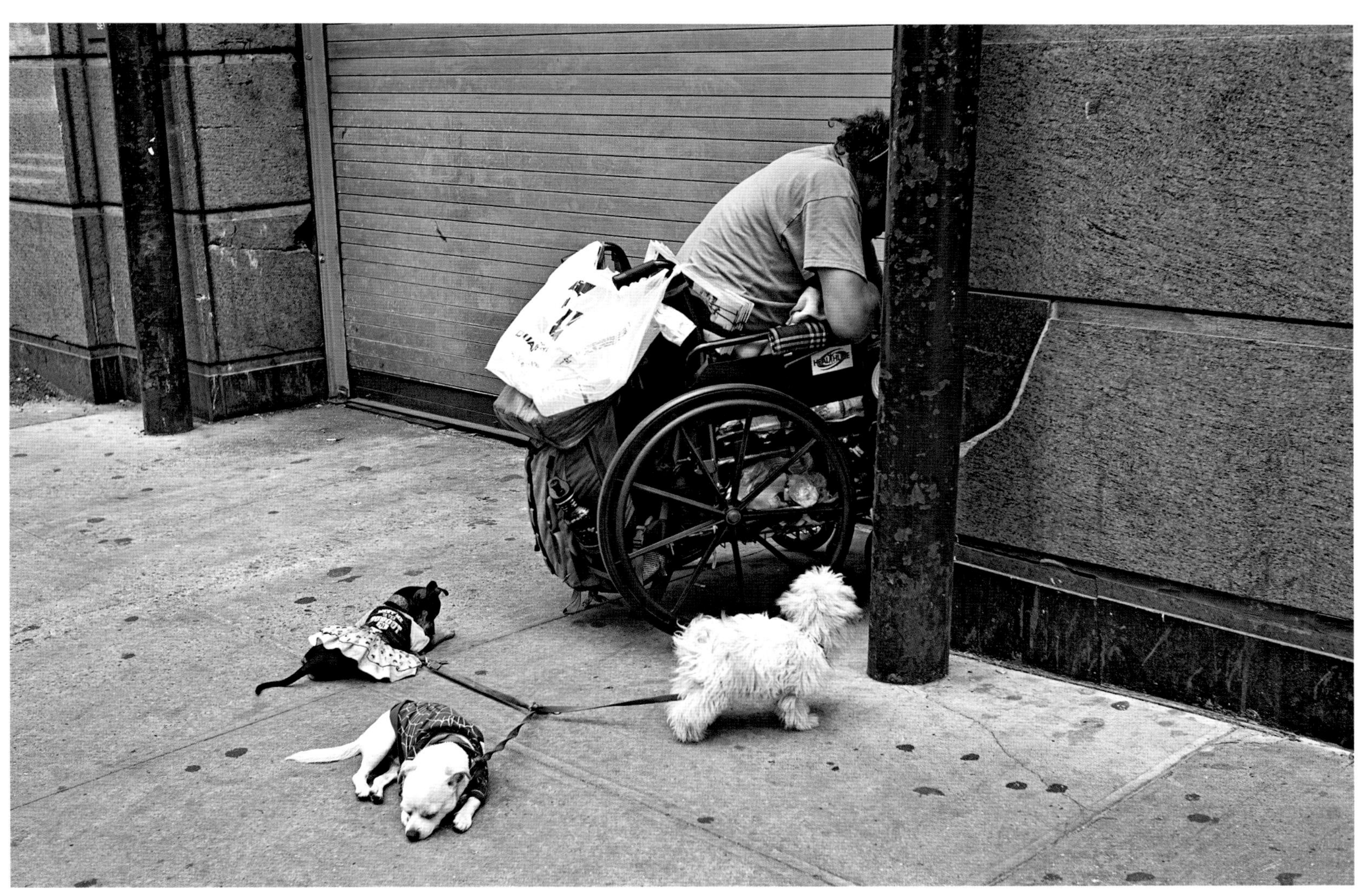

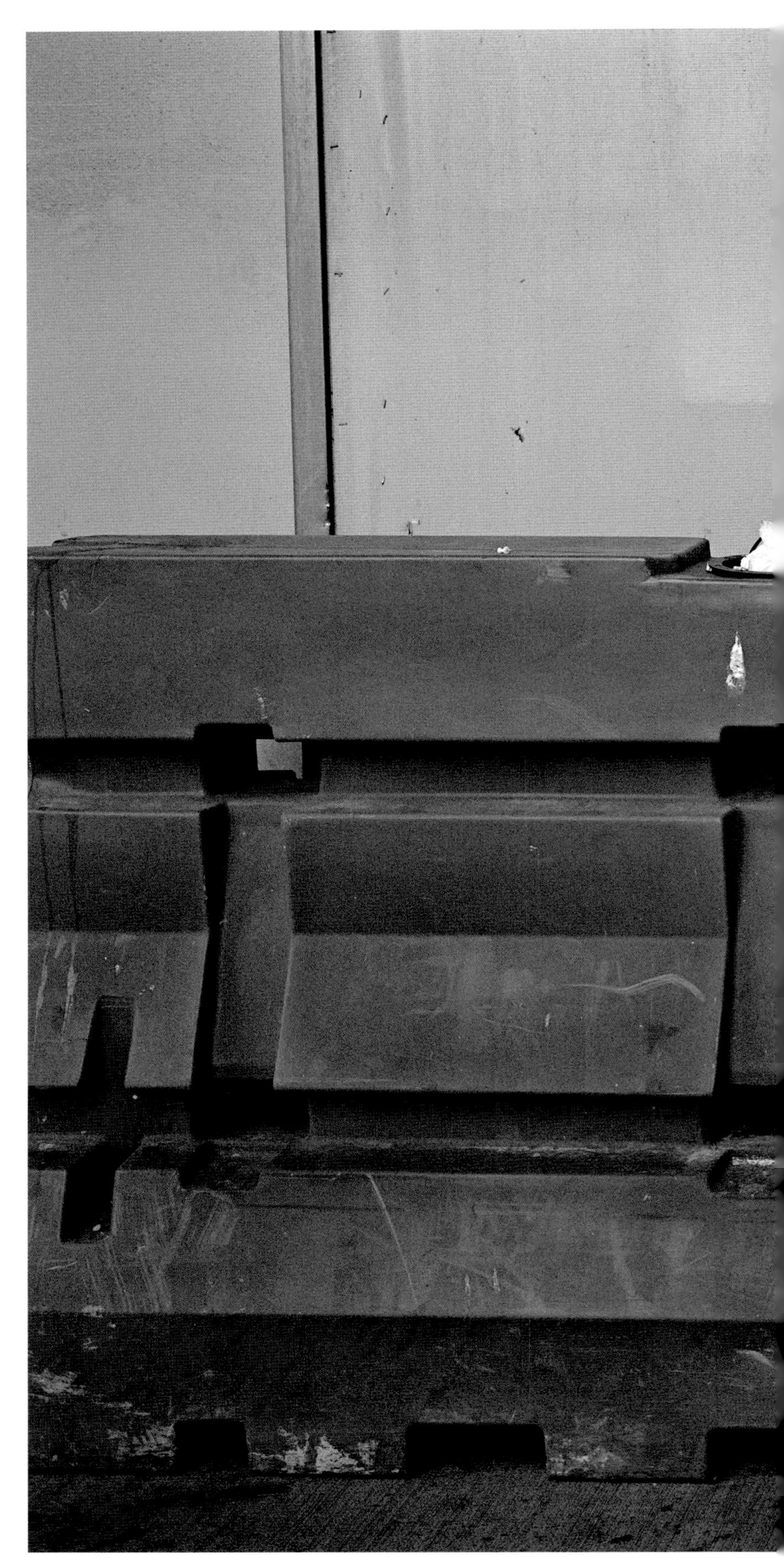

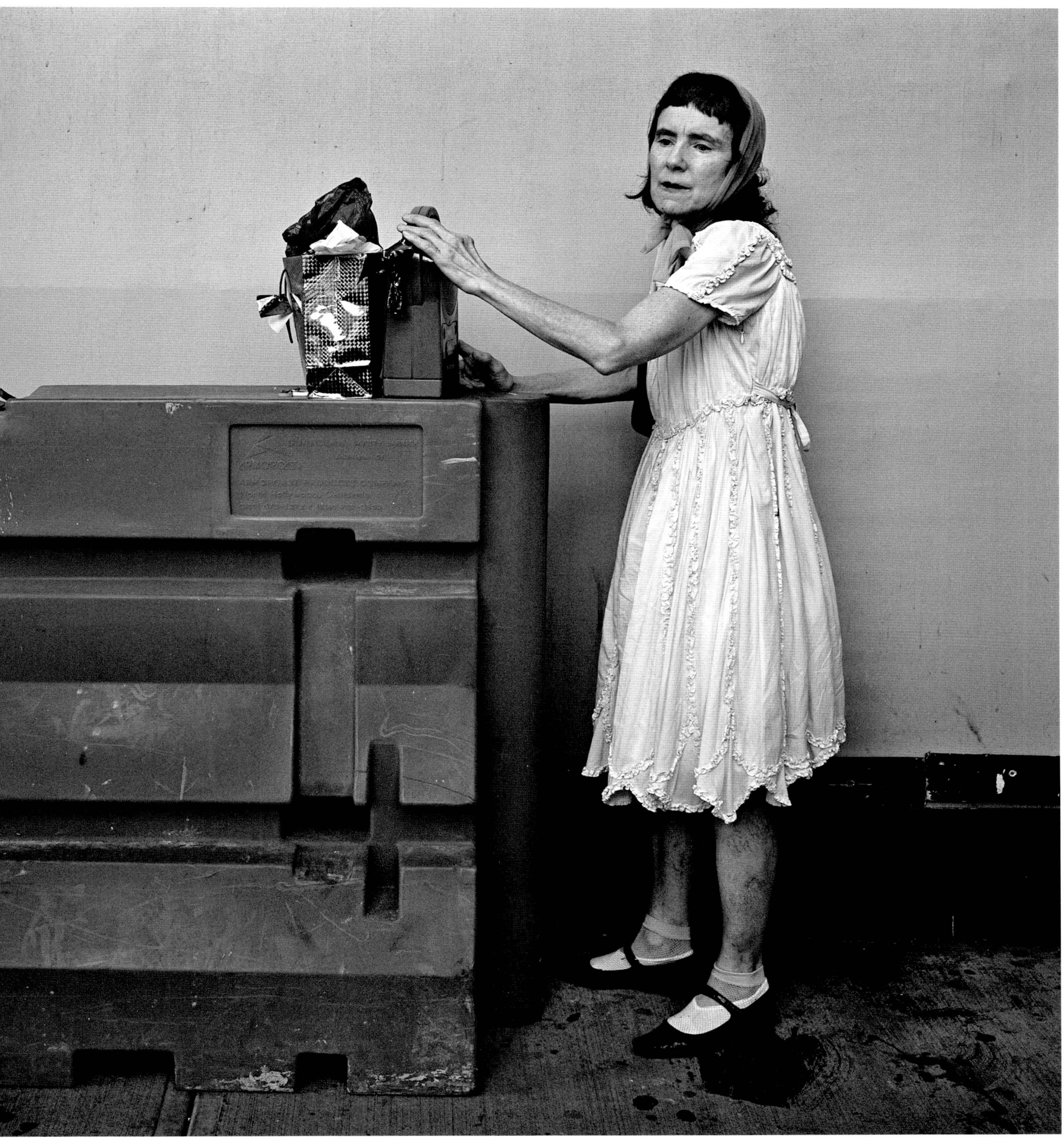

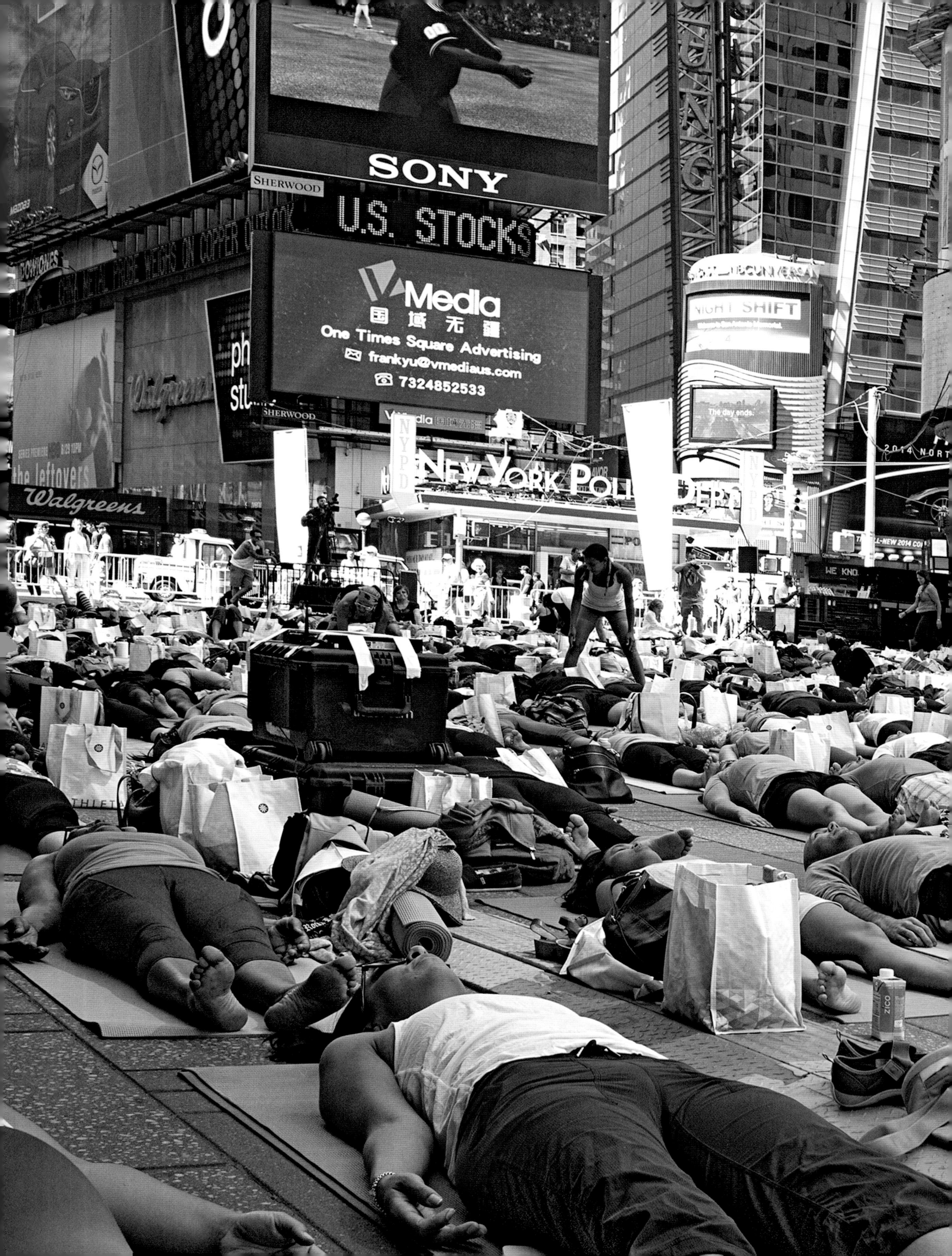
SONY
SHERWOOD
U.S. STOCKS
VMedia
国域无疆
One Times Square Advertising
frankyu@vmediaus.com
7324852533
SHERWOOD
VMedia 国域无疆
NYPD
New York Police Dep
NIGHT SHIFT
The day ends.
2014 NORT
WE KNO
Walgreens
the leftovers
THE ALL-NEW 2014 CO
zico

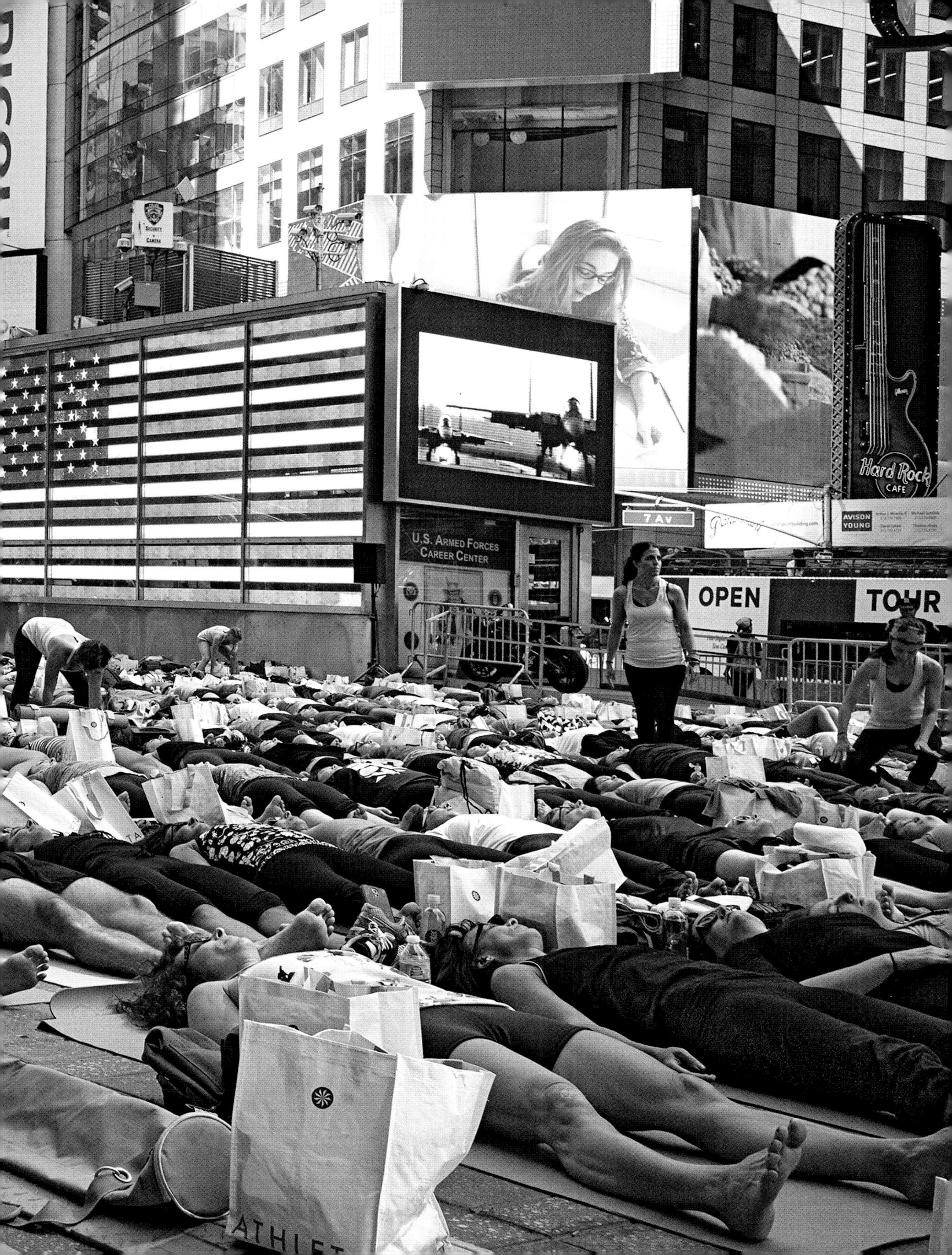

SECURITY
CAMERA
Hard Rock
CAFE
7 Av
AVISON
YOUNG
U.S. ARMED FORCES
CAREER CENTER
OPEN
TOUR
ATHLET

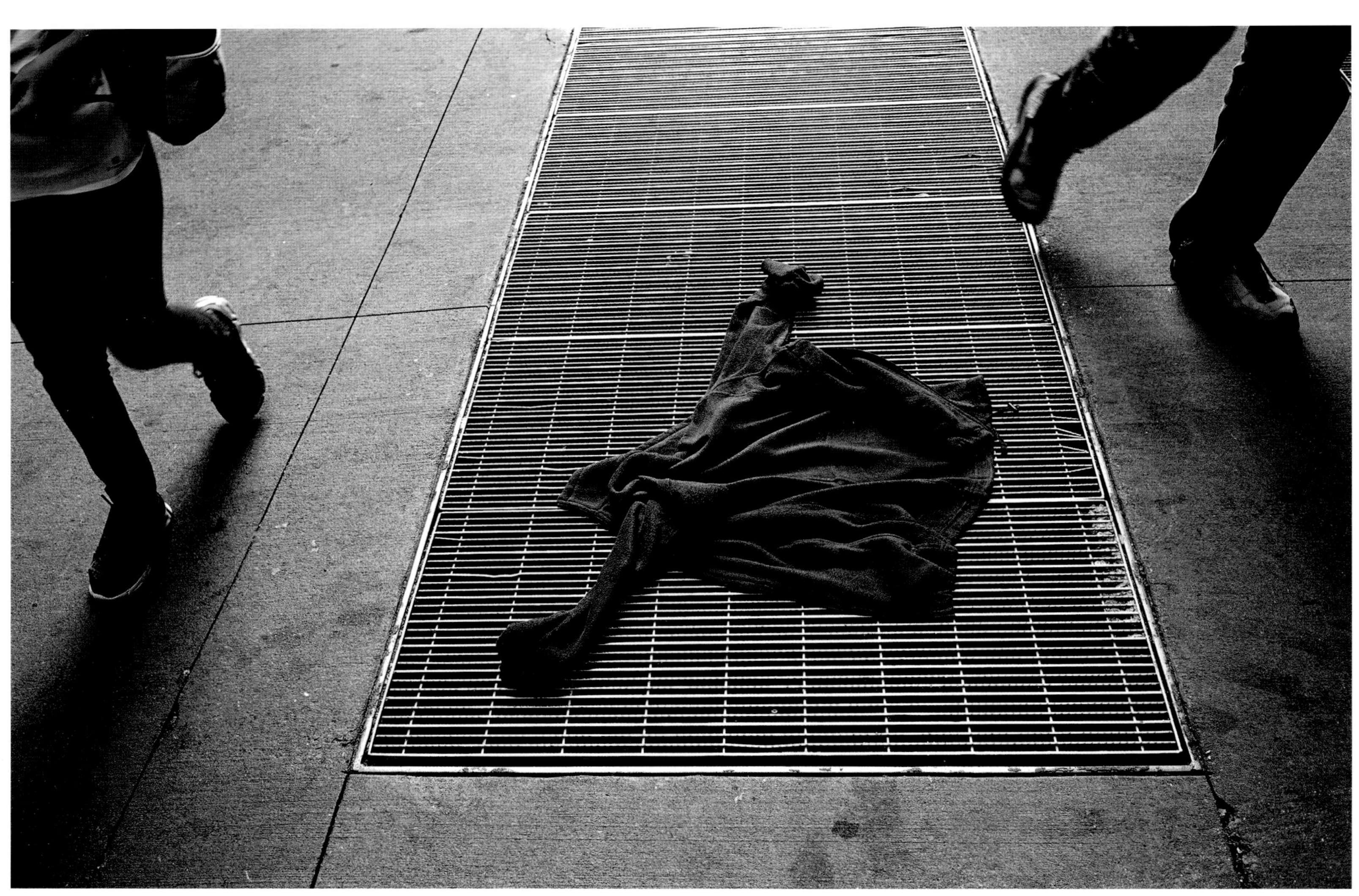

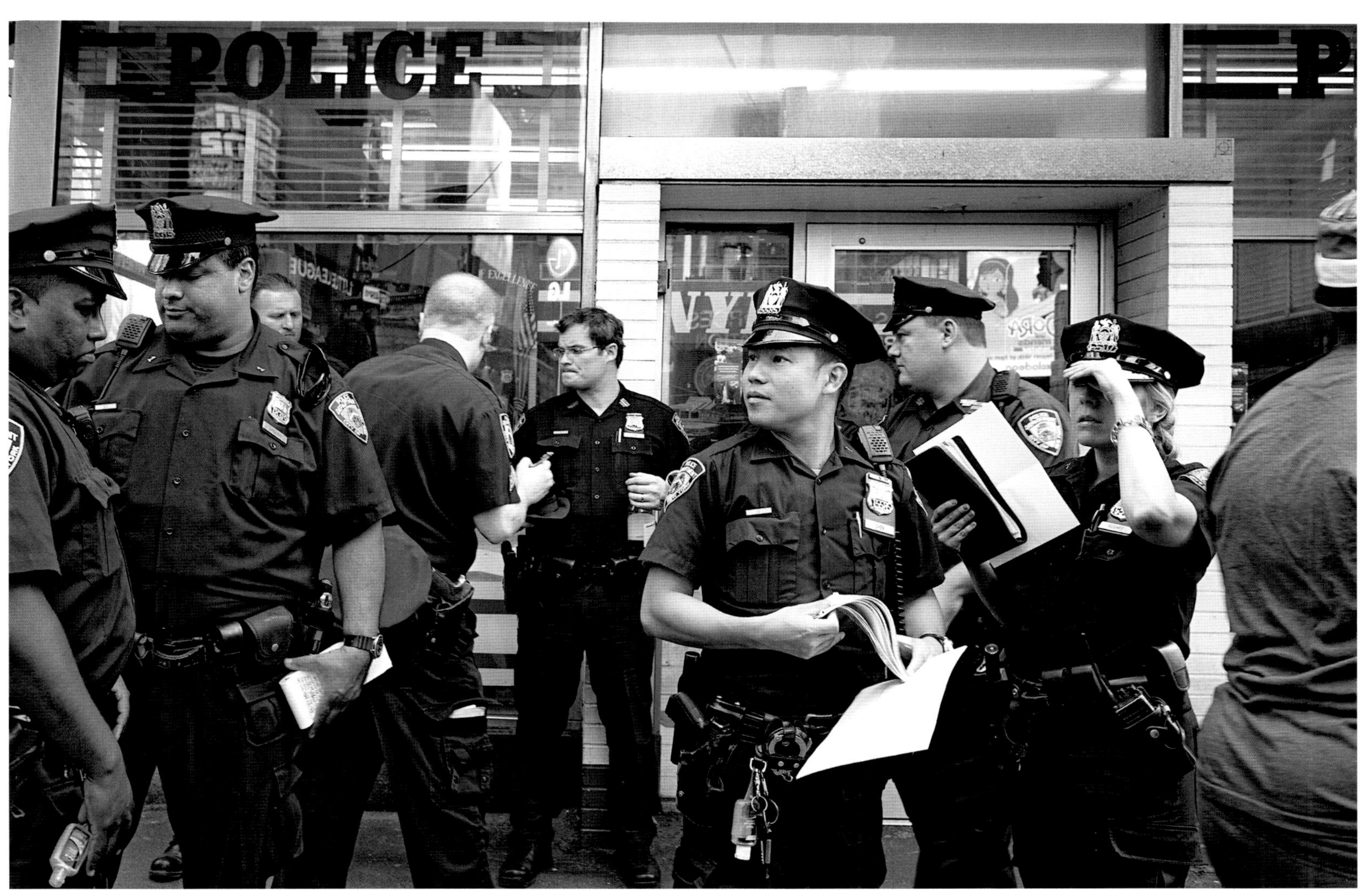

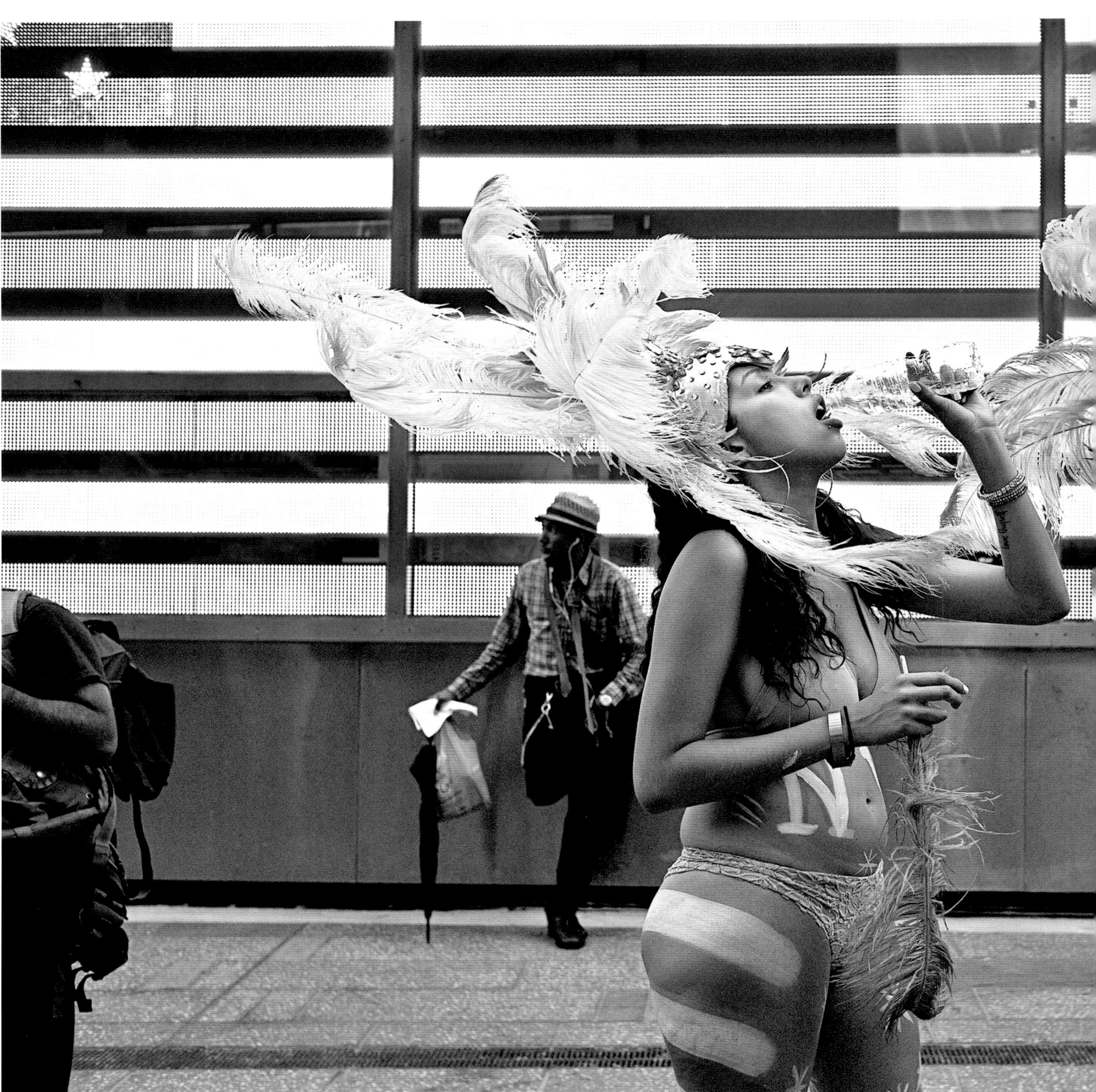

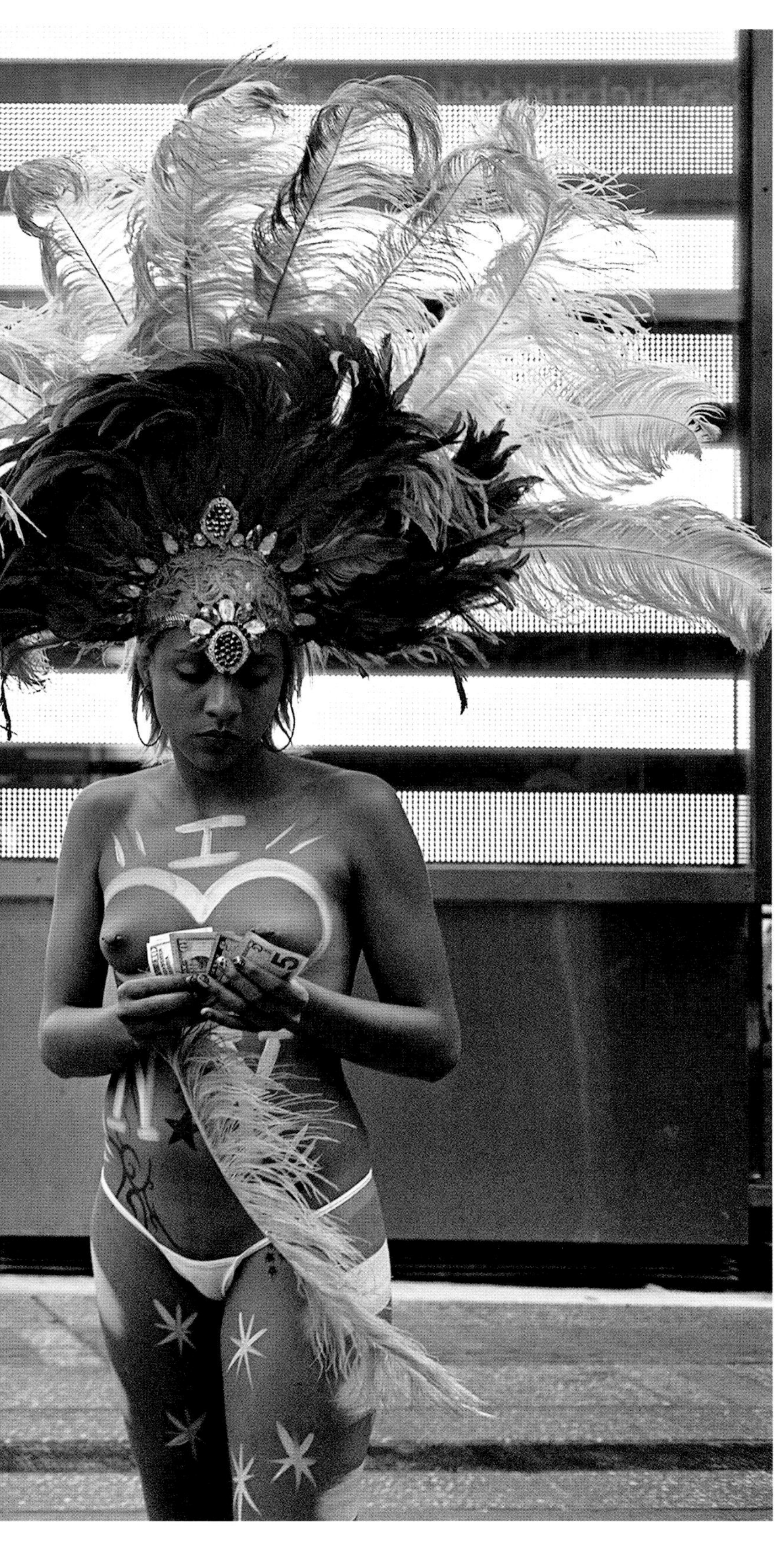

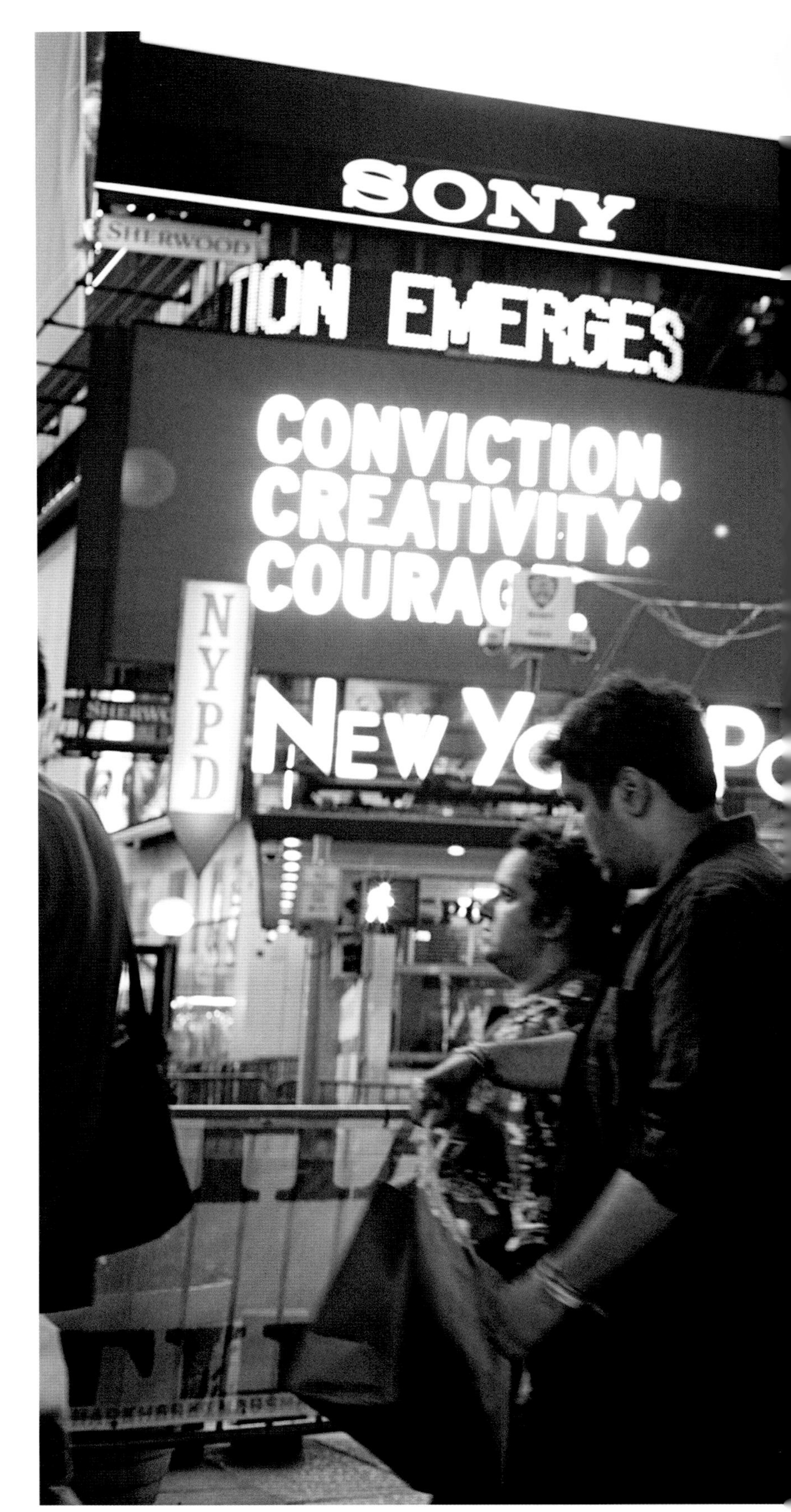
SONY
SHERWOOD
TION EMERGES
CONVICTION.
CREATIVITY.
COURAG
NYPD
New Yo
Po

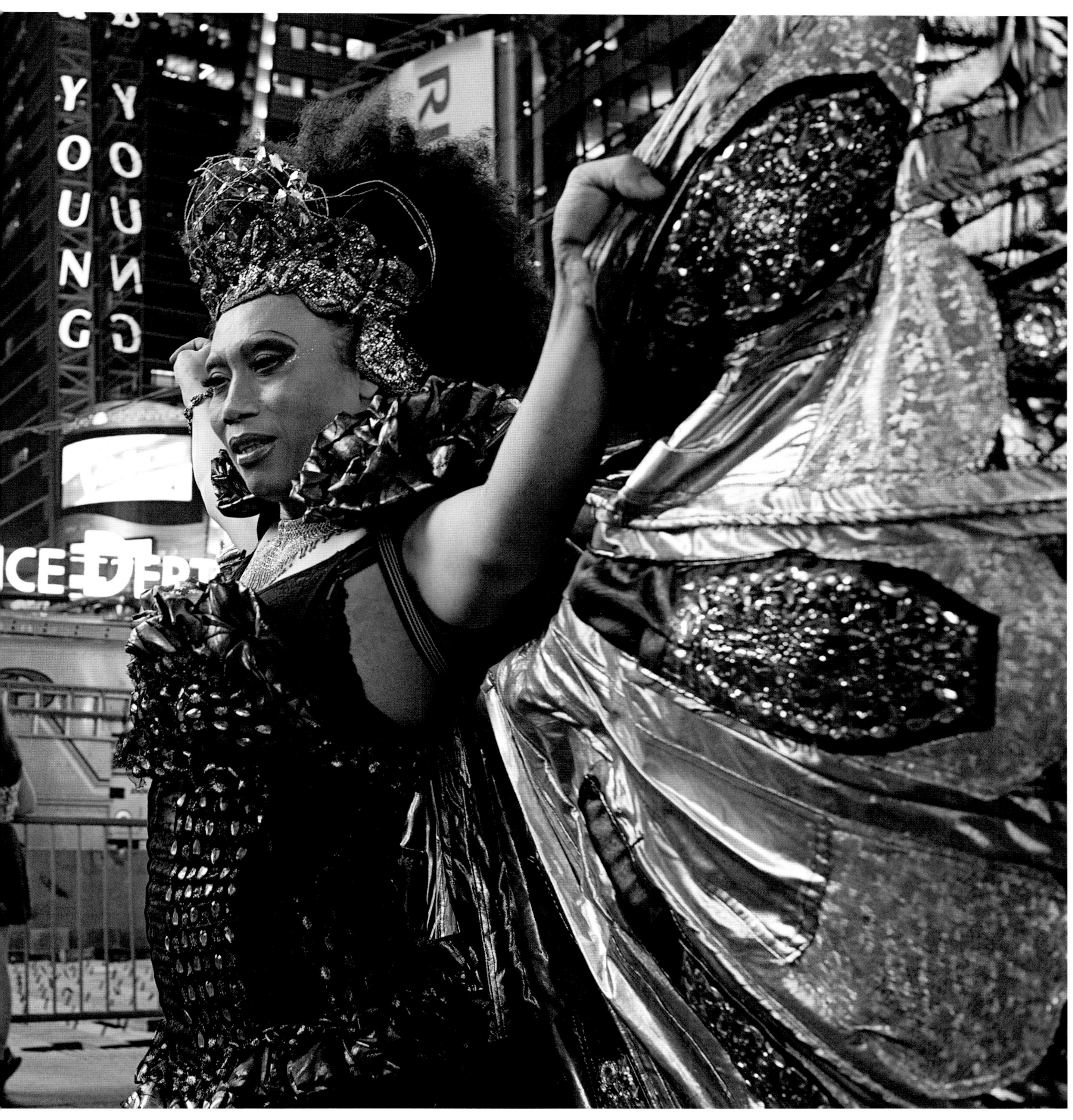

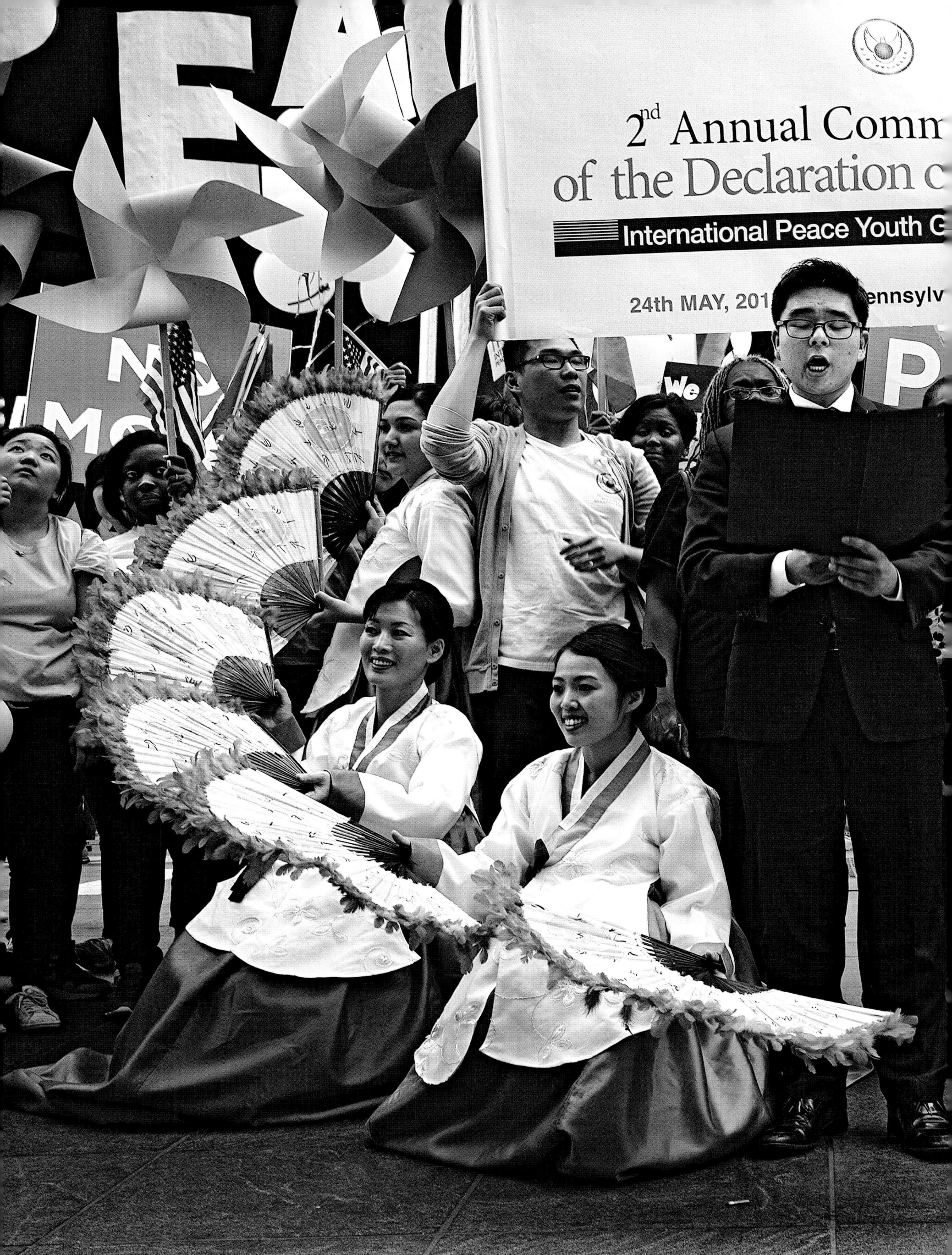

PEACE
2ⁿᵈ Annual Comm
of the Declaration c
International Peace Youth G
24th MAY, 201   ennsylv
We

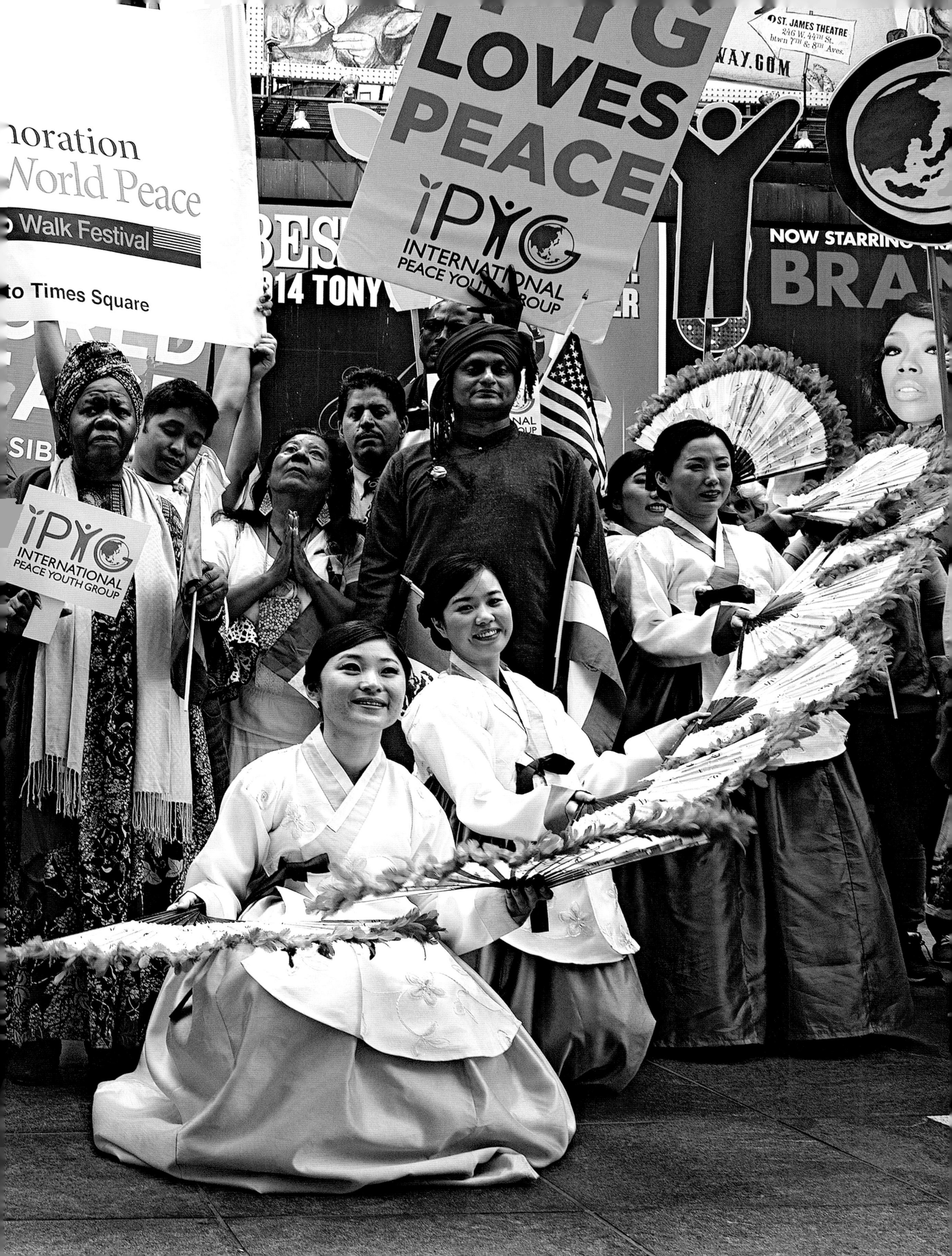
LOVES
PEACE
iPYG
INTERNATIONAL
PEACE YOUTH GROUP
iPYG
INTERNATIONAL
PEACE YOUTH GROUP
moration
World Peace
Walk Festival
to Times Square
ST. JAMES THEATRE
246 W. 44th St.
btwn 7th & 8th Aves.
WAY.COM
2014 TONY
NOW STARRING
BRA

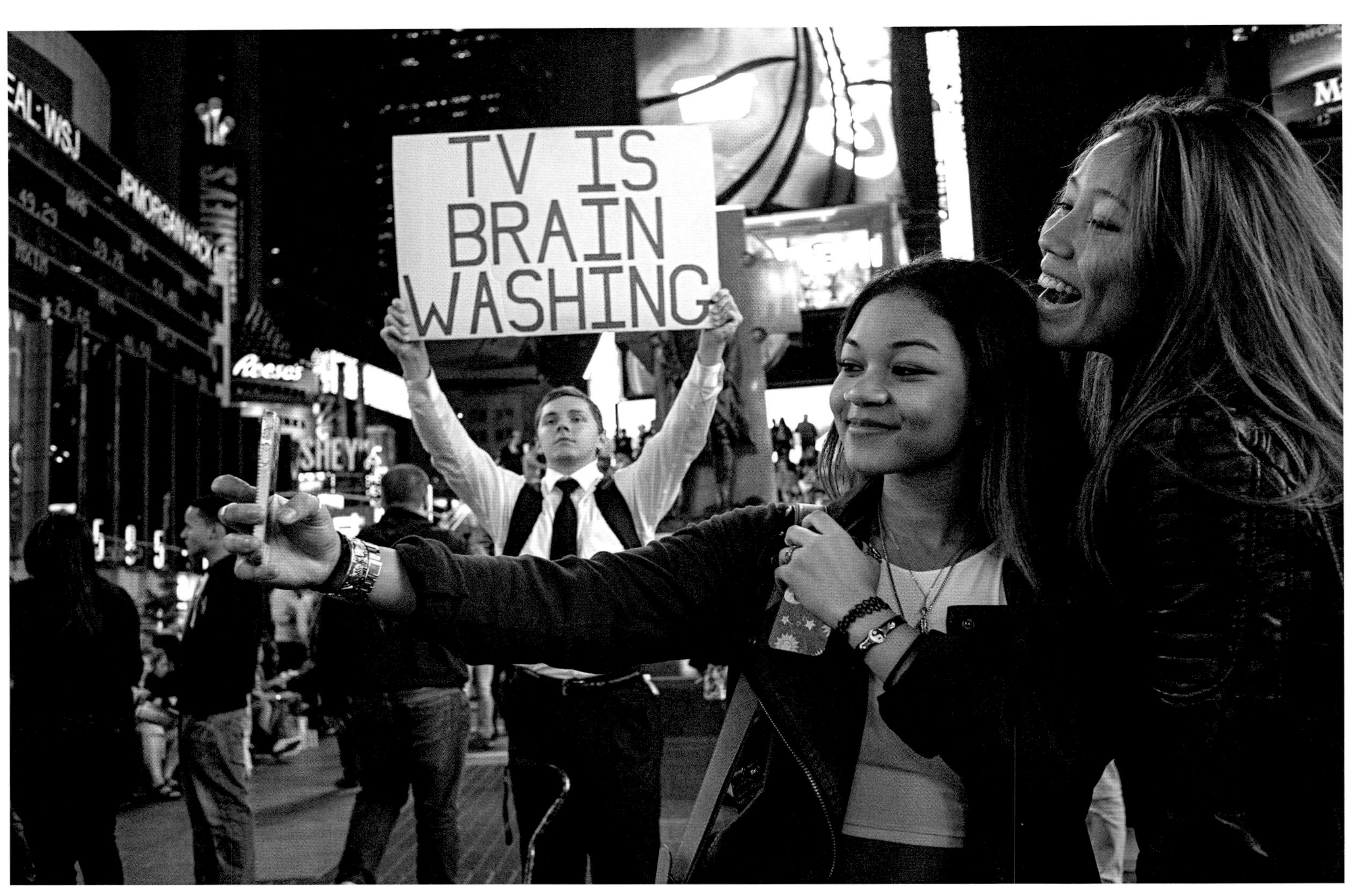

TV IS
BRAIN
WASHING

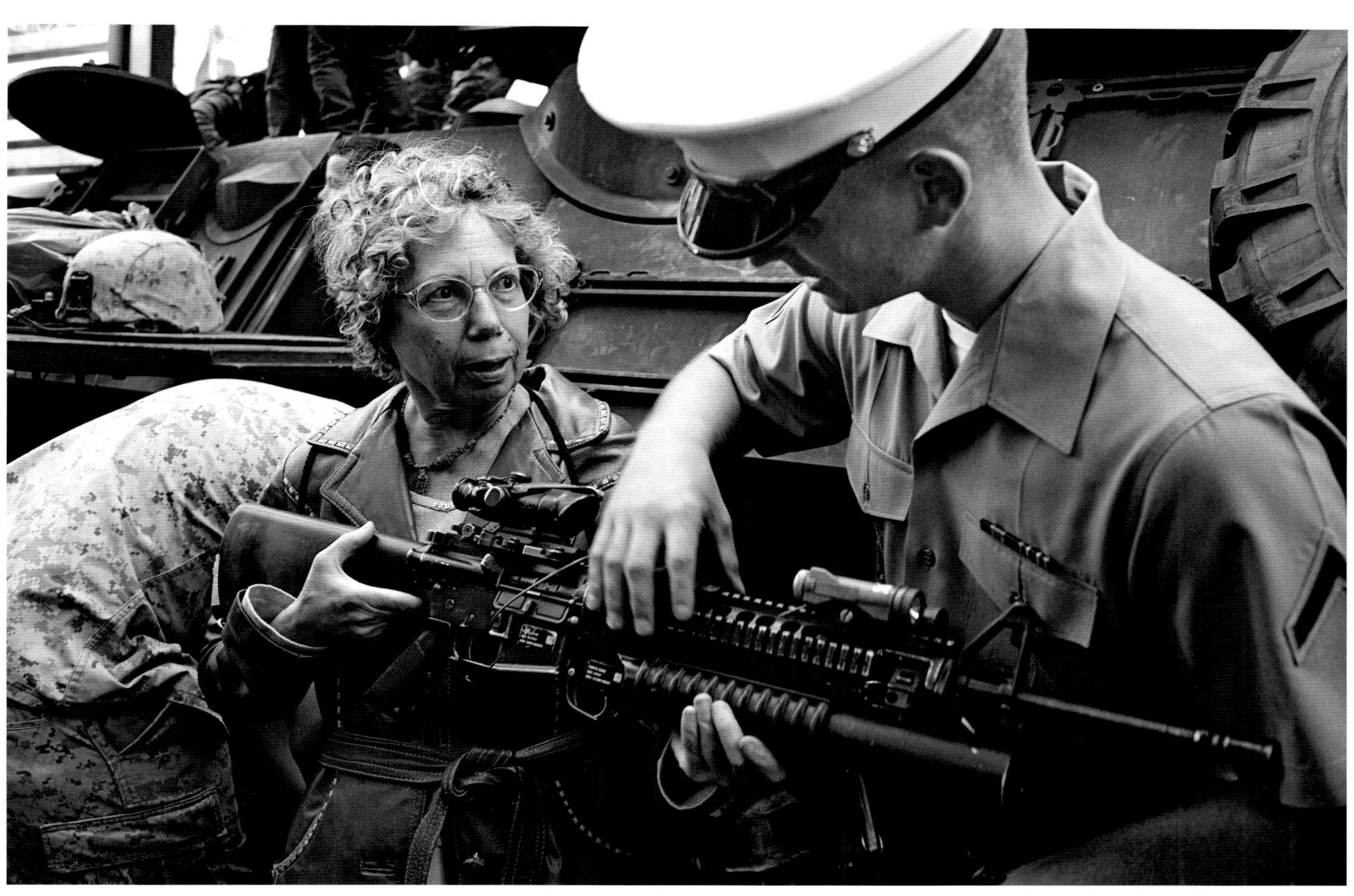

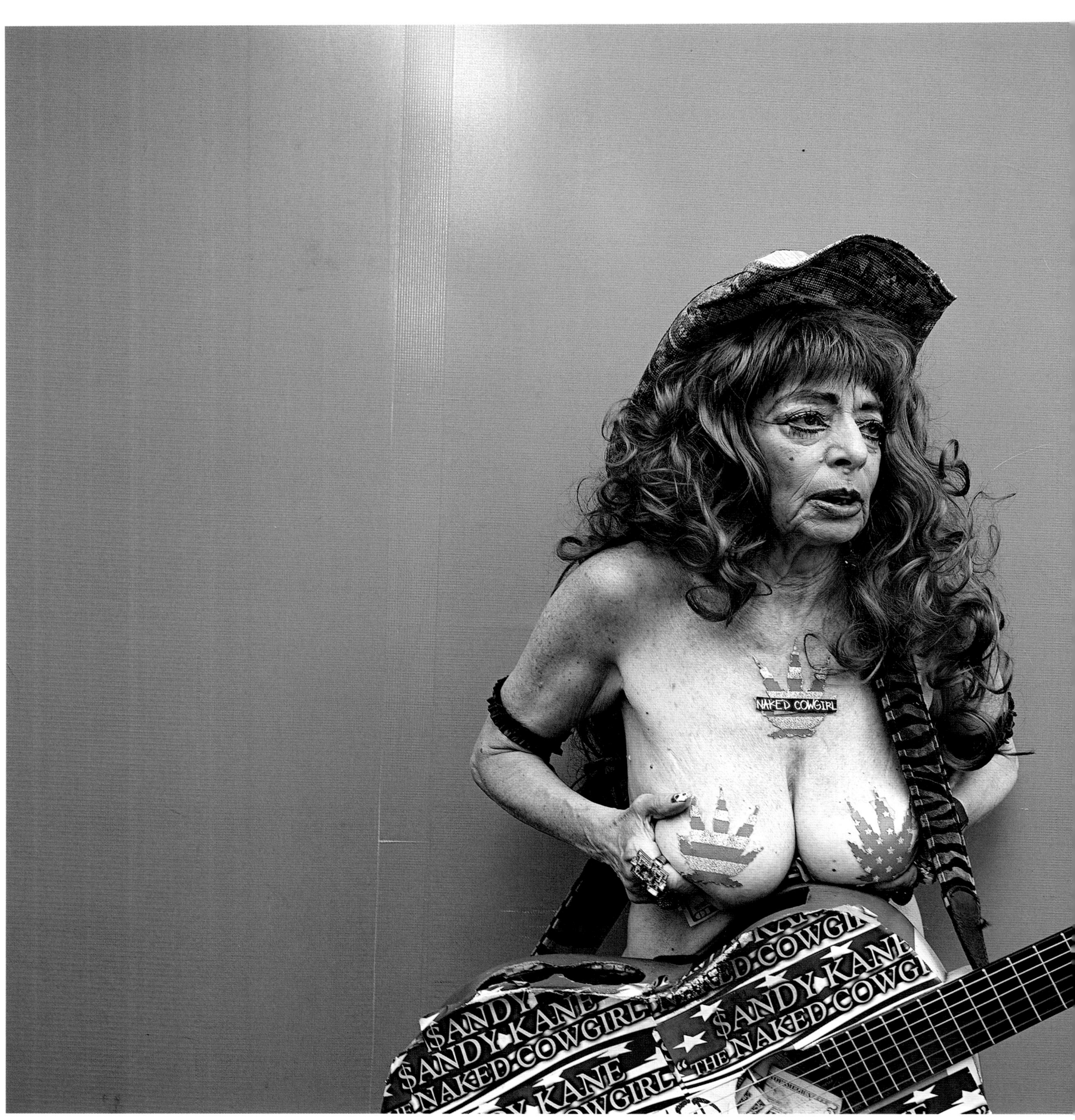

NAKED COWGIRL
$ANDY KANE
$ANDY KANE
THE NAKED COWGIRL
SANDY KANE
COWGIRL THE NAKED COWGI

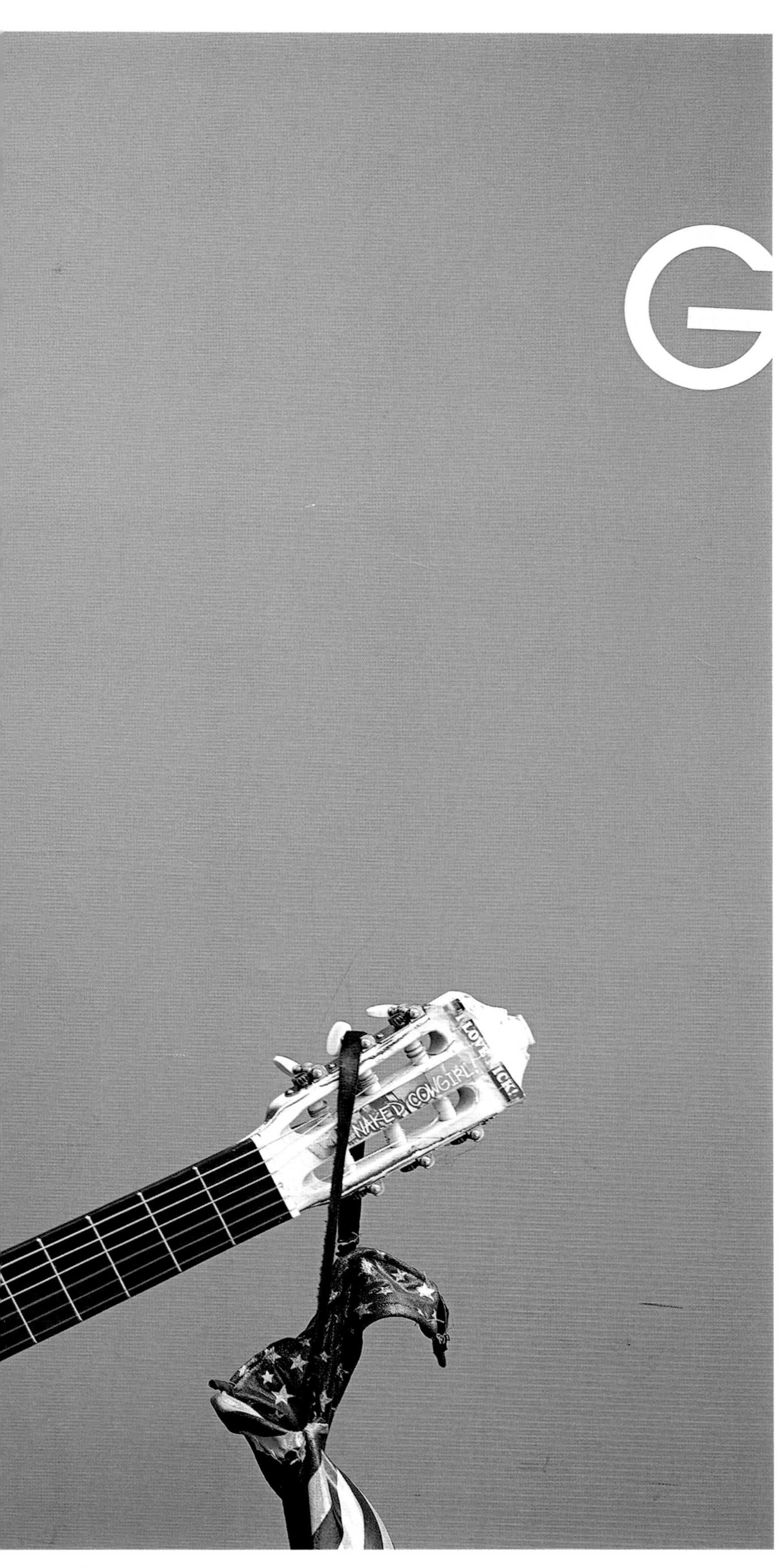
NAKED COWGIRL

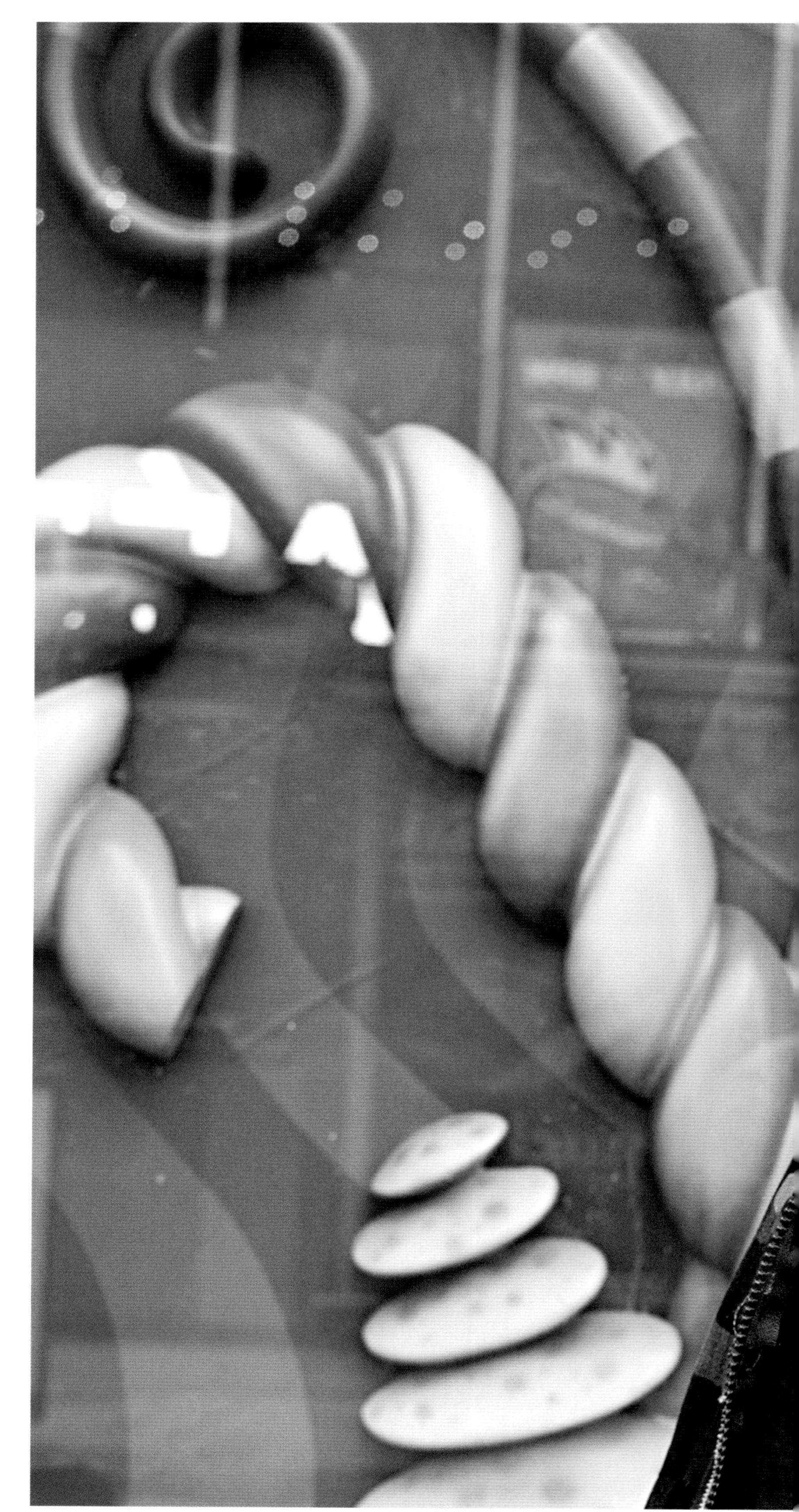

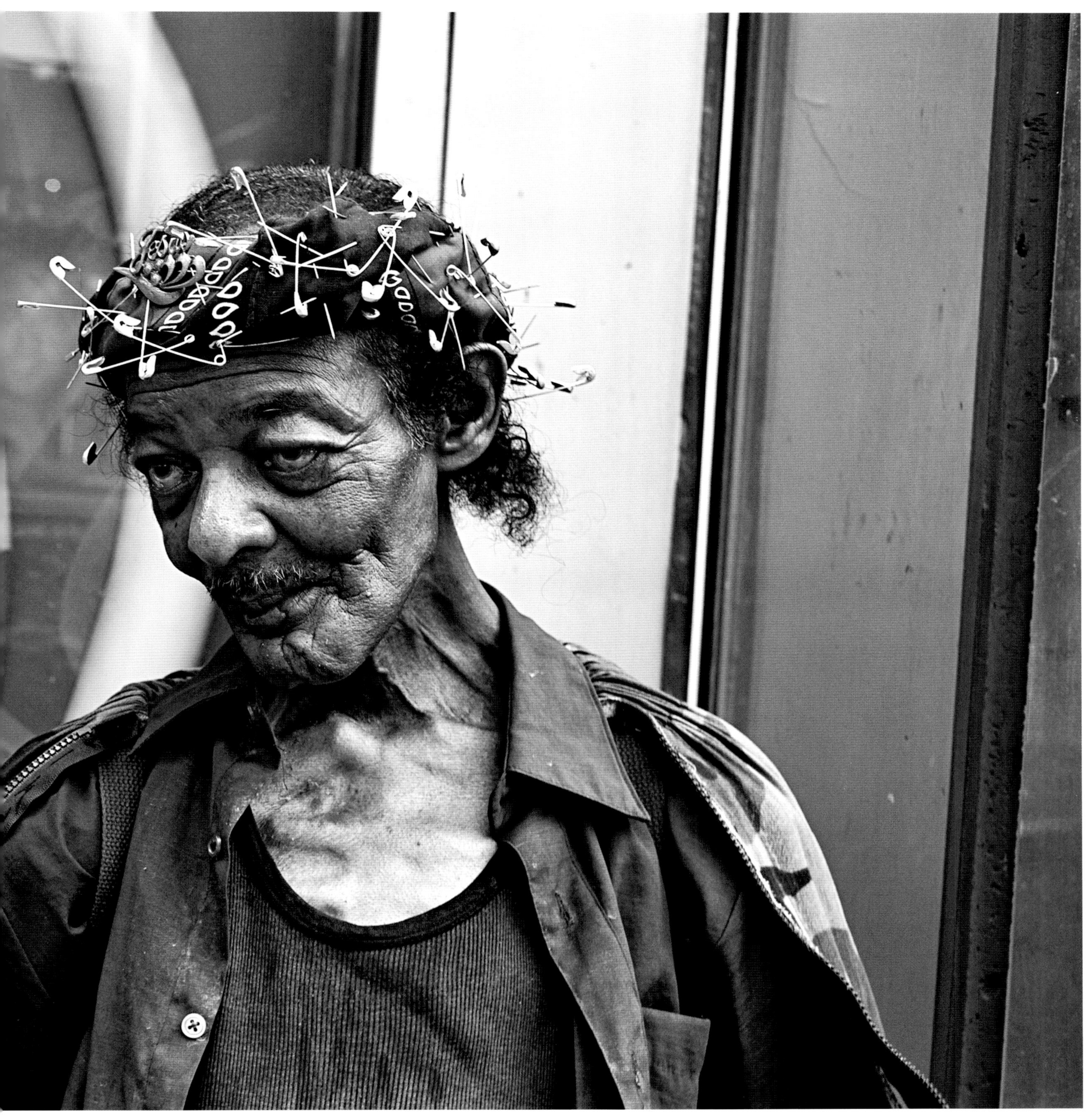

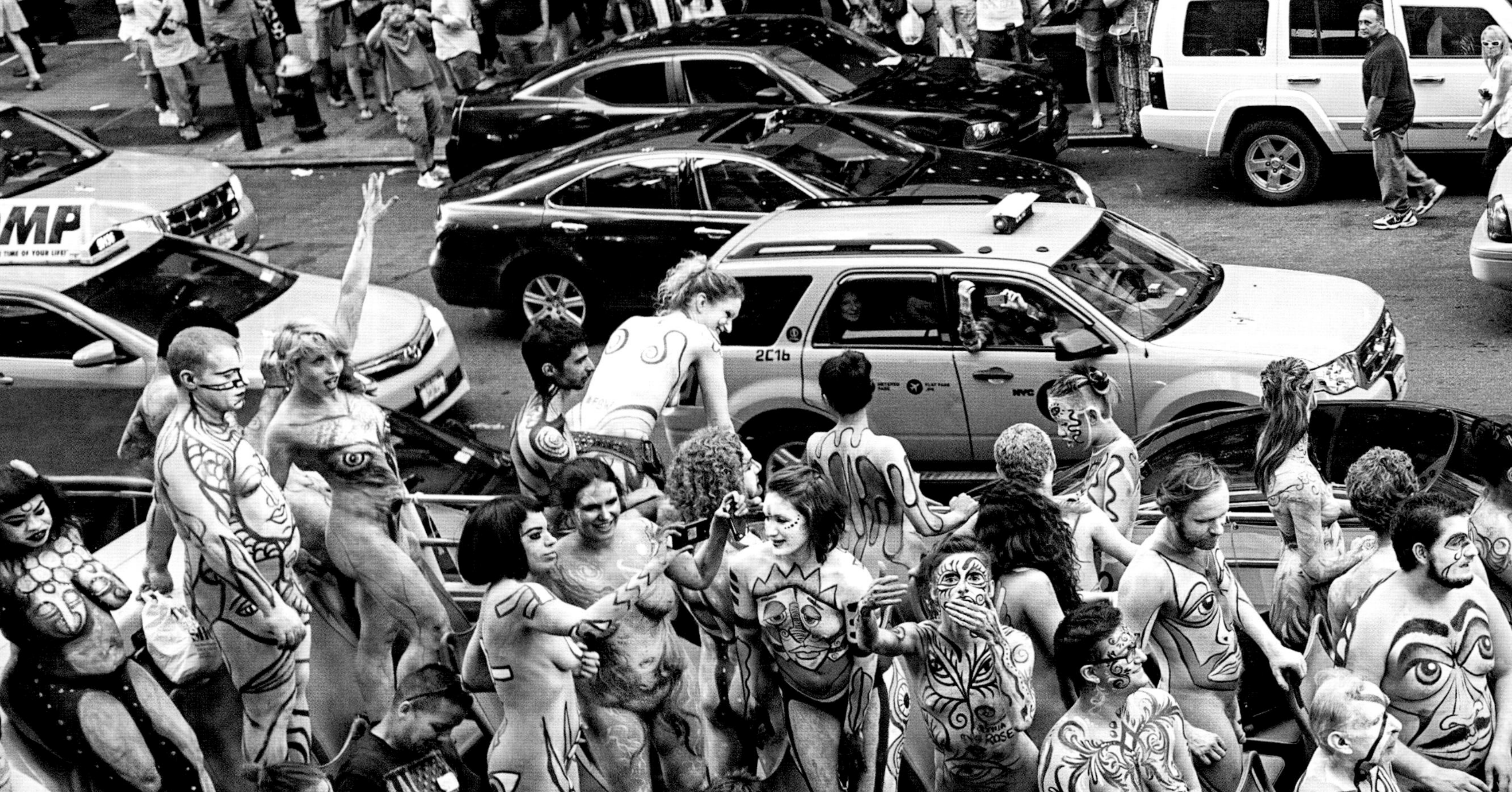

BRUNCH · DINNER
Bud & Bud Li...
$4 Pints
all day all night
TAVERN
AR · RESTAURANT · KARA
723
MP
2C16
NYC · BODYPA
hosted by: Andy Golub
KRYOLAN
PROFESSIONAL MAKE-UP
JERRY'S
International Palette Shop
YOUNG NATURIST

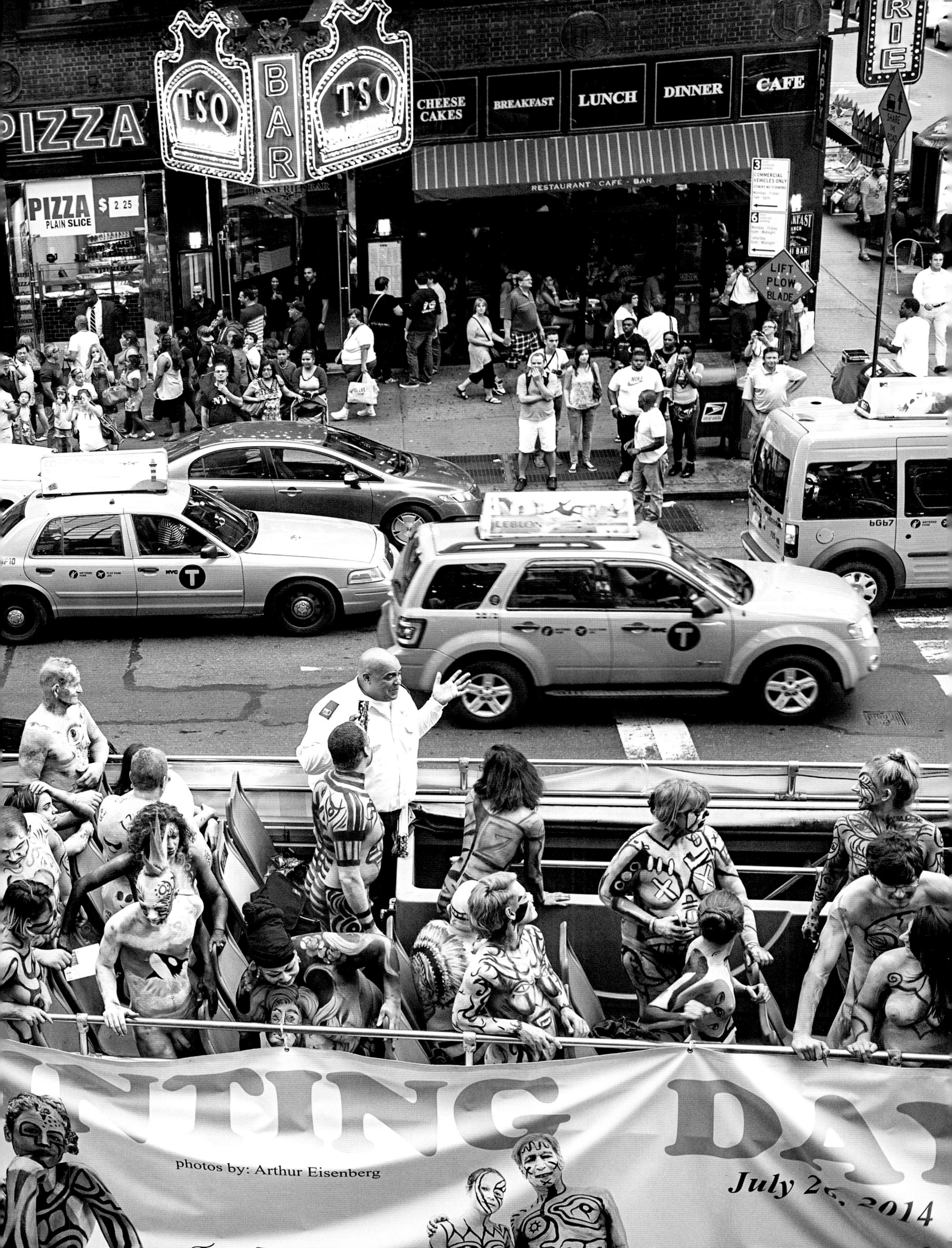

PIZZA
TSQ BAR TSQ
CHEESE CAKES
BREAKFAST
LUNCH
DINNER
CAFE
RIE
PIZZA
PLAIN SLICE
$2.25
RESTAURANT · CAFE · BAR
LIFT PLOW BLADE
SHARE THE ROAD
COMMERCIAL VEHICLES ONLY
NYC T
photos by: Arthur Eisenberg
July 26, 2014

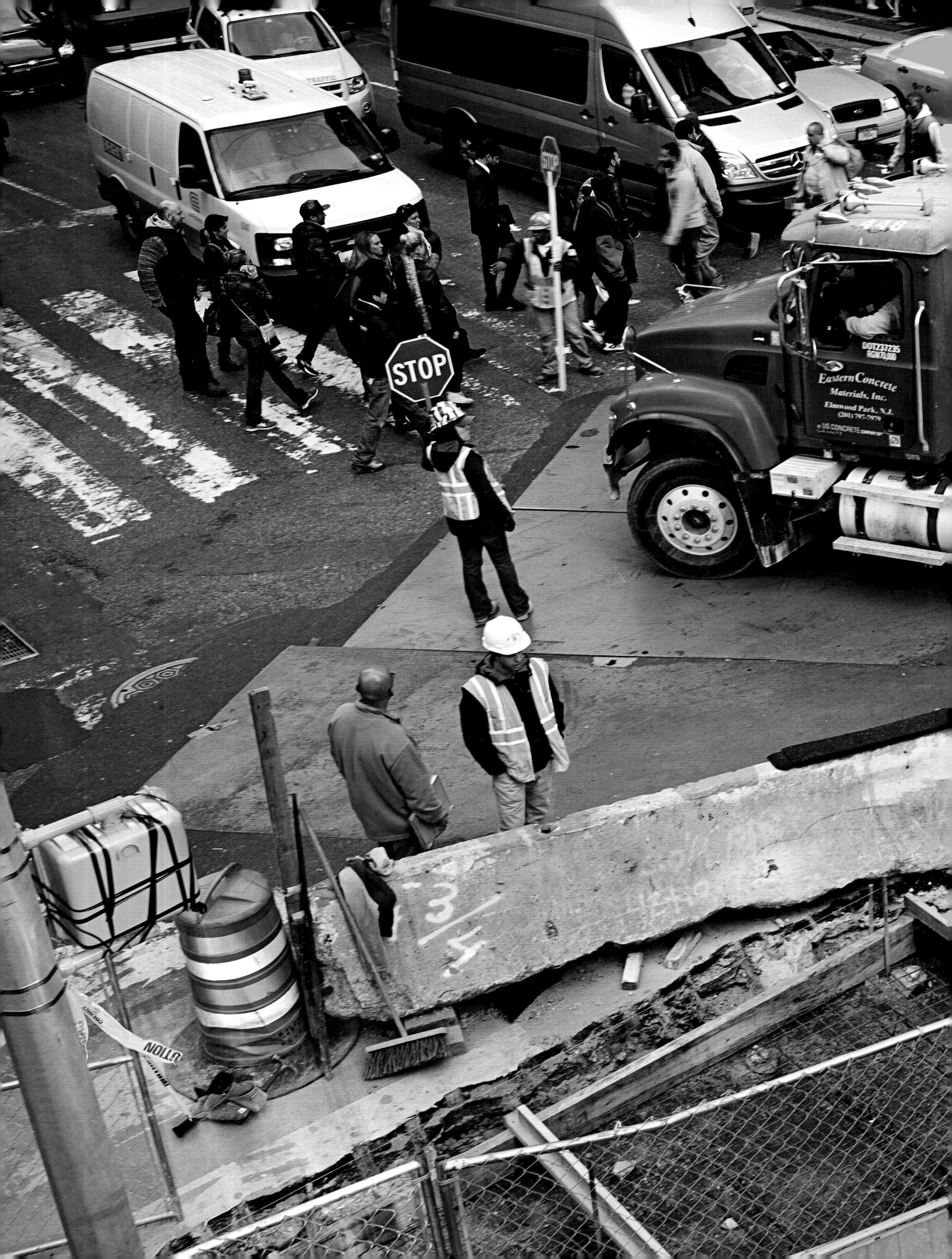

STOP
Eastern Concrete
Materials, Inc.
Elmwood Park, N.J.
448
CAUTION

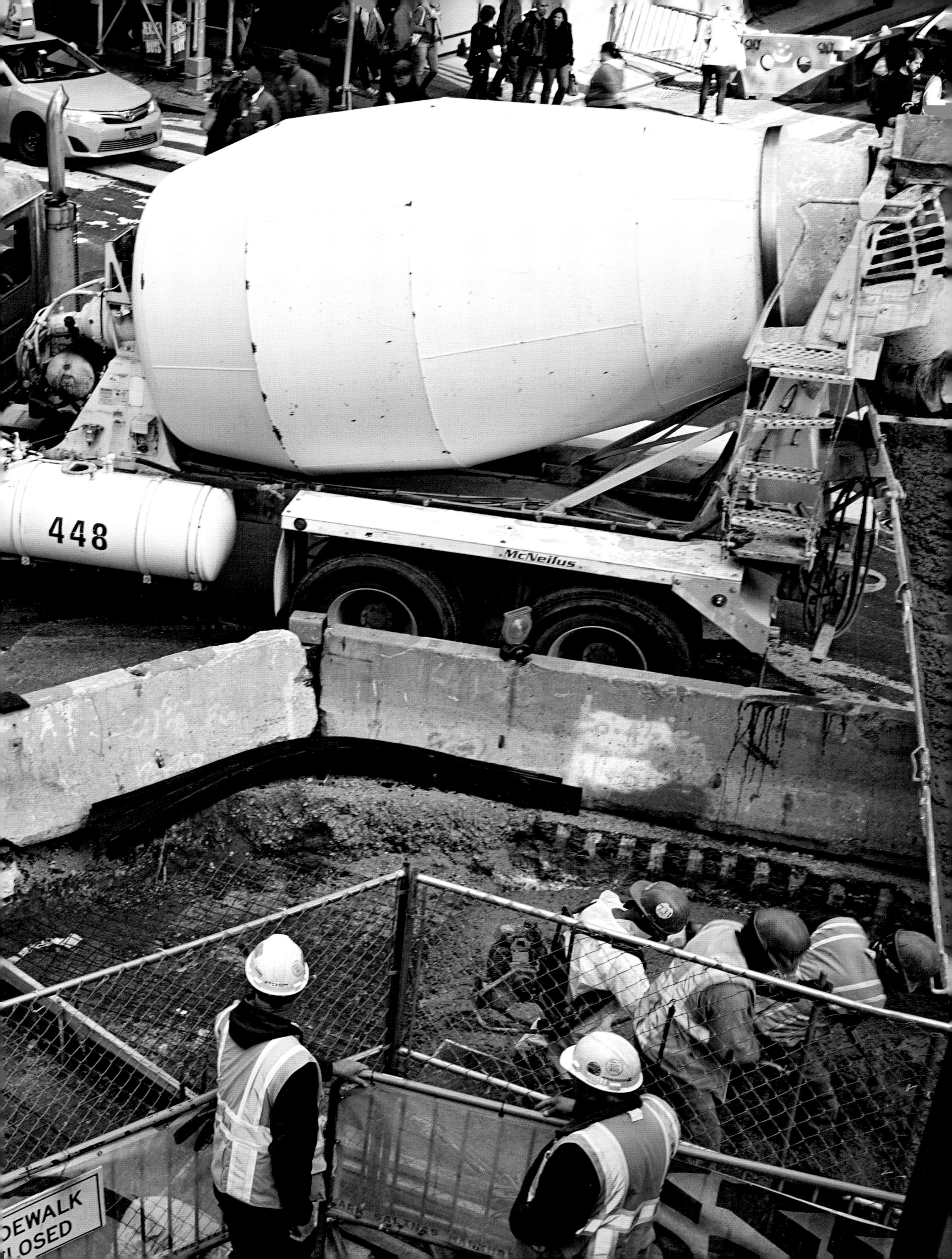
448
McNeilus
CITY
CITY
SIDEWALK
CLOSED

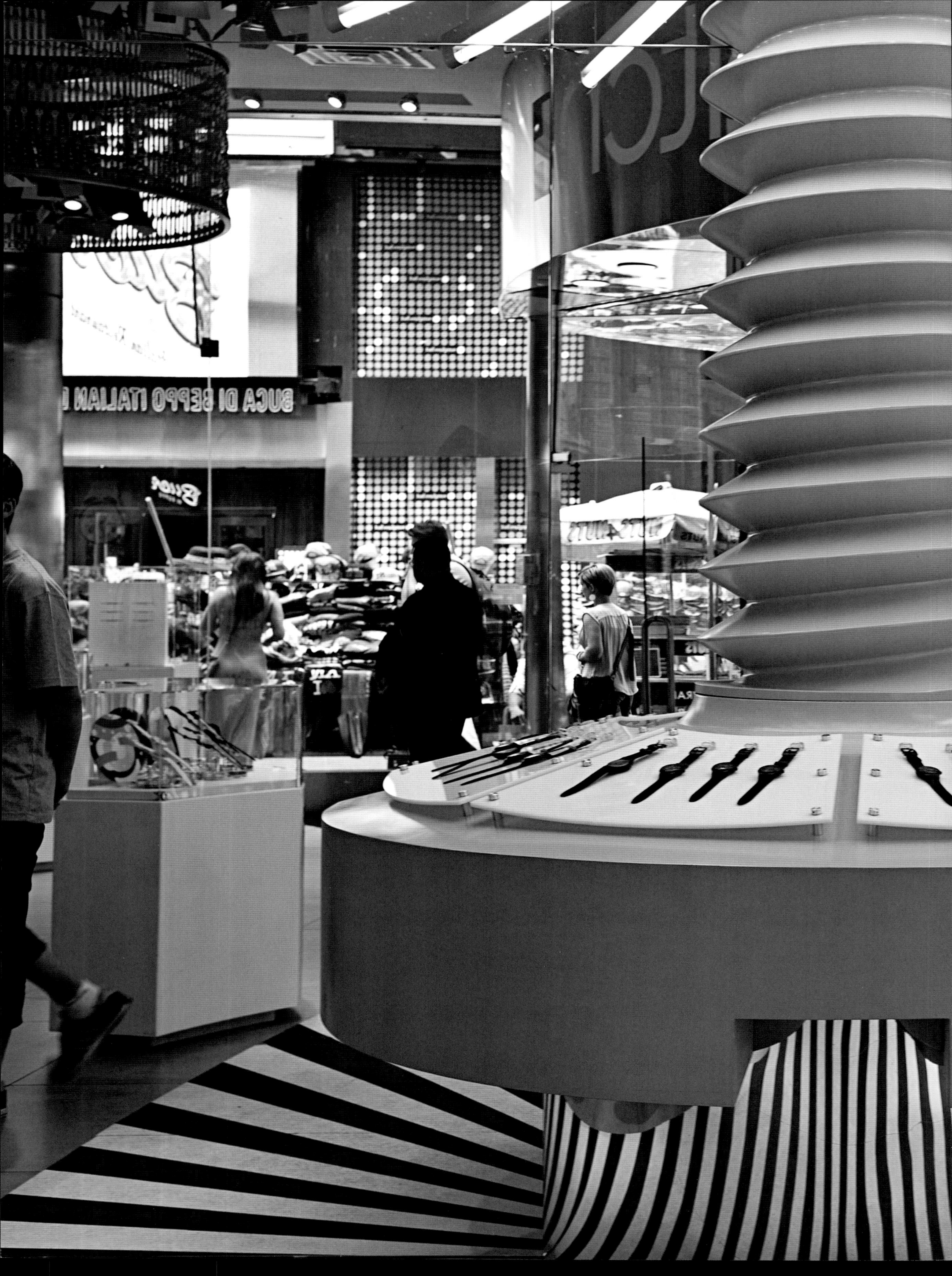

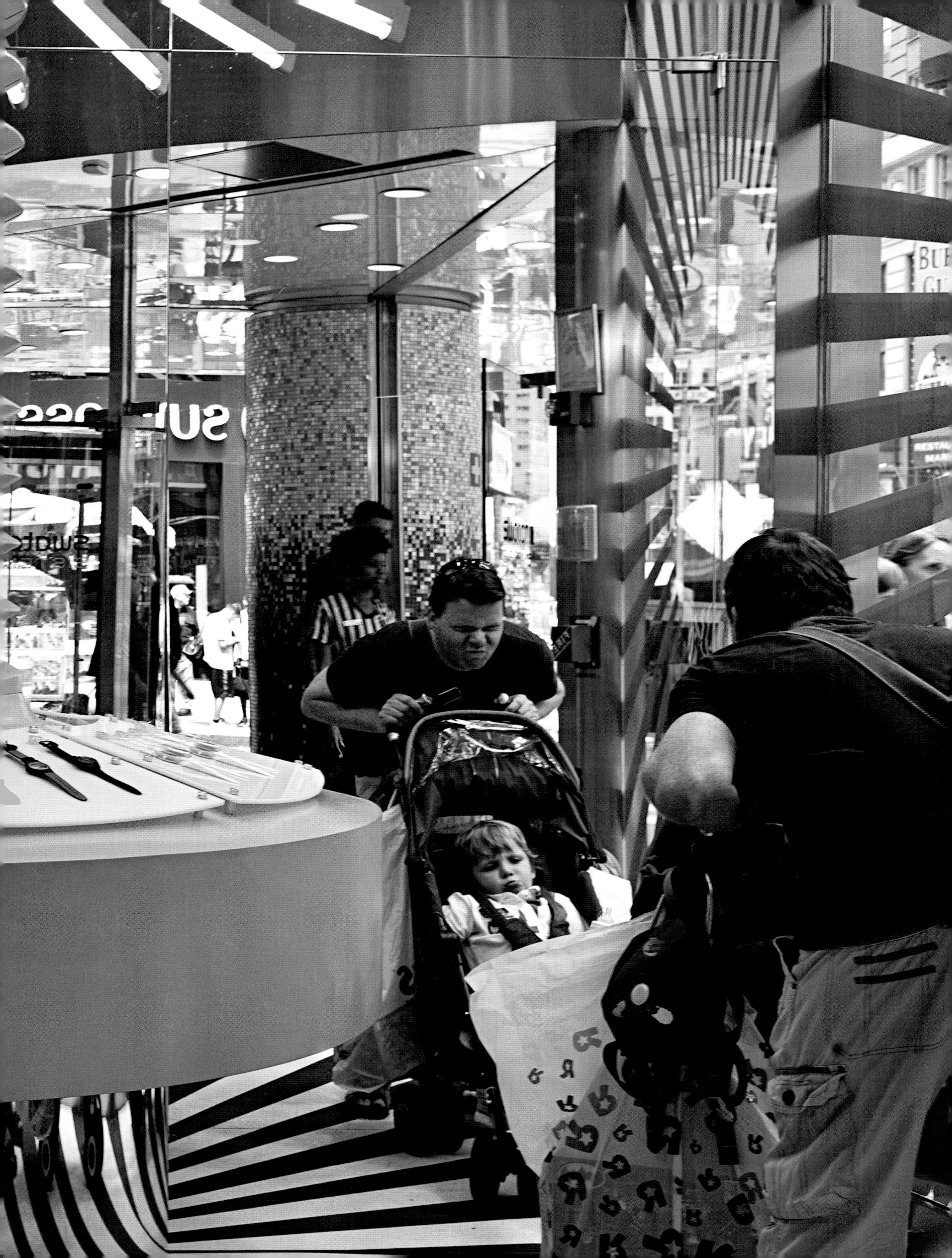

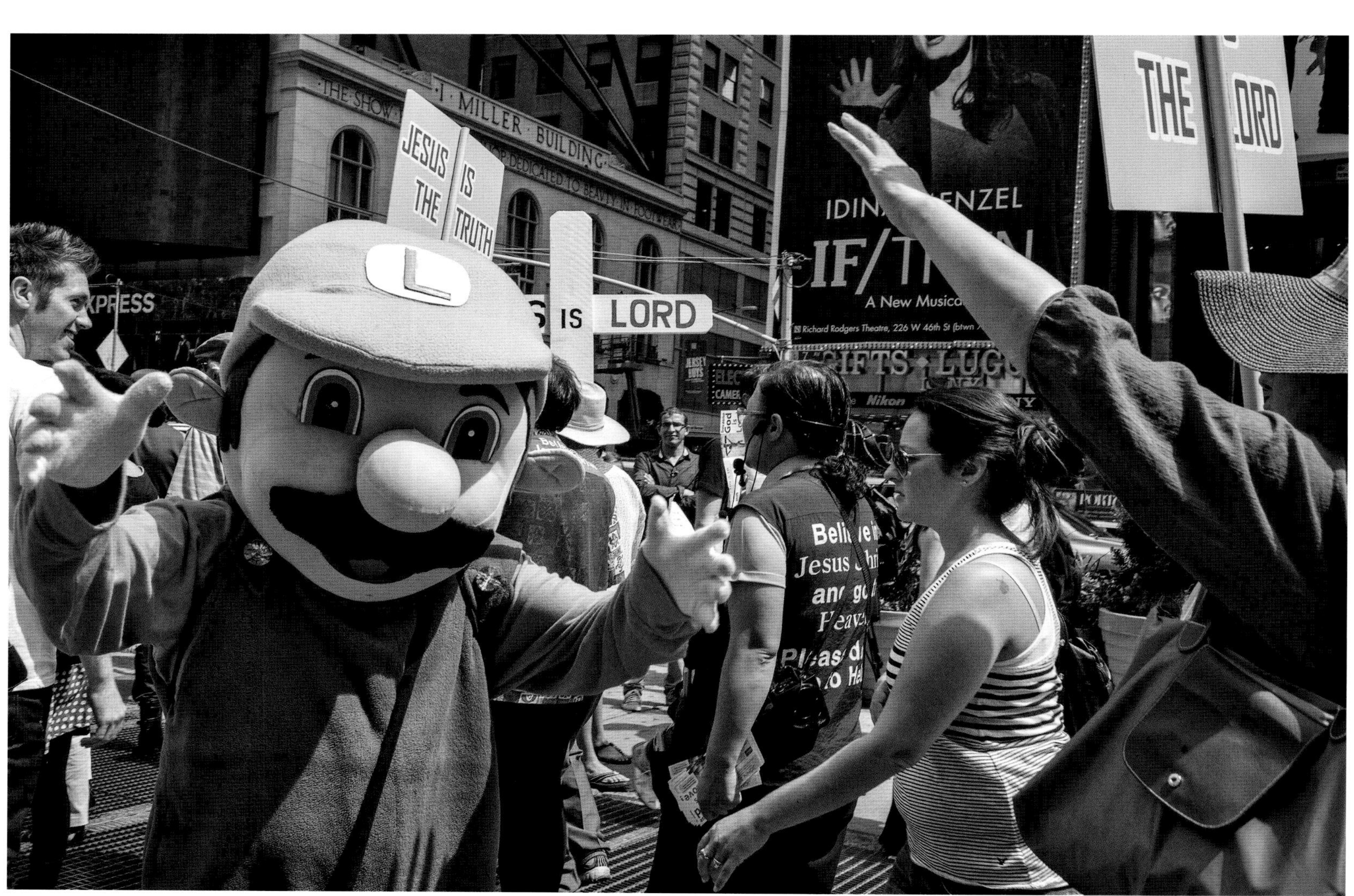

THE SHOW
I · MILLER · BUILDING
DEDICATED TO BEAUTY IN FOOTWEAR
JESUS IS THE TRUTH
IS LORD
THE LORD
IDINA MENZEL
IF/THEN
A New Musical
Richard Rodgers Theatre, 226 W 46th St
GIFTS · LUGG
CAMER
Nikon
EXPRESS
Believe
Jesus Chr
and go
Pleas
Please d
No Ha

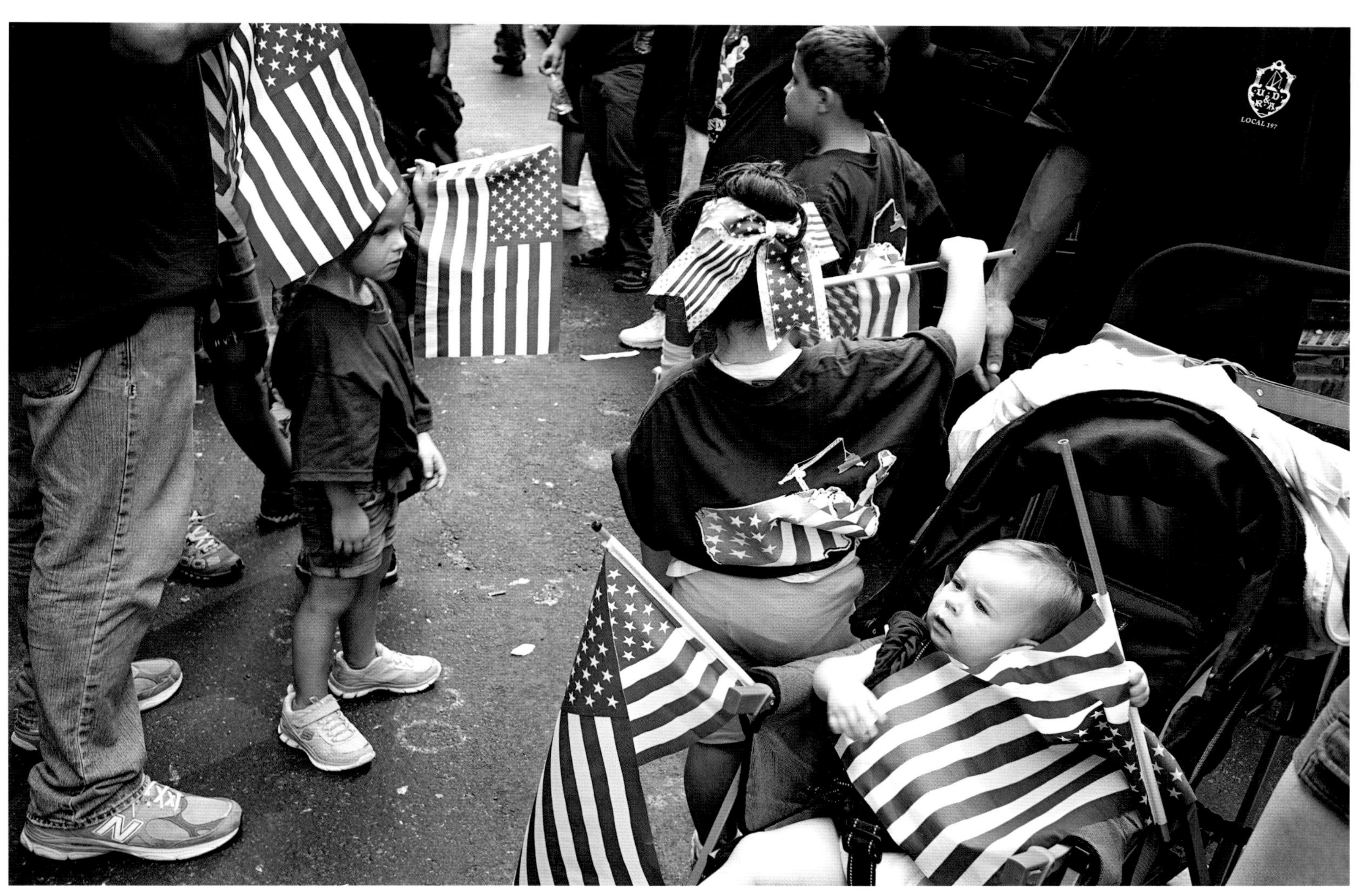

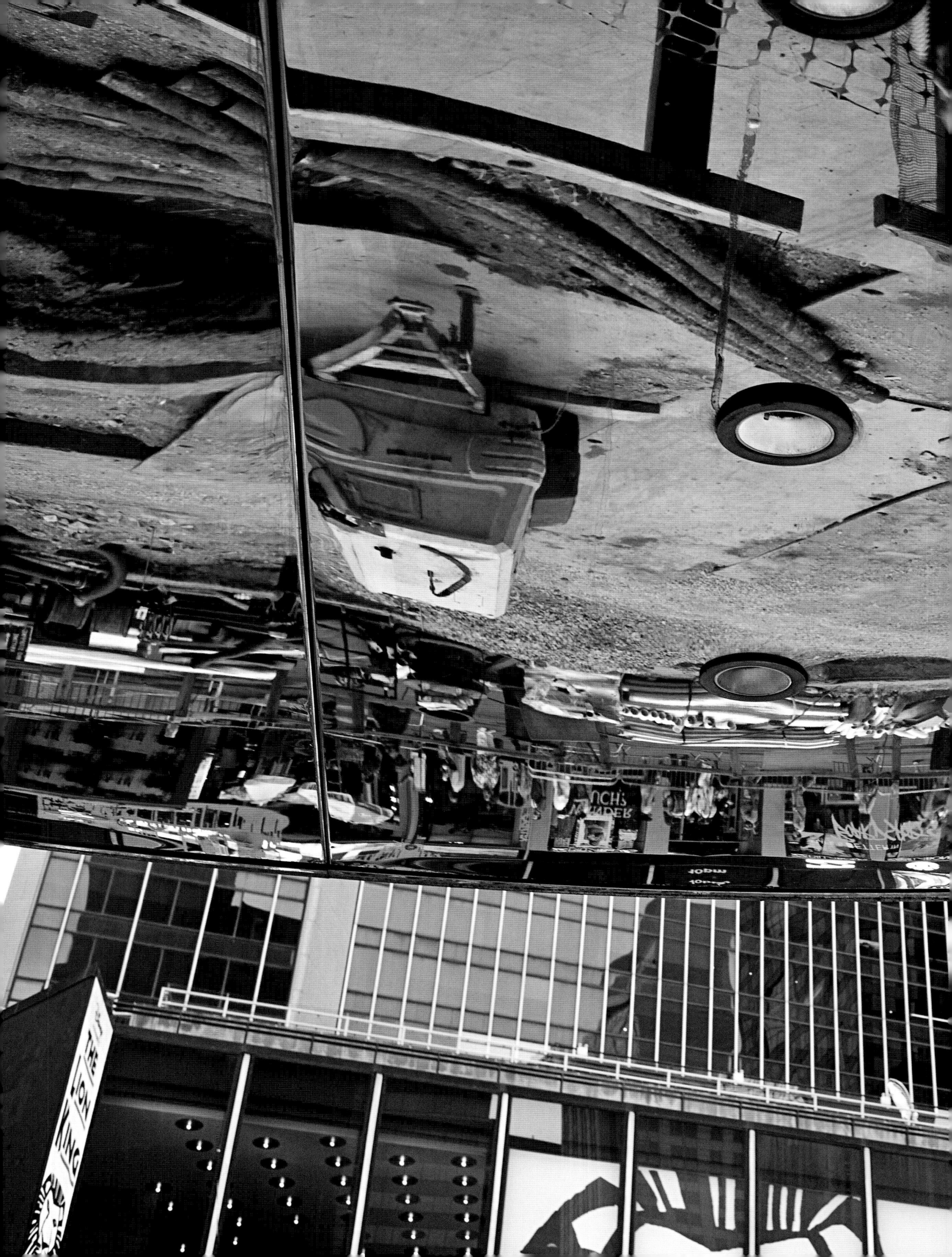

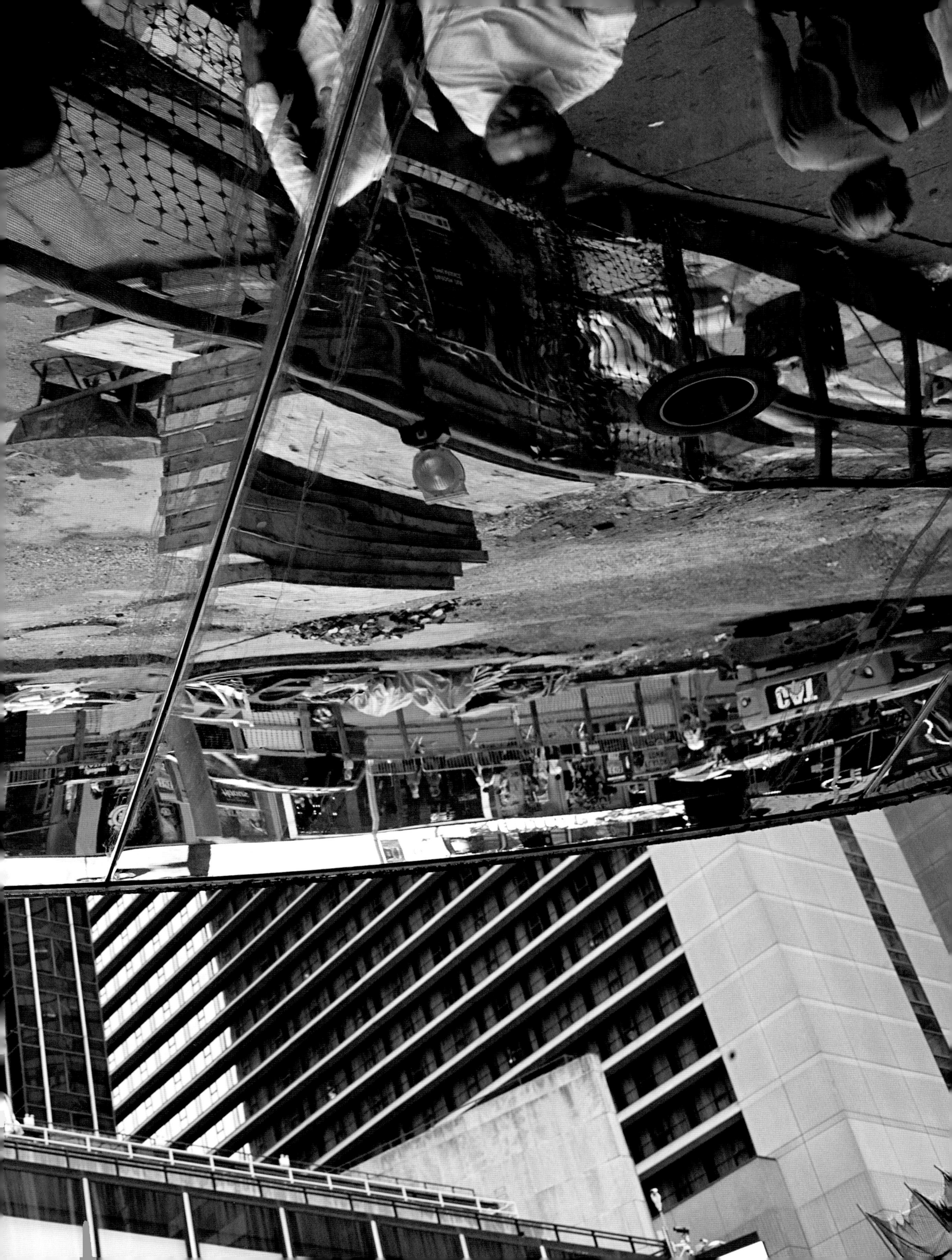

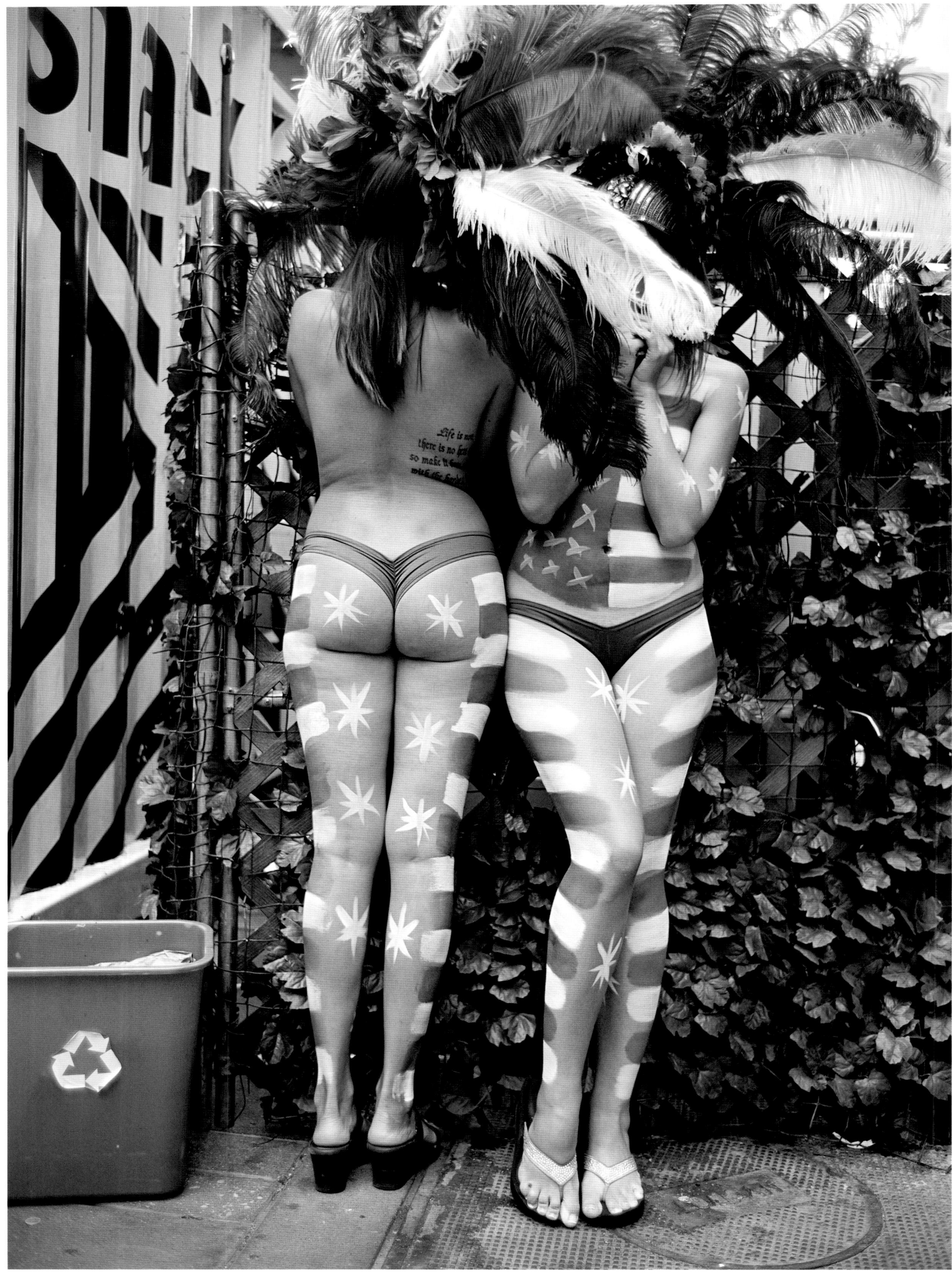

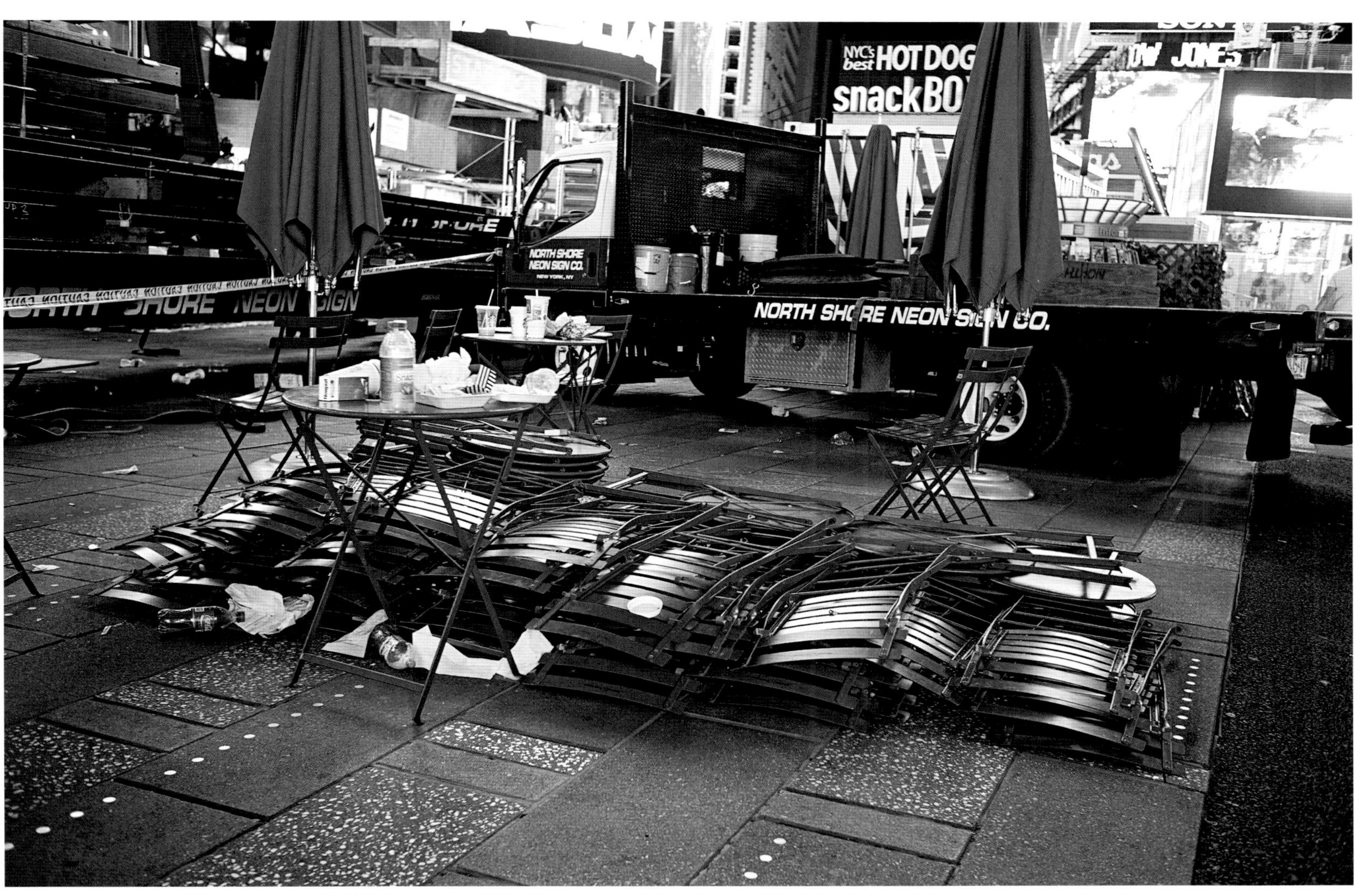

NYC's best HOT DOG
snackBOX
DOW JONES
NORTH SHORE NEON SIGN CO.
NORTH SHORE NEON SIGN CO. NEW YORK, NY
CAUTION

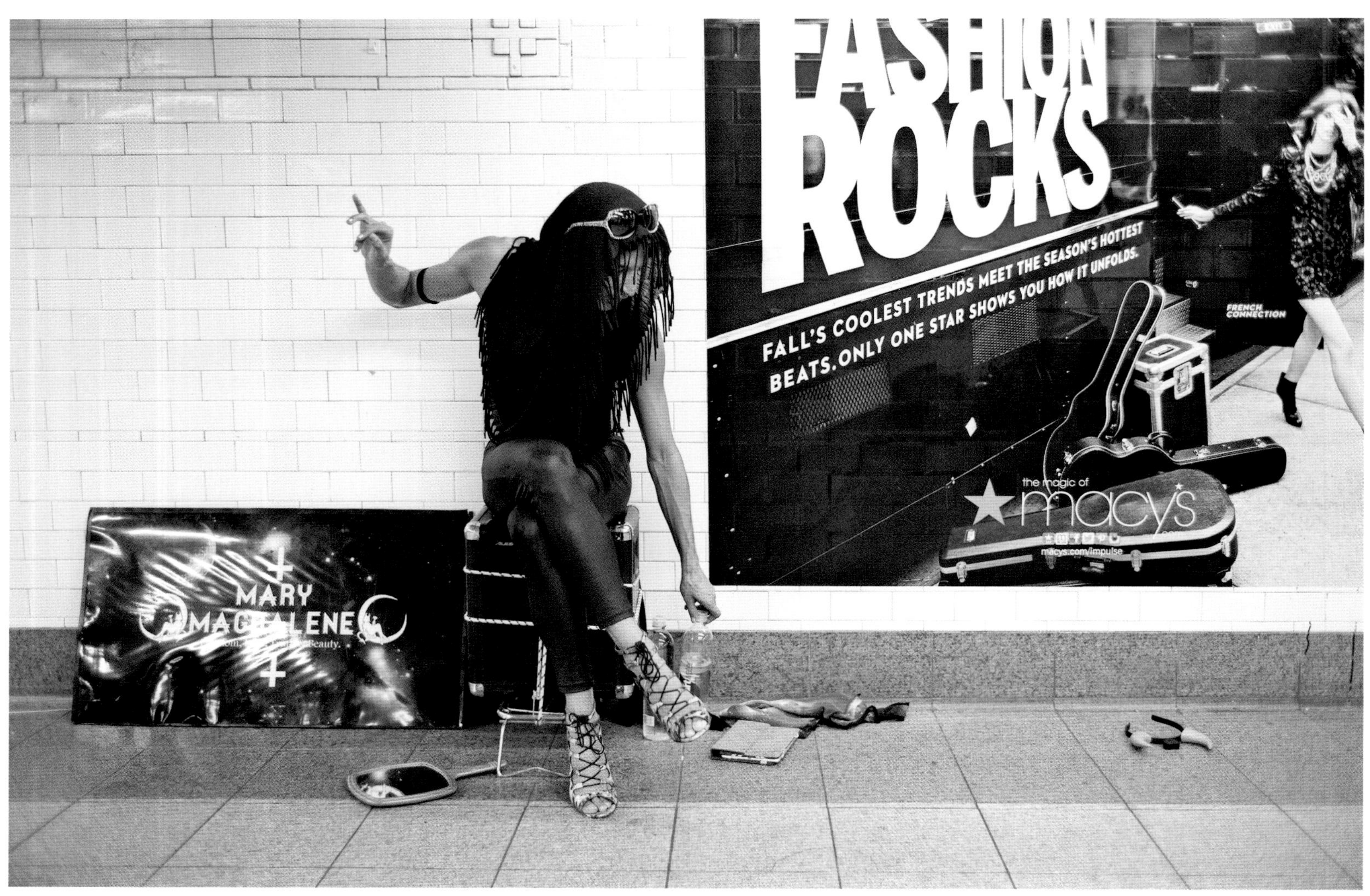
FASHION
ROCKS
FALL'S COOLEST TRENDS MEET THE SEASON'S HOTTEST
BEATS. ONLY ONE STAR SHOWS YOU HOW IT UNFOLDS.
FRENCH
CONNECTION
the magic of
macy's
macys.com/impulse
MARY
MAGDALENE

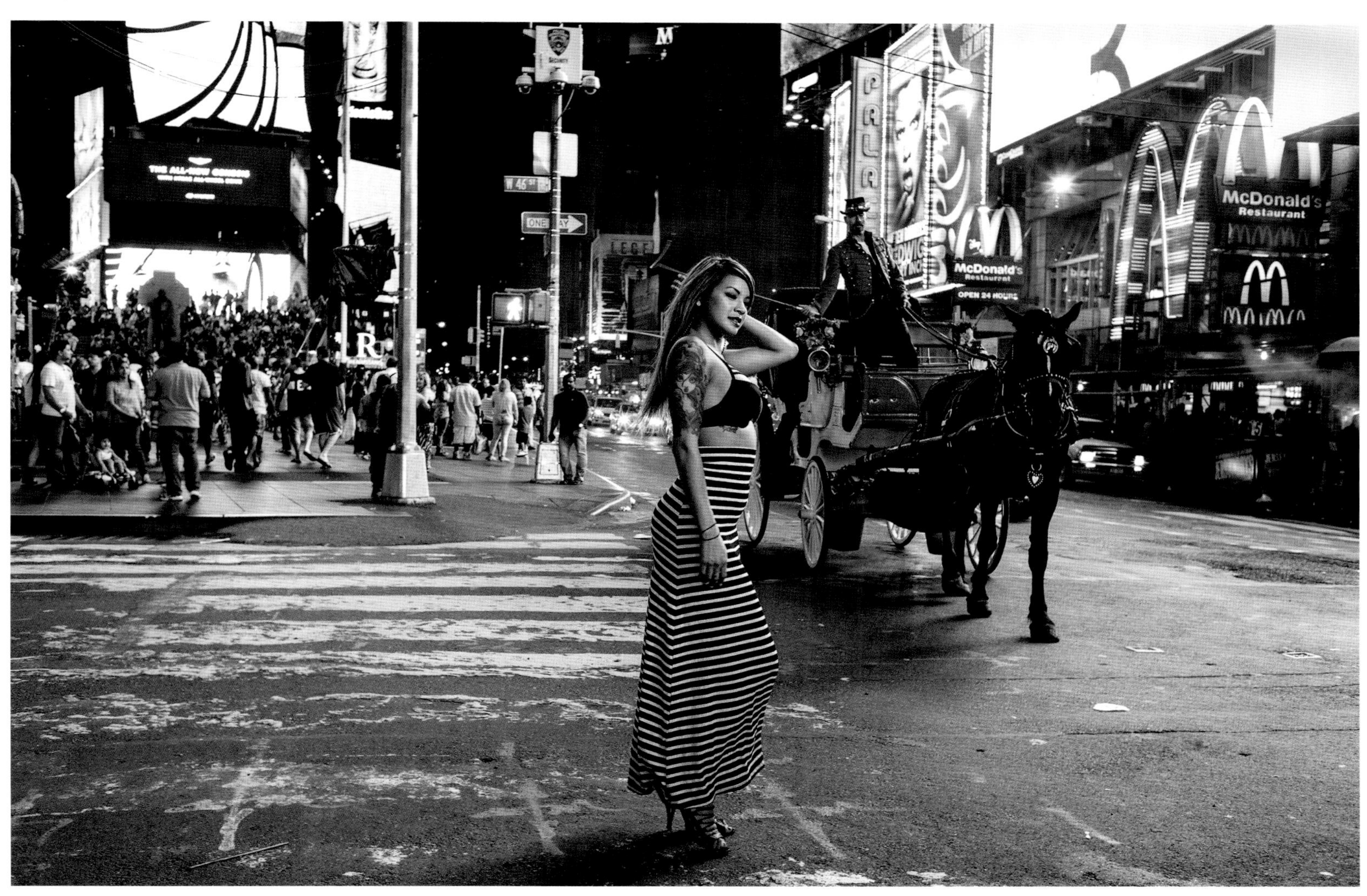

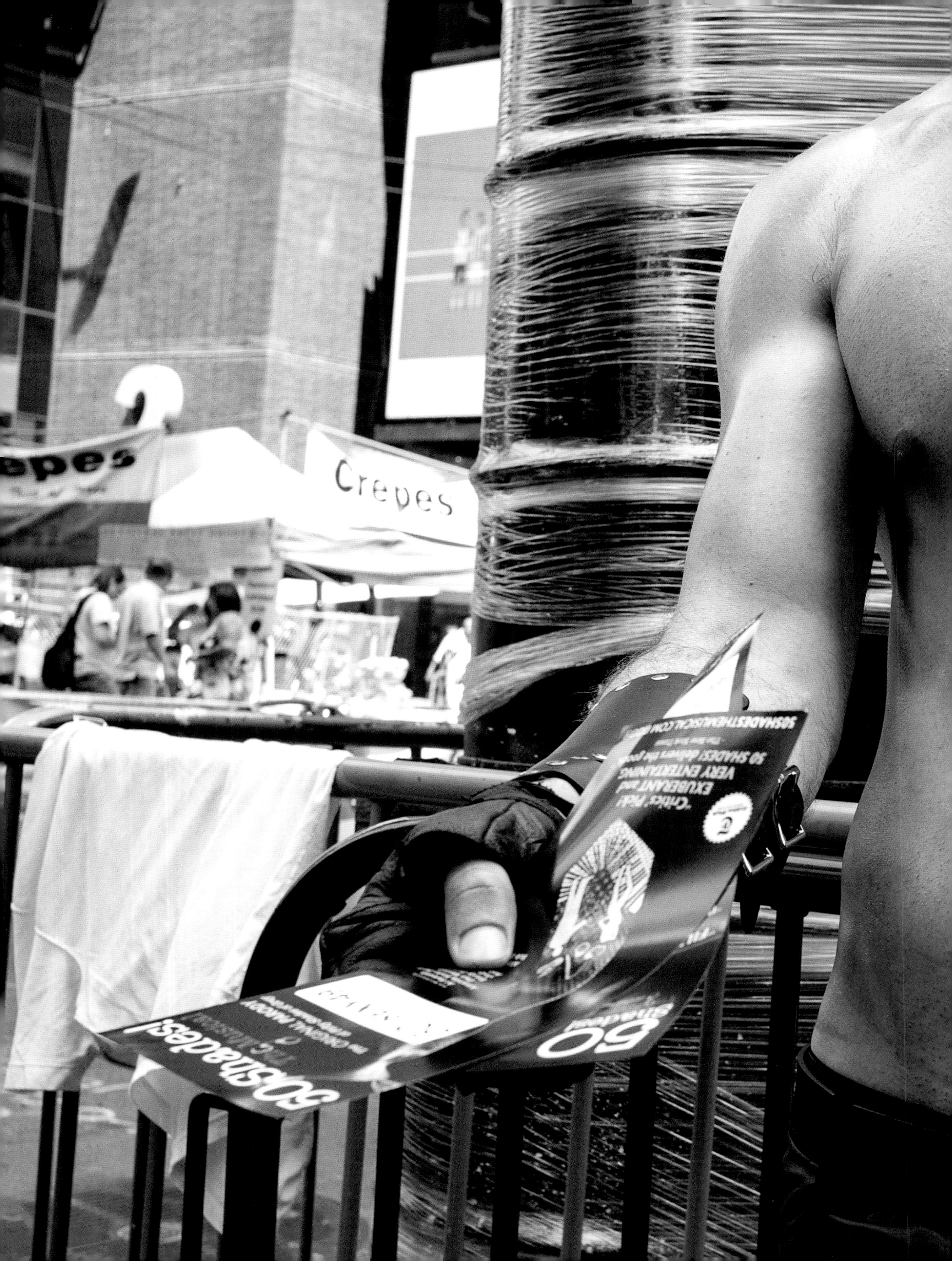
Crepes
Crepes
50SHADESTHEMUSICAL.COM
50 SHADES! delivers the goods
VERY ENTERTAINING
EXUBERANT and
"Critic's Pick"
50 SHADES!
THE MUSICAL
The ORIGINAL PARODY

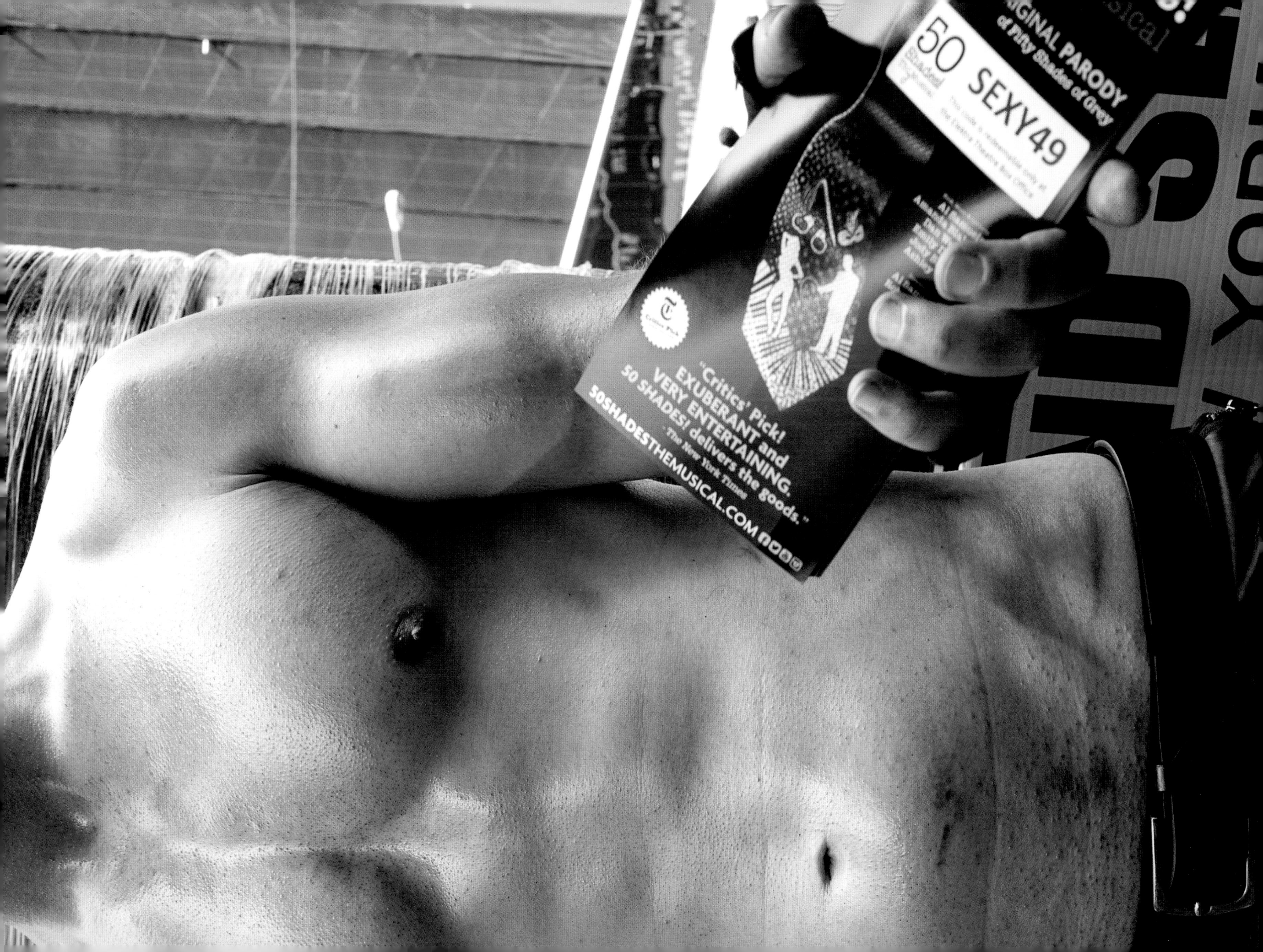
ORIGINAL PARODY
of Fifty Shades of Grey
50 SEXY49
Critics' Pick!
"Critics' Pick!
EXUBERANT and
VERY ENTERTAINING.
50 SHADES! delivers the goods."
- The New York Times
50SHADESTHEMUSICAL.COM

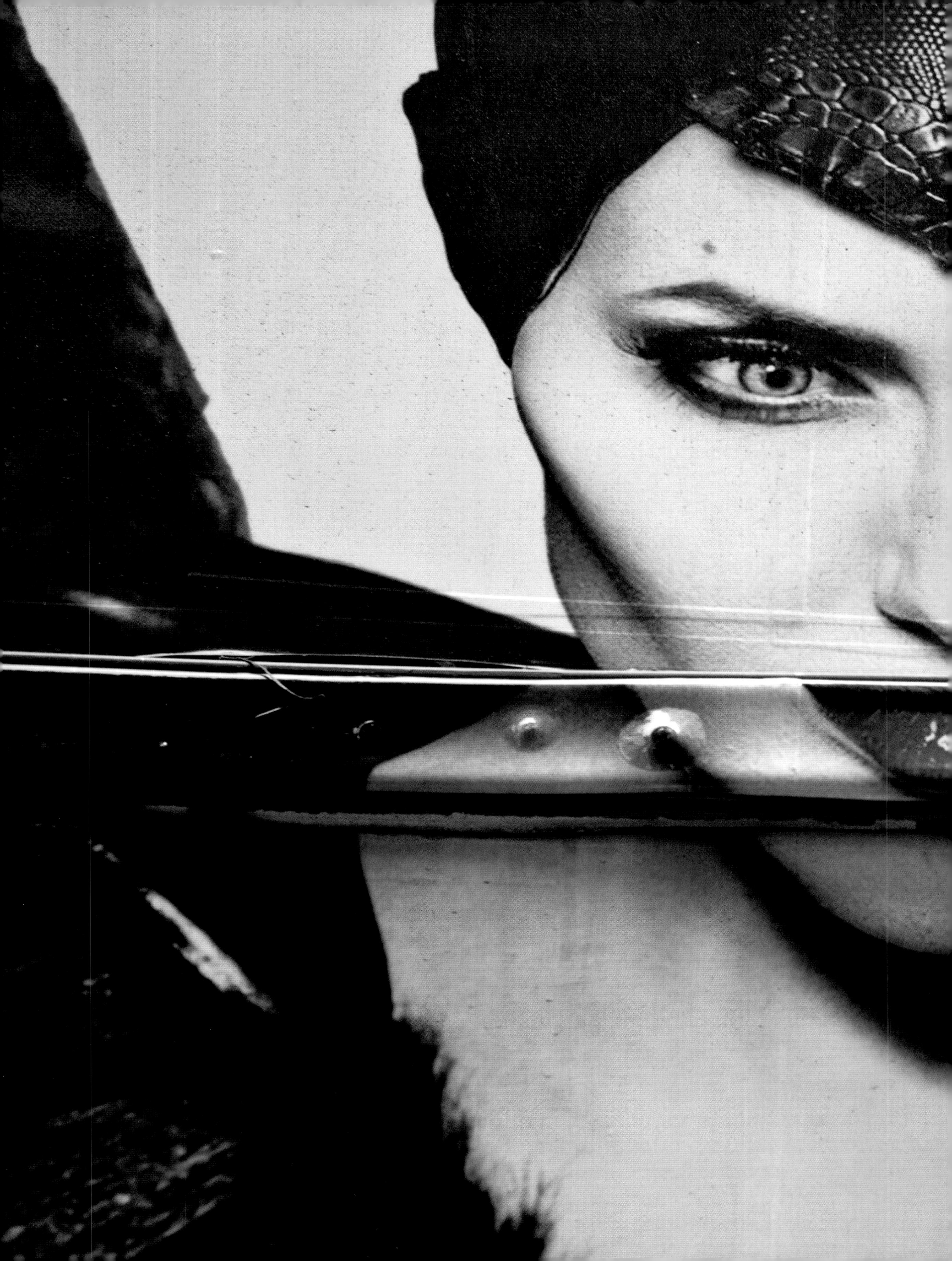

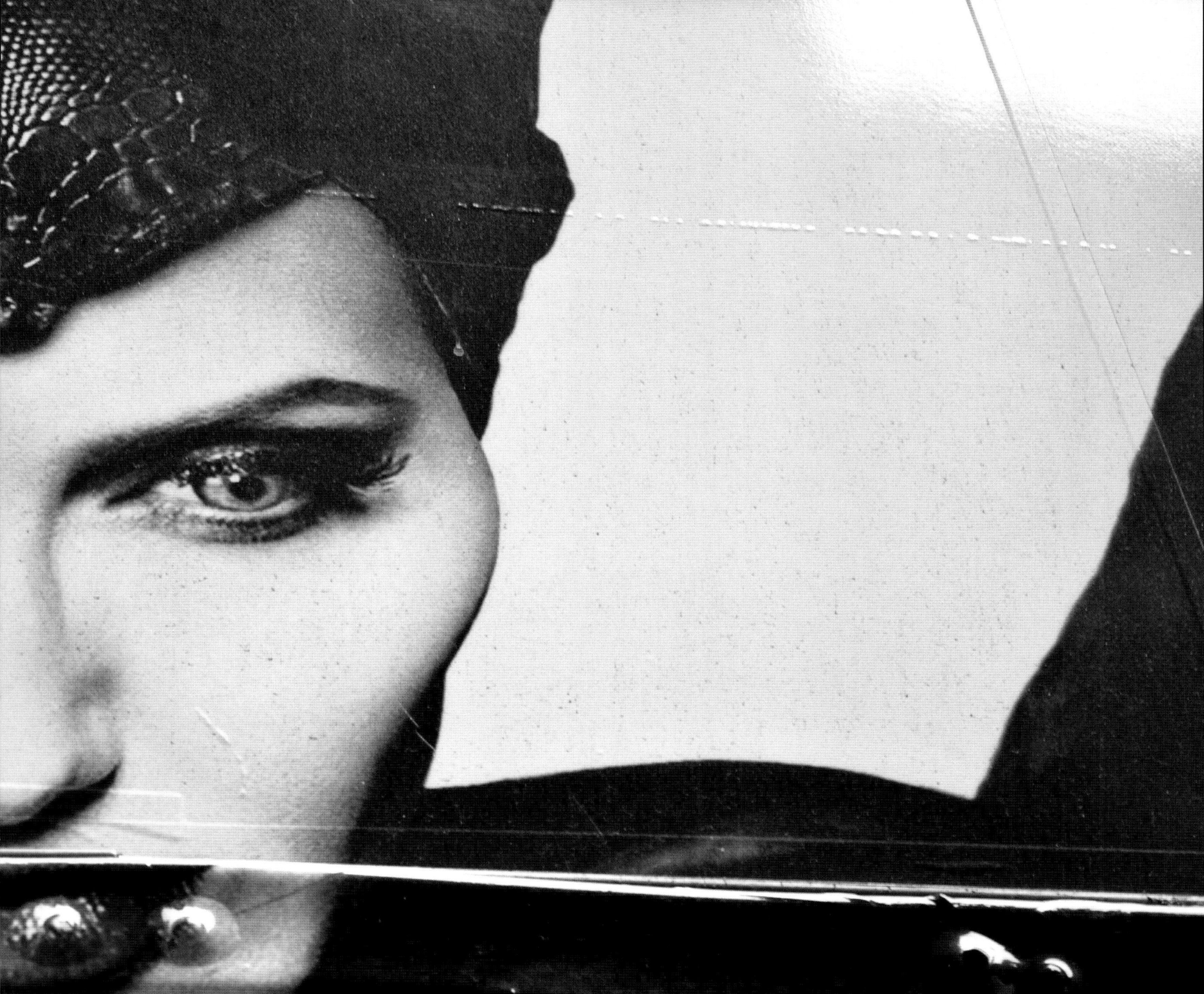

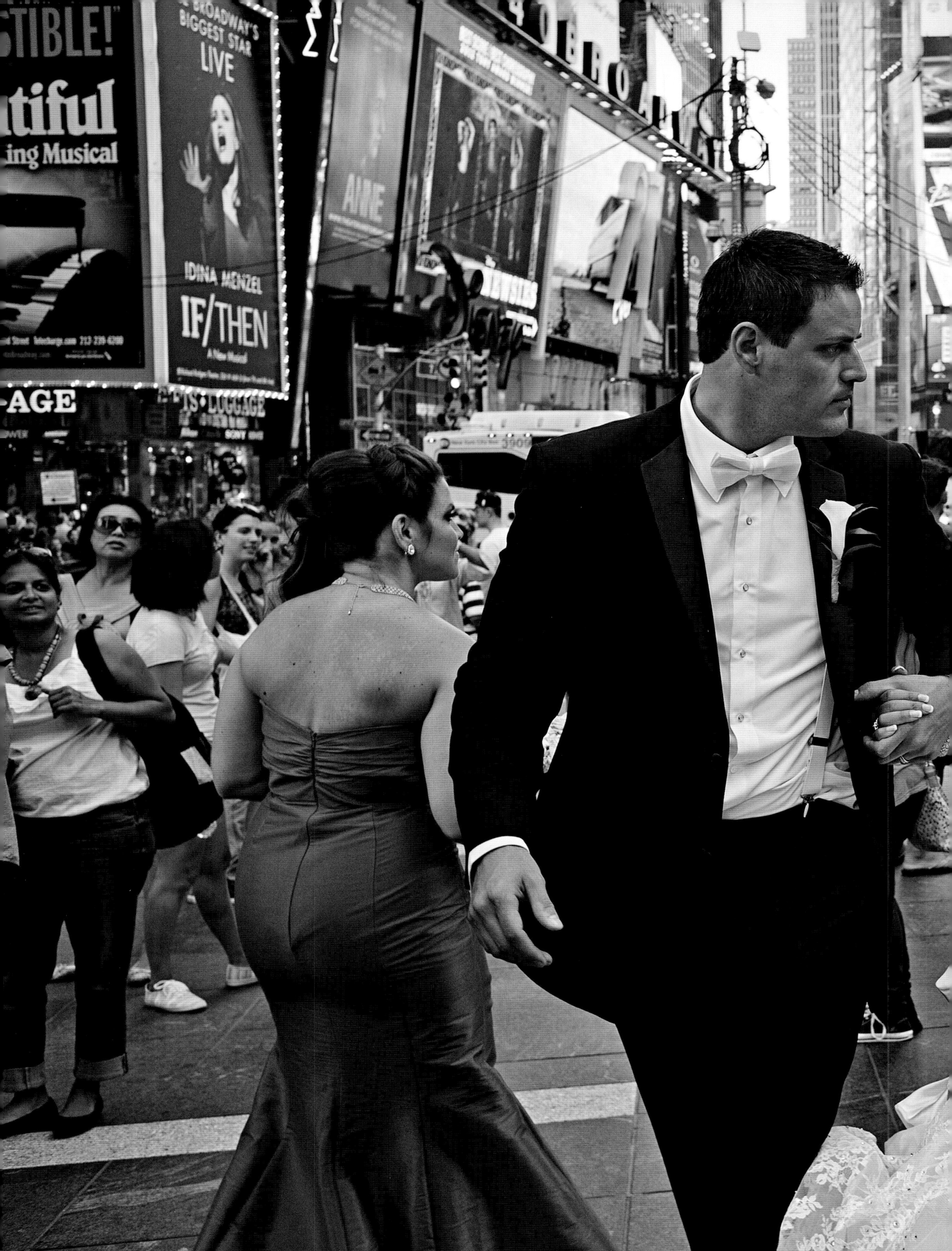
STIBLE!"
tiful
ing Musical
BROADWAY'S
BIGGEST STAR
LIVE
ANIE
IDINA MENZEL
IF/THEN
A New Musical
AGE
LUGGAGE
OBRO

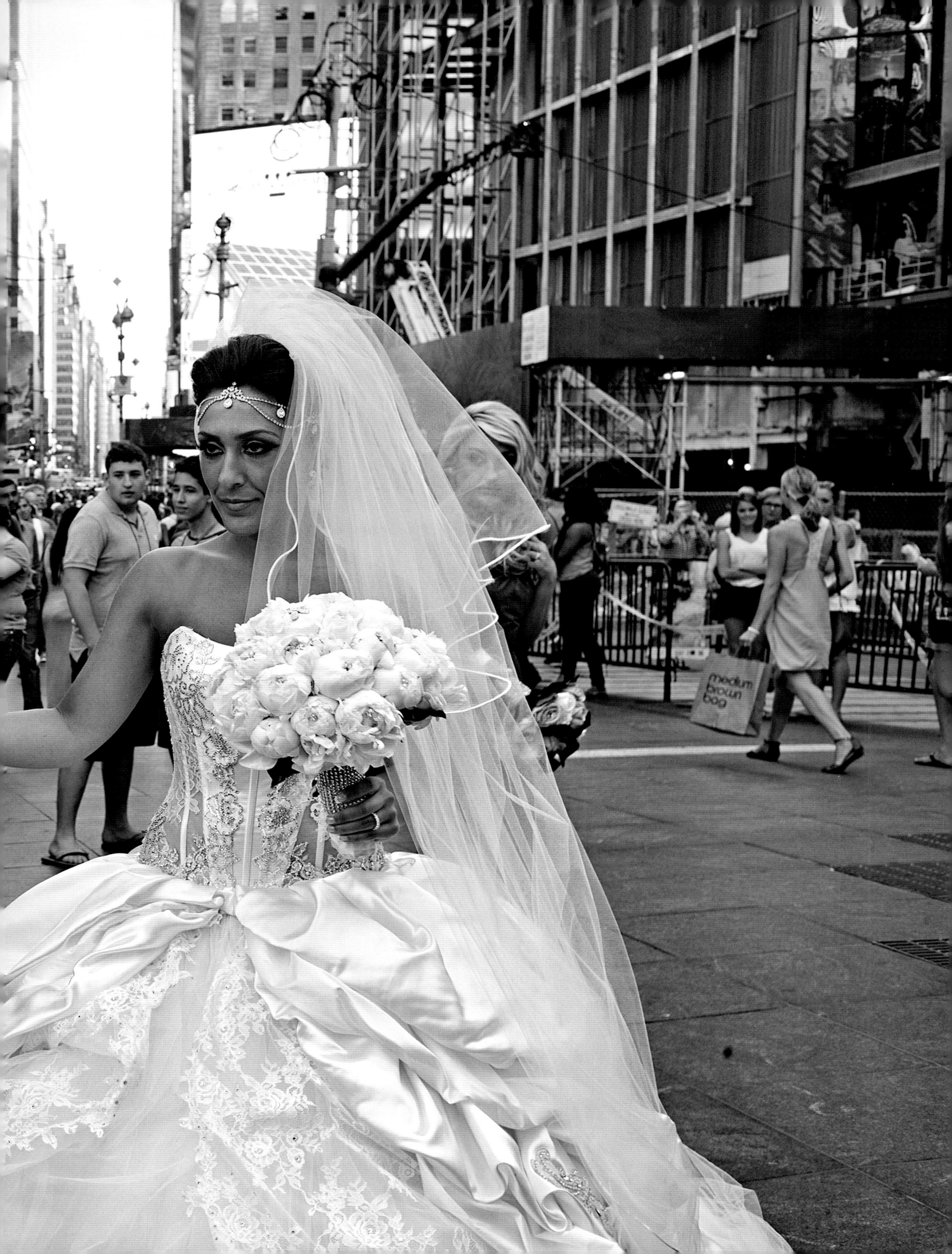

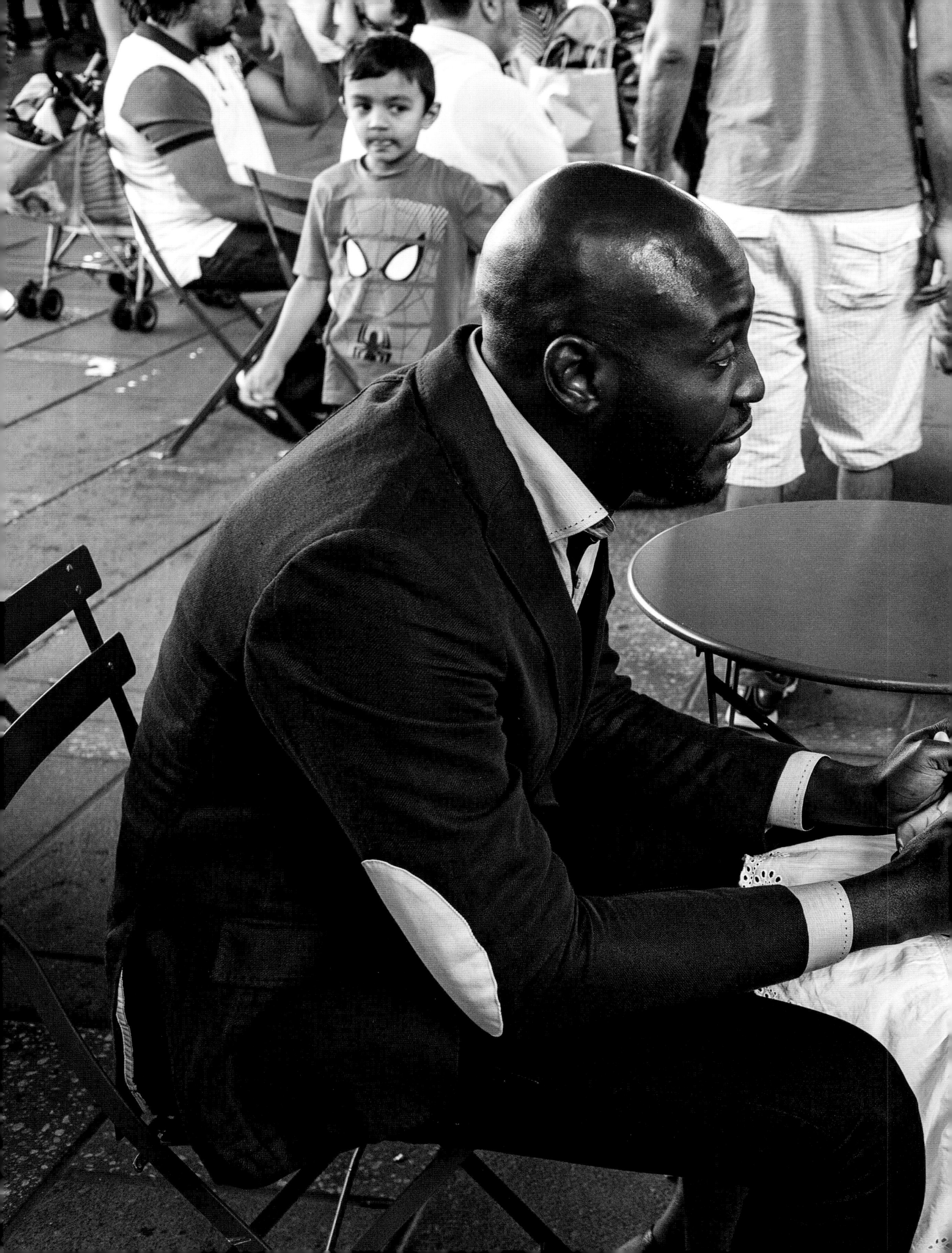

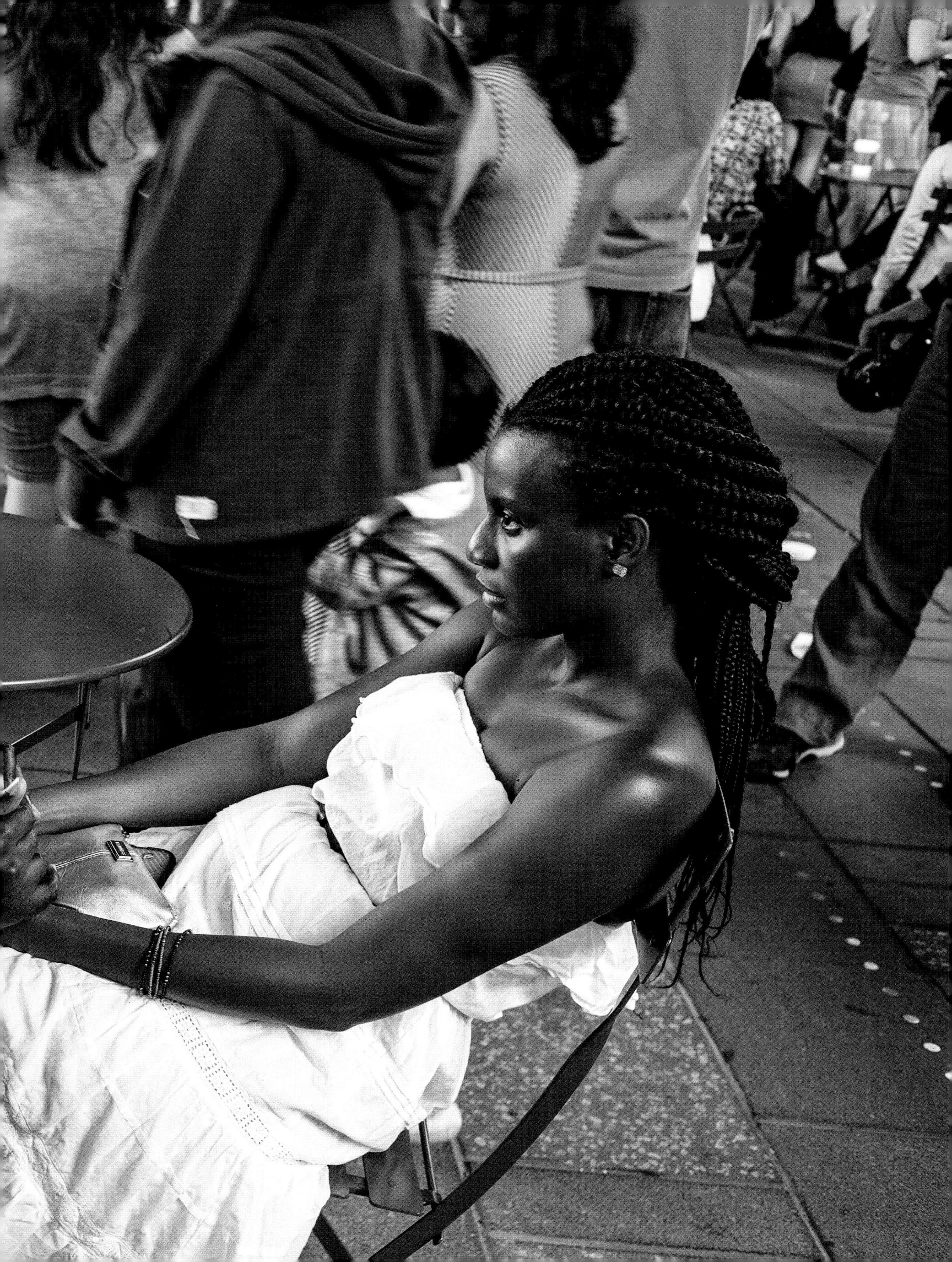

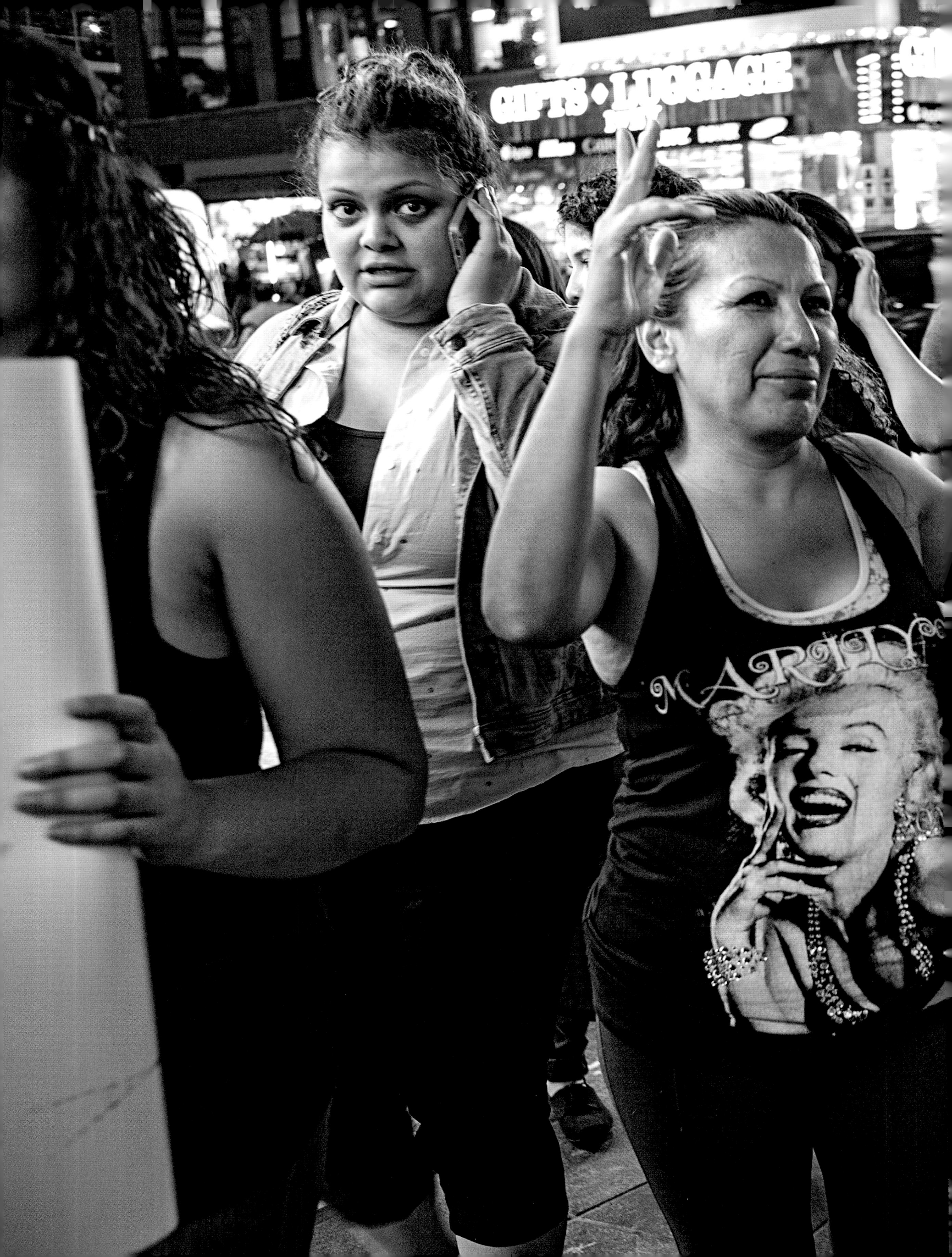

GIFTS · LUGGAGE
MARILYN

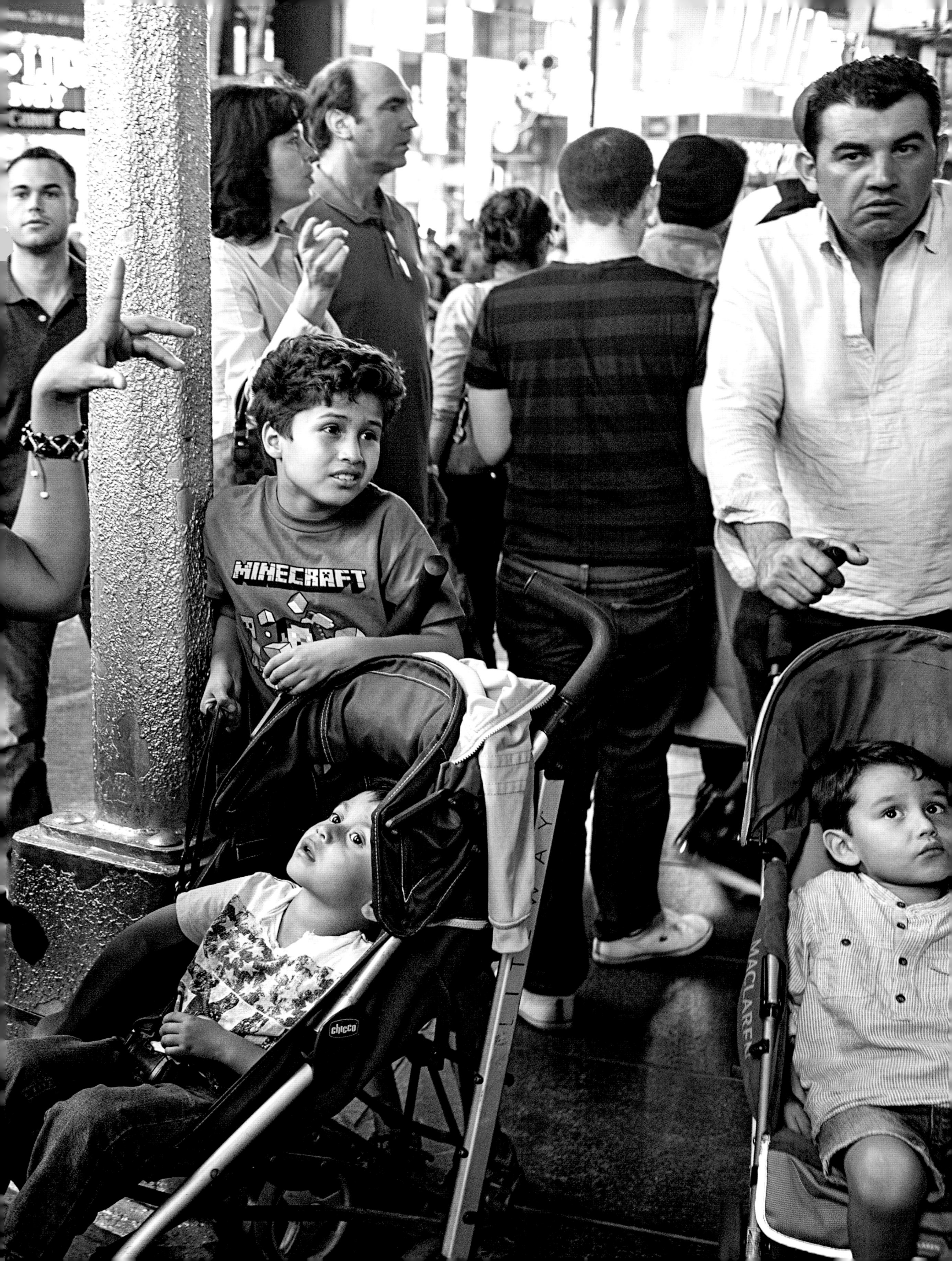

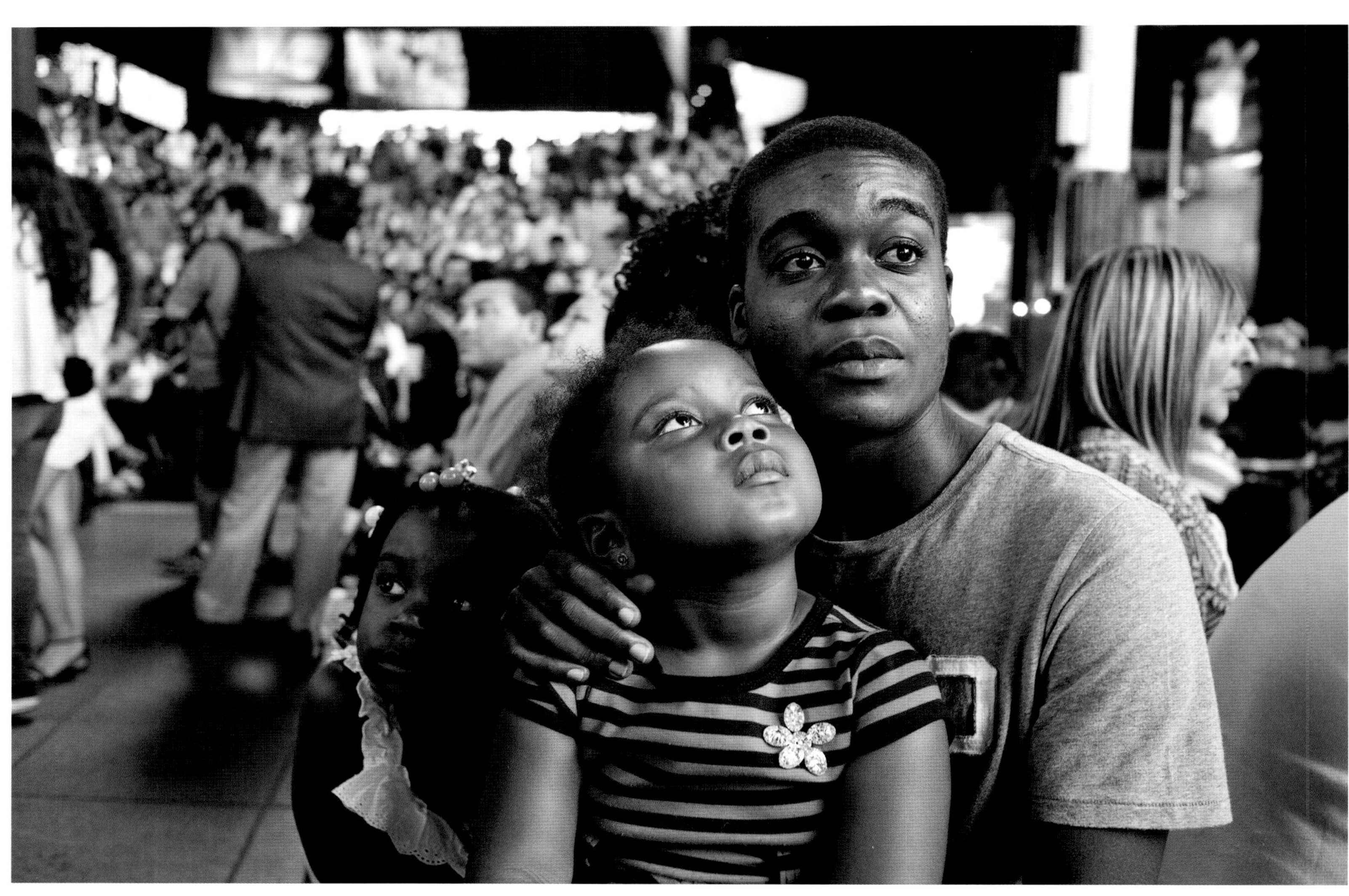

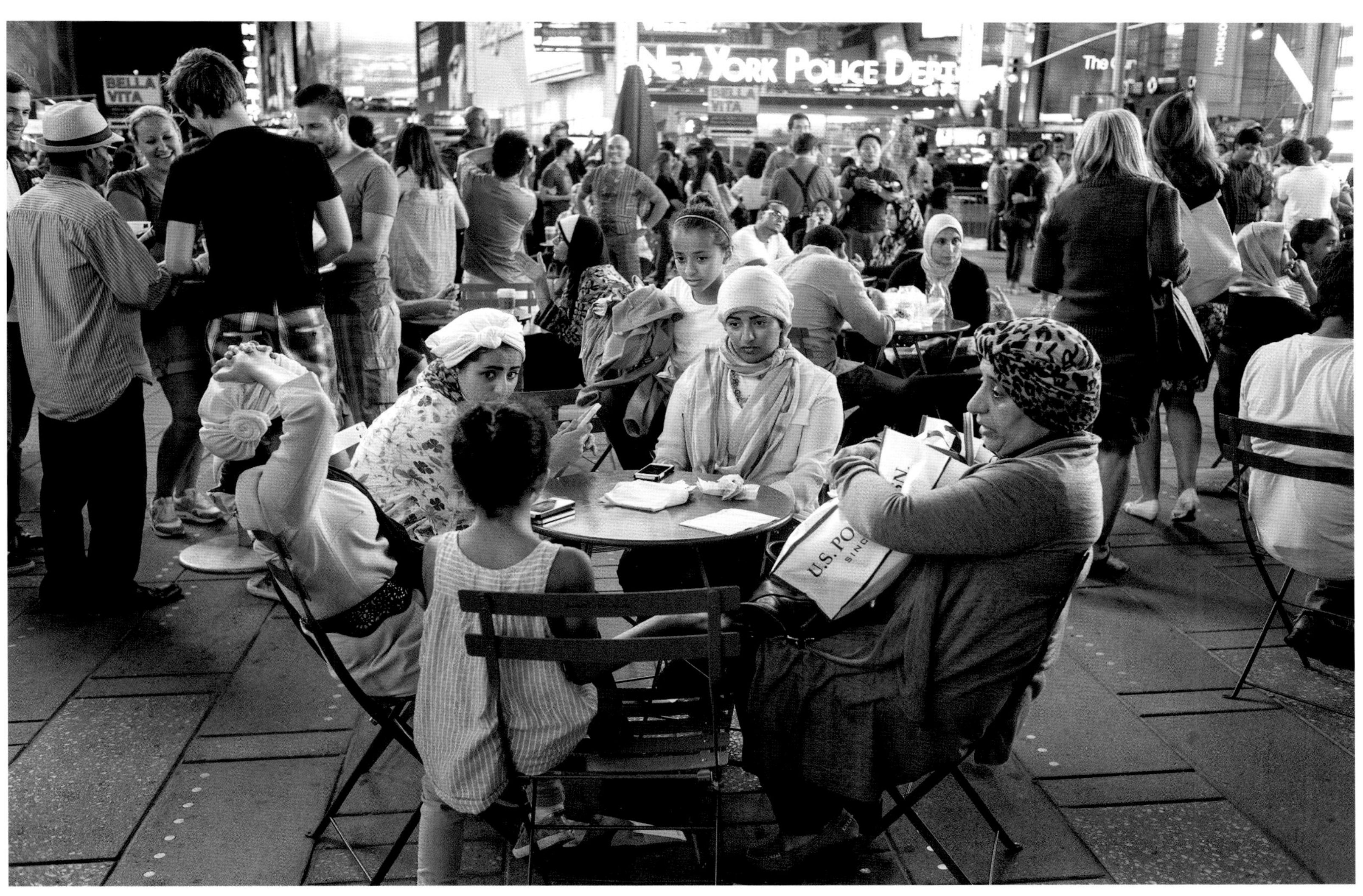
NEW YORK POLICE DEPT
BELLA VITA
BELLA VITA
U.S. PO

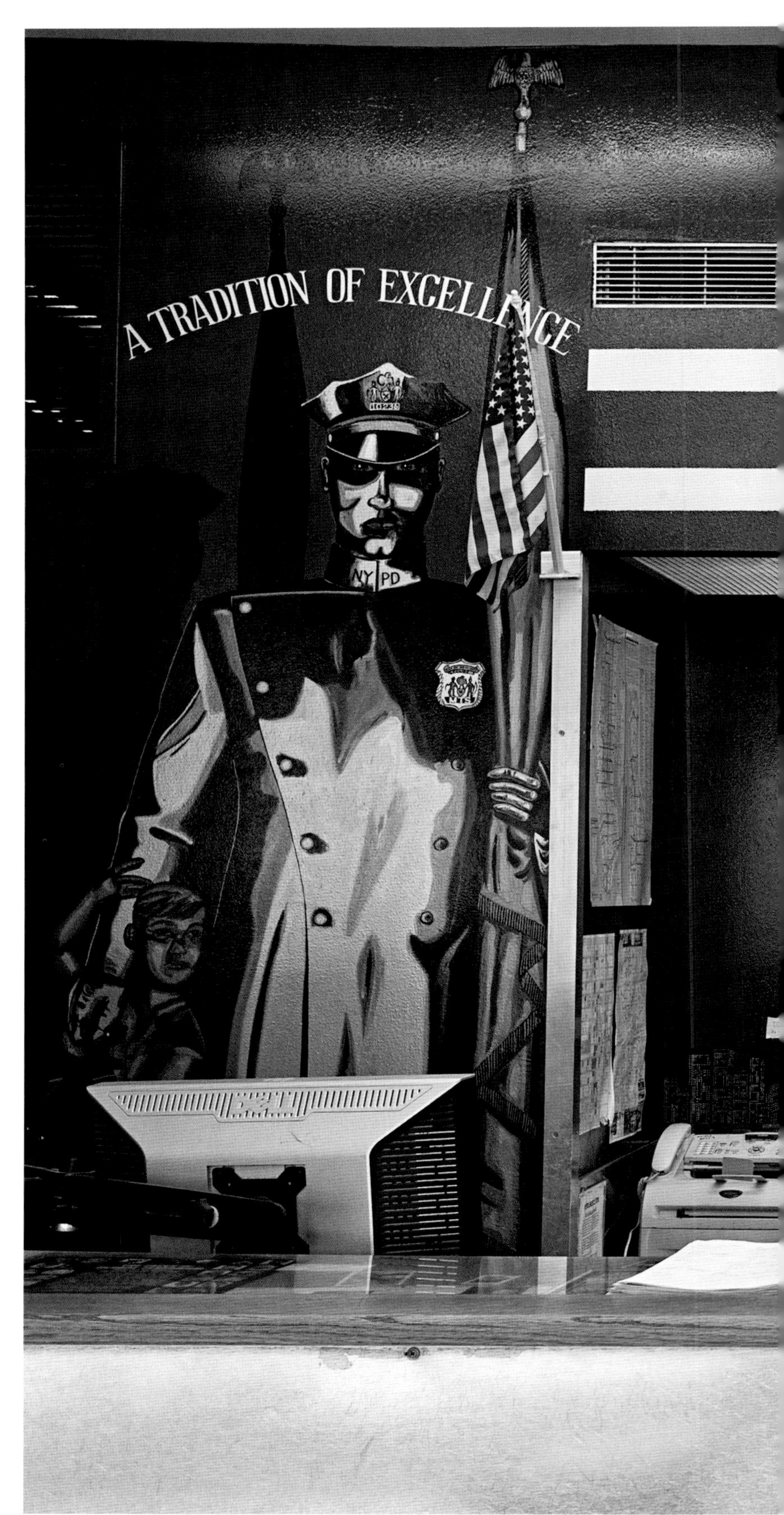
A TRADITION OF EXCELLENCE
NY PD

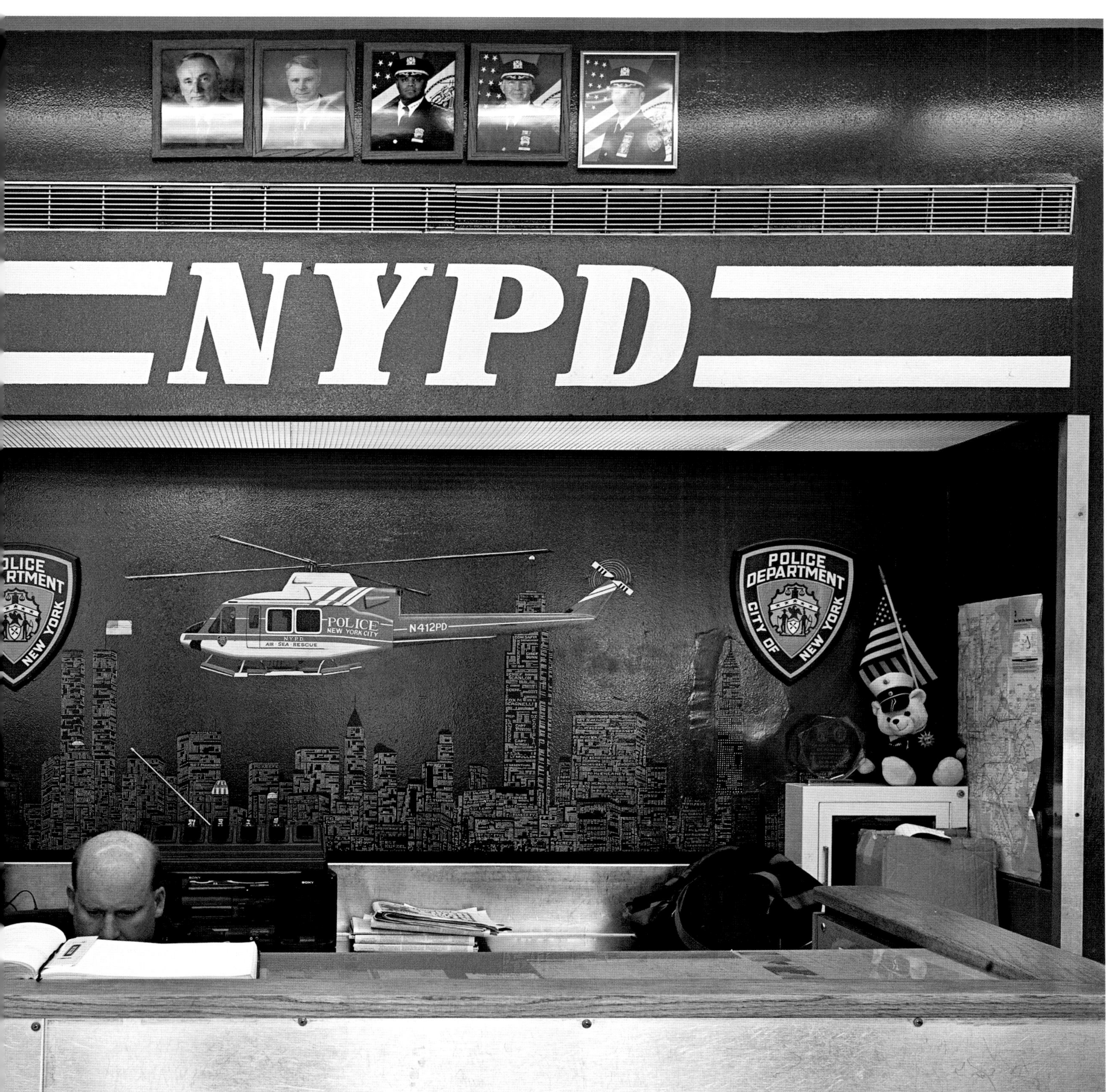

NYPD
POLICE DEPARTMENT CITY OF NEW YORK
POLICE DEPARTMENT CITY OF NEW YORK
POLICE NEW YORK CITY
N412PD
N.Y.P.D. AIR·SEA·RESCUE

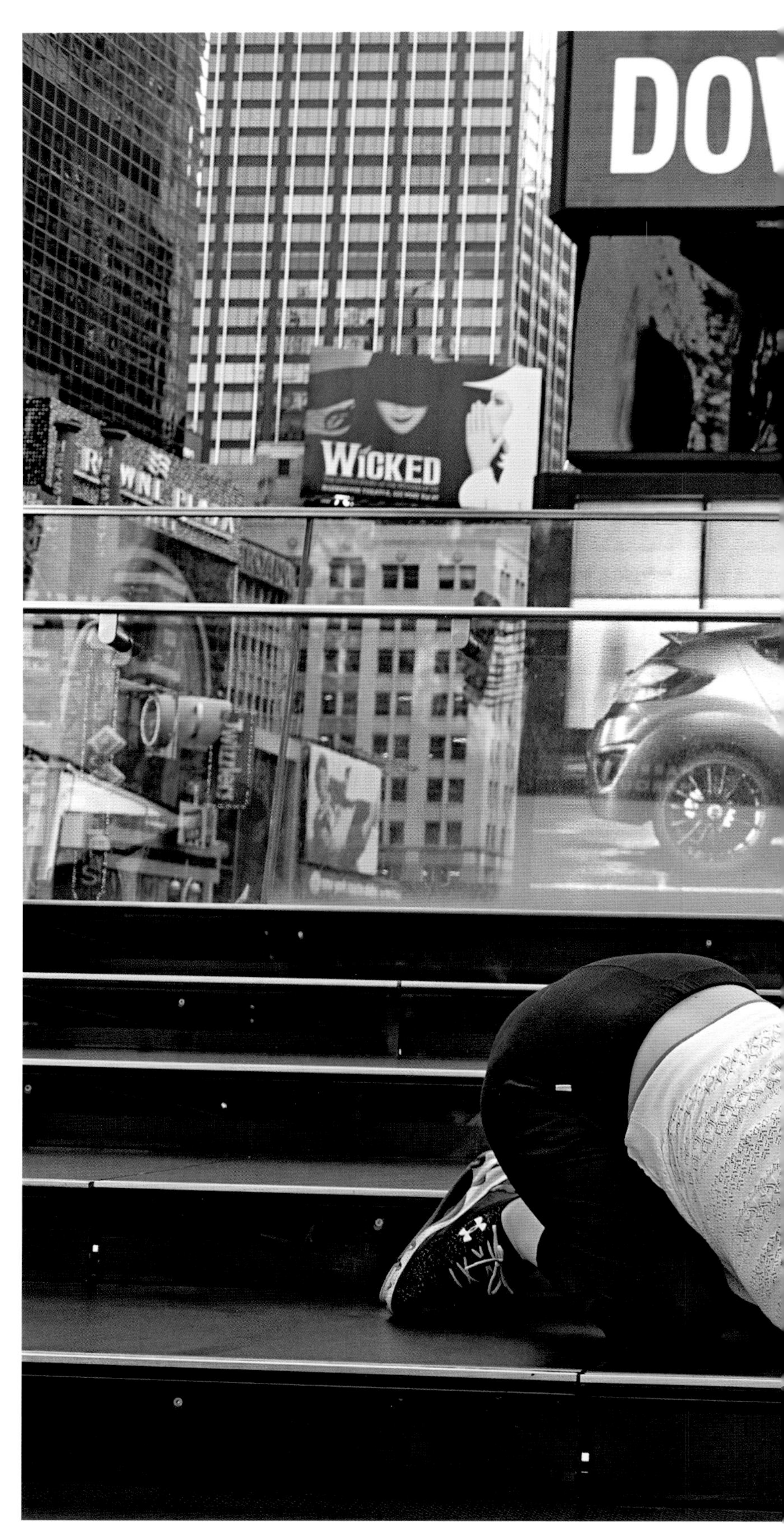

DO
WiCKED

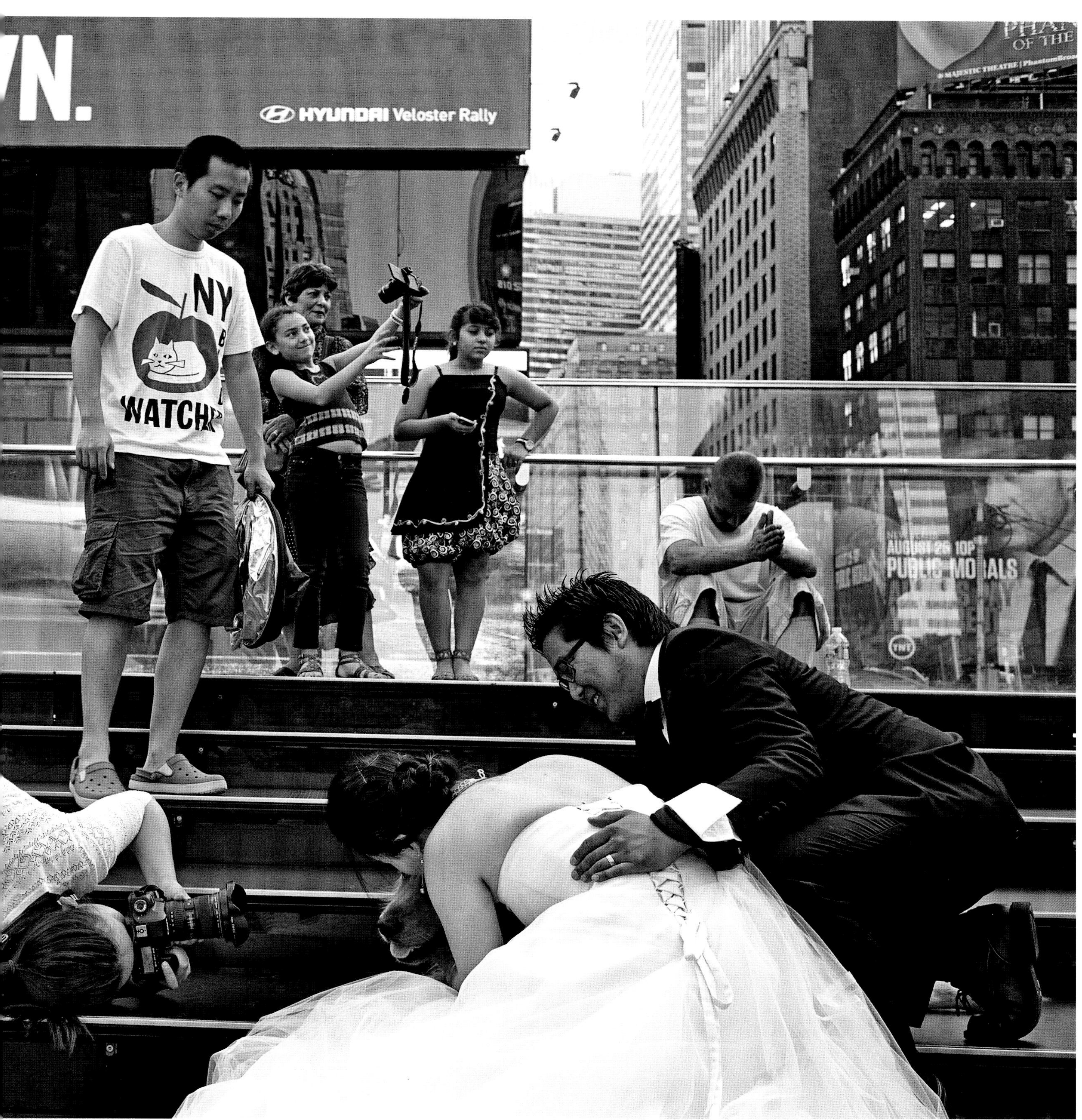
WN.
HYUNDAI Veloster Rally
NY
WATCH
PHANTOM
OF THE
MAJESTIC THEATRE | PhantomBroad
AUGUST 26 10P
PUBLIC MORALS
TNT

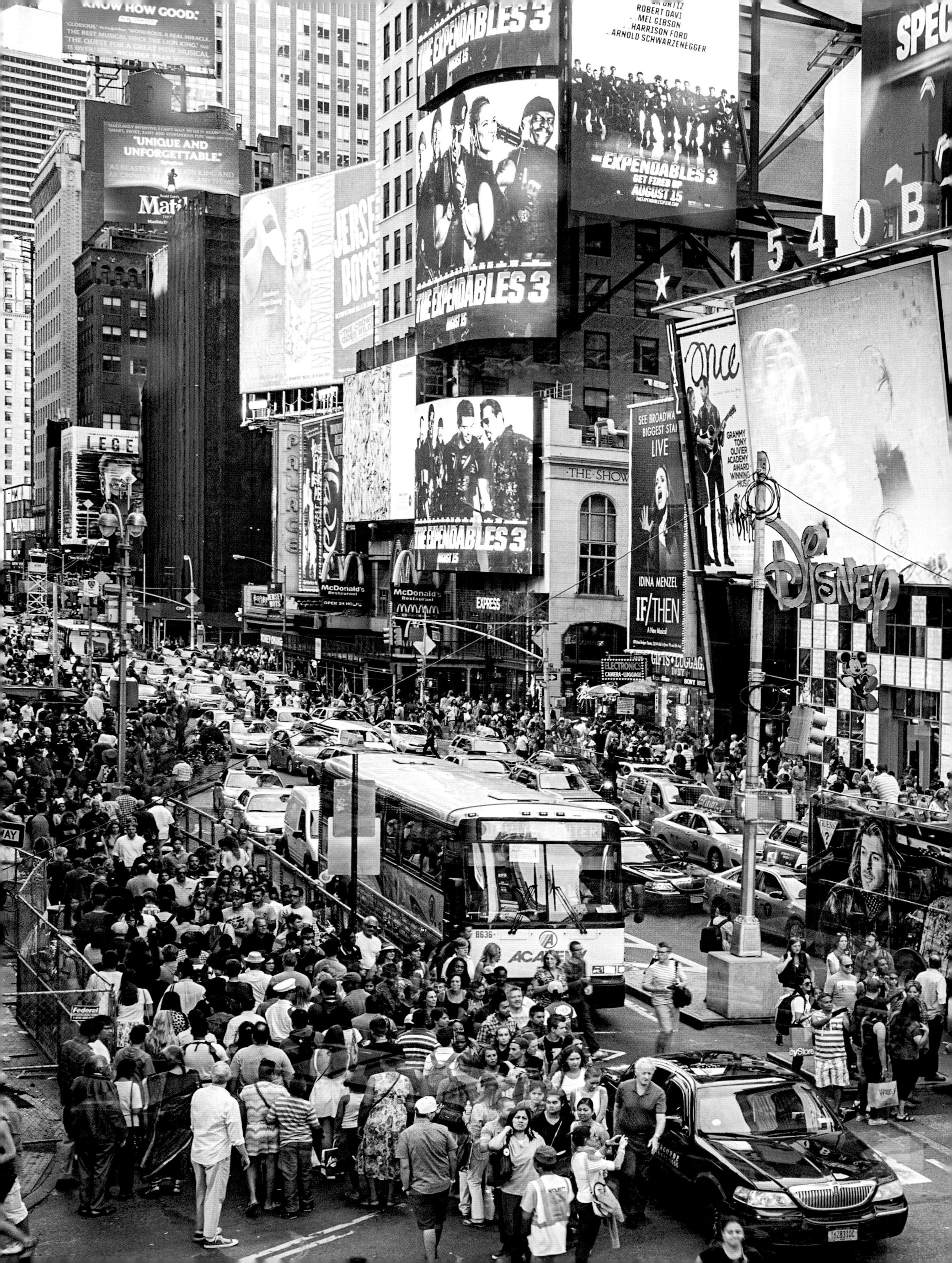

KNOW HOW GOOD.
UNIQUE AND UNFORGETTABLE
Matilda
THE EXPENDABLES 3
ROBERT DAVI
MEL GIBSON
HARRISON FORD
ARNOLD SCHWARZENEGGER
THE EXPENDABLES 3
GET FIRED UP
AUGUST 15
THEEXPENDABLESFILM.COM
SPEC
1 5 4 0 B
JERSEY BOYS
MAMMA MIA!
LEGE
once
SEE BROADWAY'S BIGGEST STARS
LIVE
IF/THEN
A New Musical
IDINA MENZEL
Disney
THE SHOW
McDonald's
Restaurant
OPEN 24 HOURS
McDonald's
Restaurant
EXPRESS
ELECTRONICS
CAMERA · LUGGAGE
GIFTS · LUGGAGE
SONY
ACADEMY
8636
GUESS

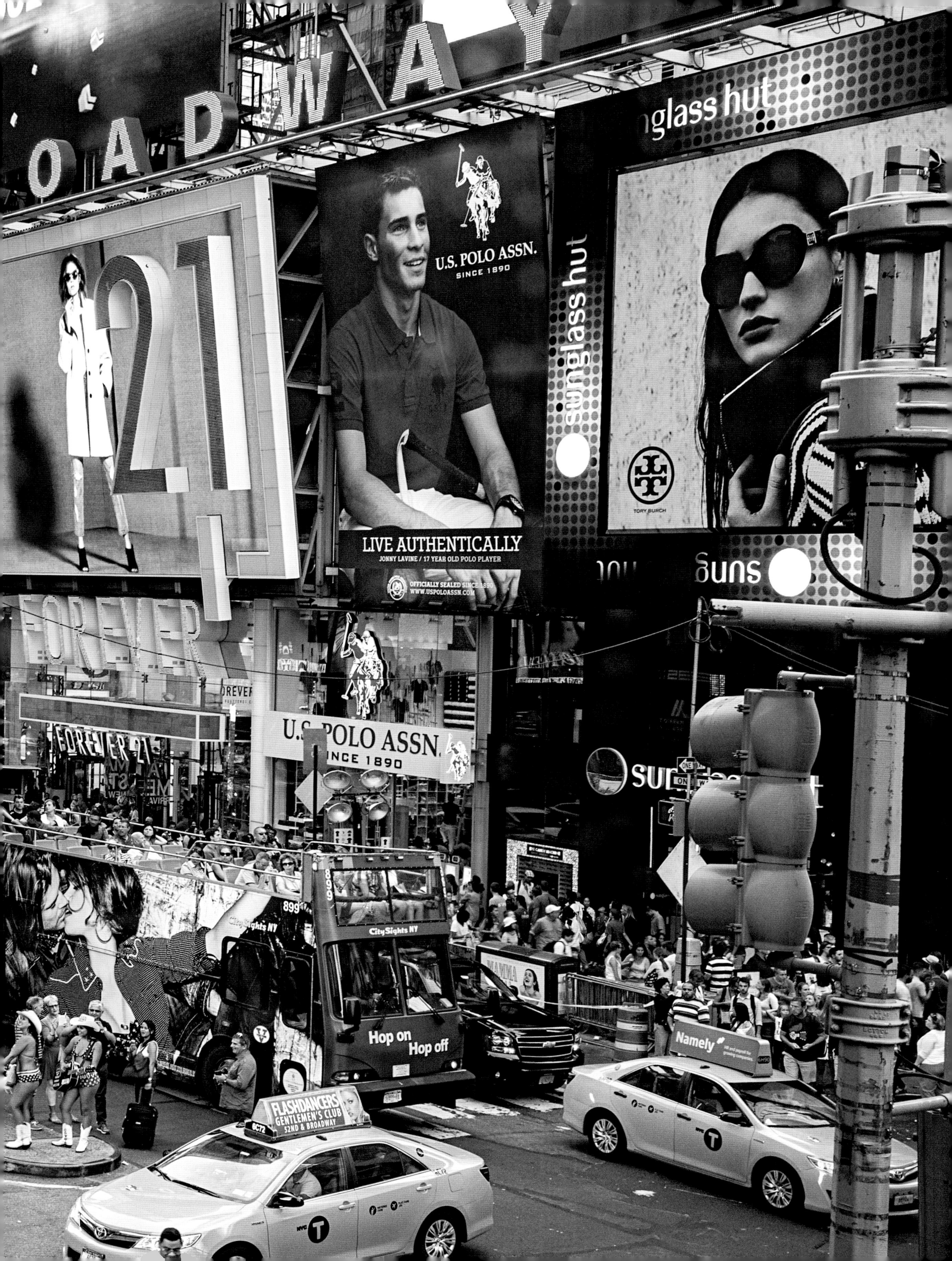
OADWAY
21
FOREVER
U.S. POLO ASSN.
SINCE 1890
LIVE AUTHENTICALLY
JONNY LAVINE / 17 YEAR OLD POLO PLAYER
OFFICIALLY SEALED SINCE 1890
WWW.USPOLOASSN.COM
sunglass hut
nglass hut
TORY BURCH
suns
U.S. POLO ASSN.
SINCE 1890
su
ONE WAY
Hop on Hop off
CitySights NY
899
Namely
FLASHDANCERS
GENTLEMEN'S CLUB
52ND & BROADWAY
NYC
T

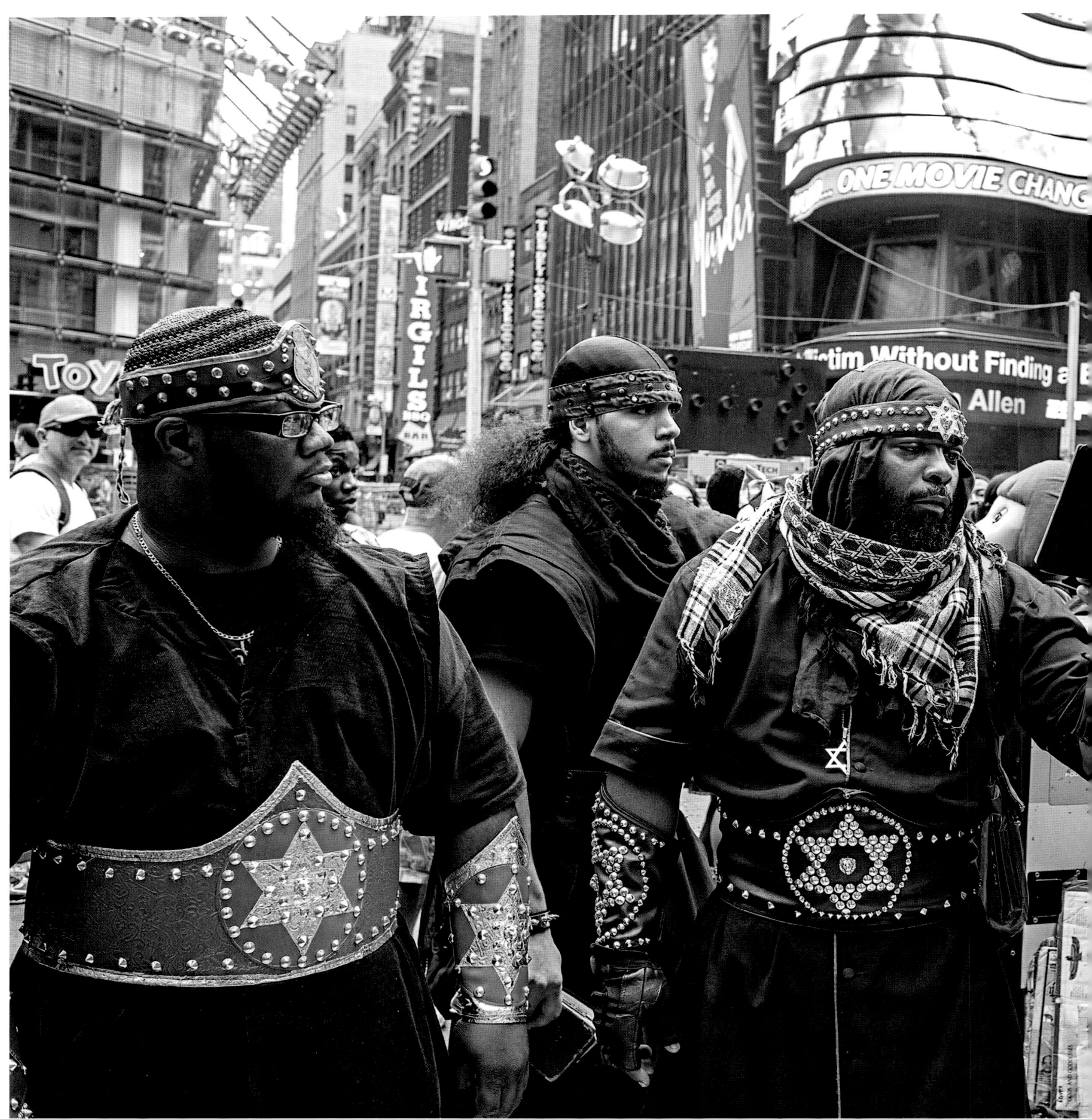

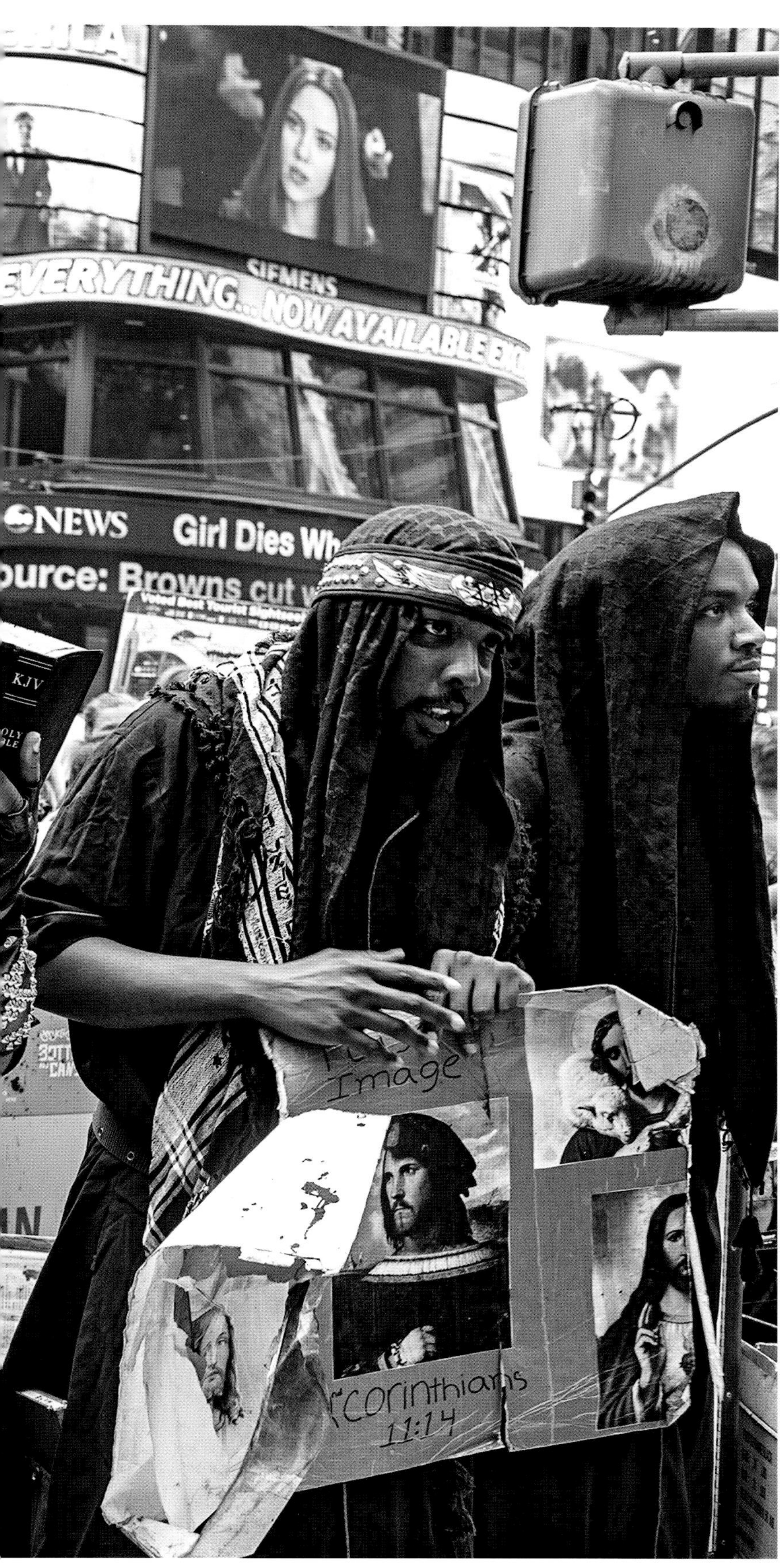
SIEMENS
EVERYTHING... NOW AVAILABLE EX
NEWS
Girl Dies Wh
ource: Browns cut
KJV
HOLY BIBLE
Image
corinthians
11:14

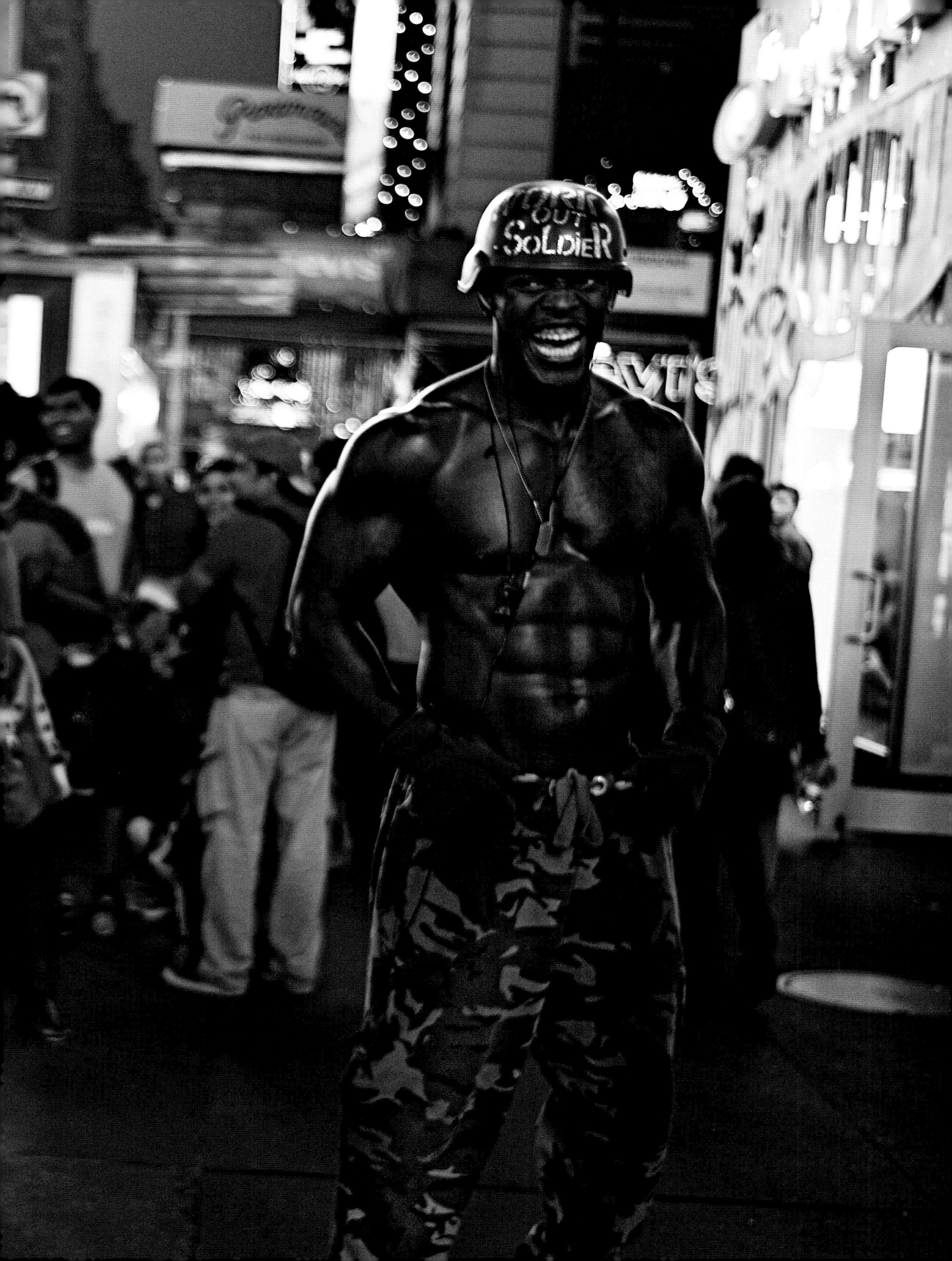
WORK
OUT
SoldieR

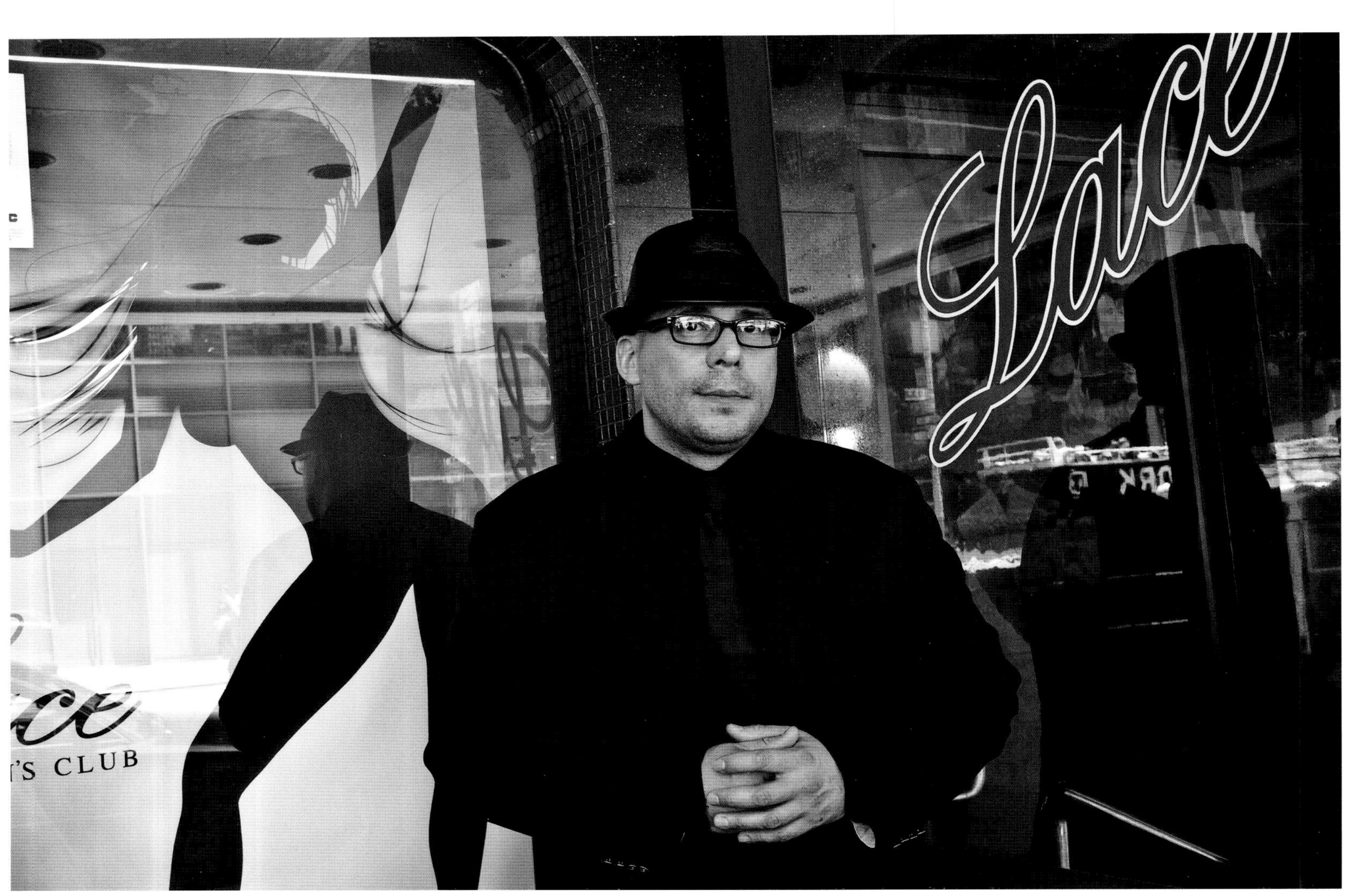

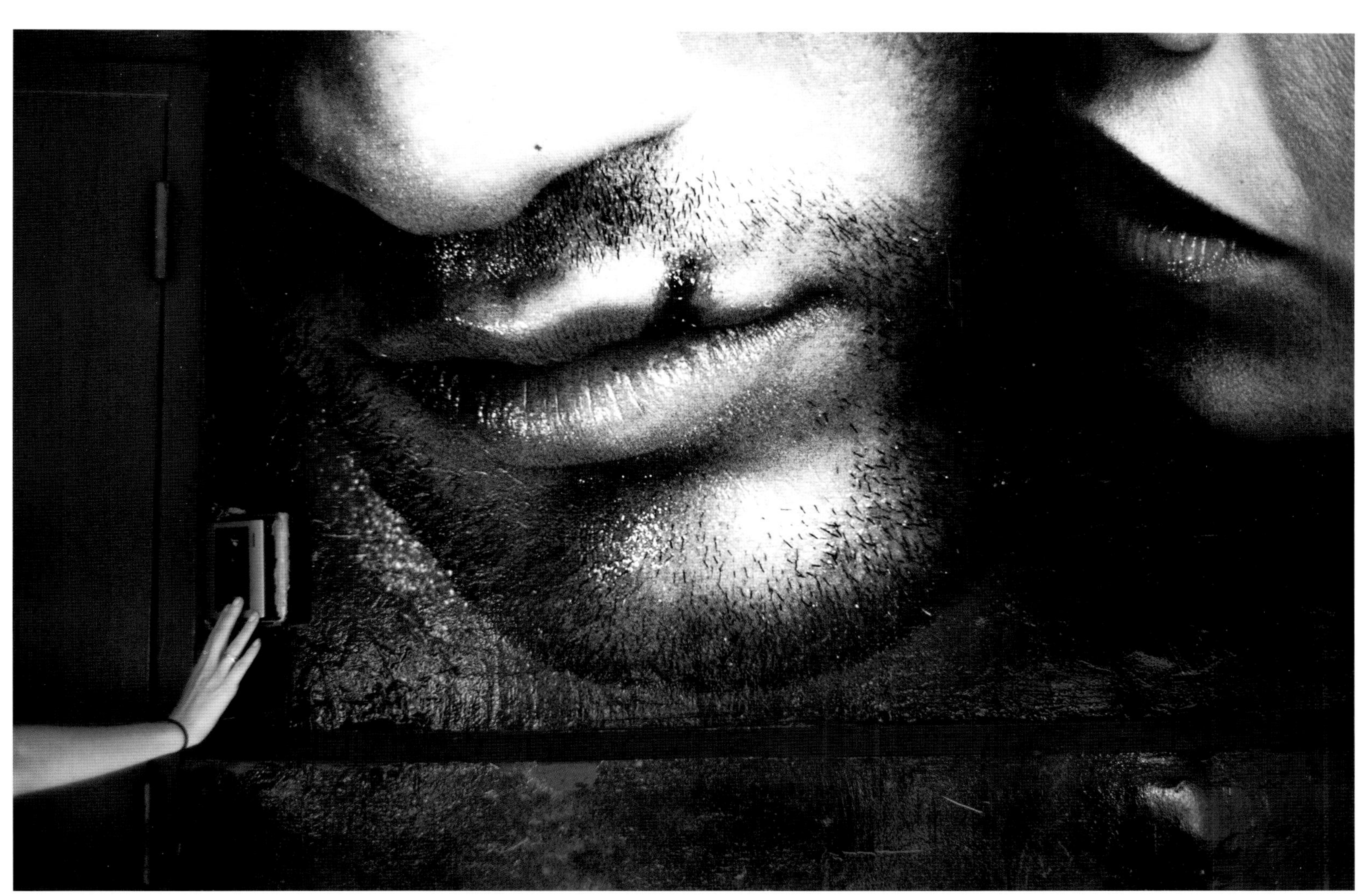

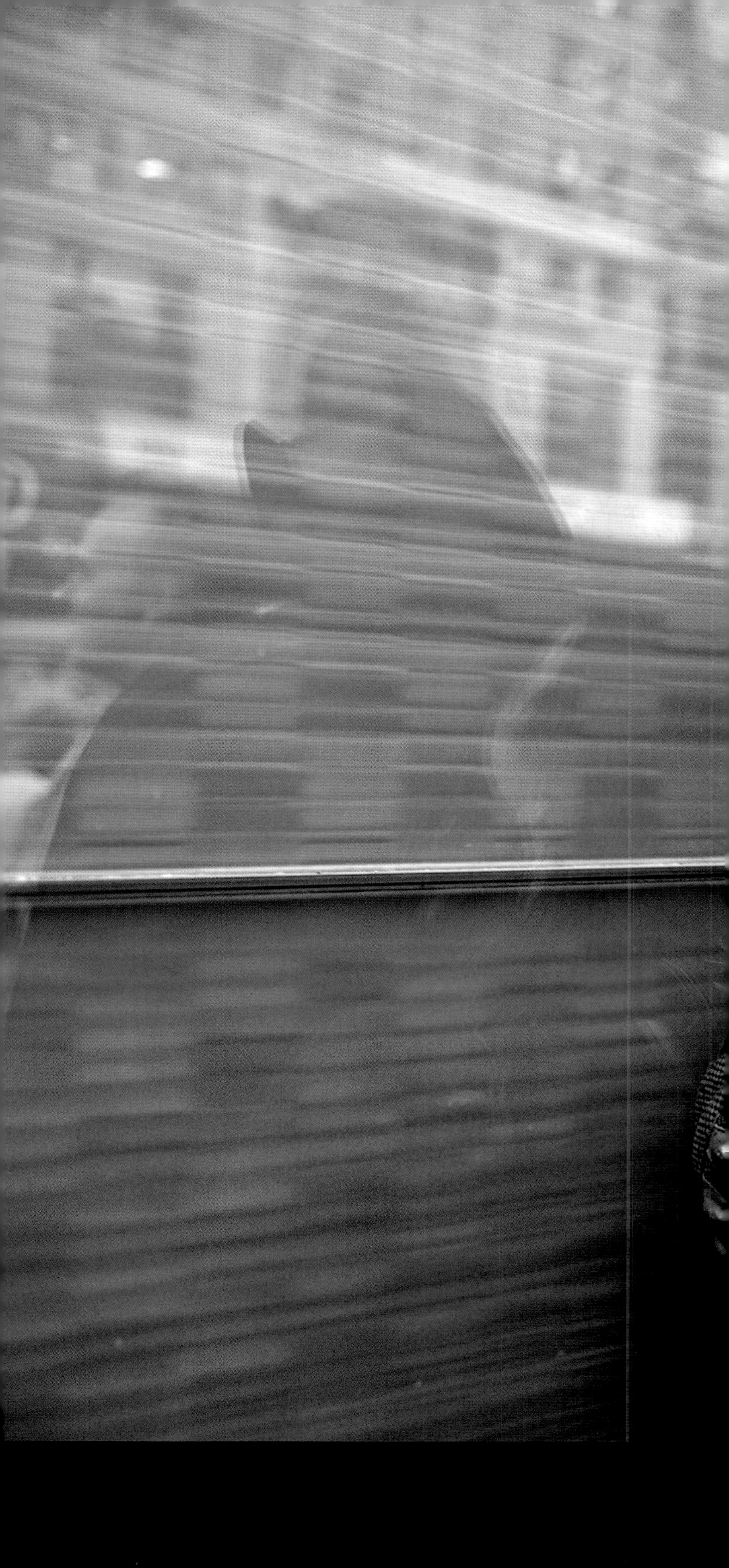

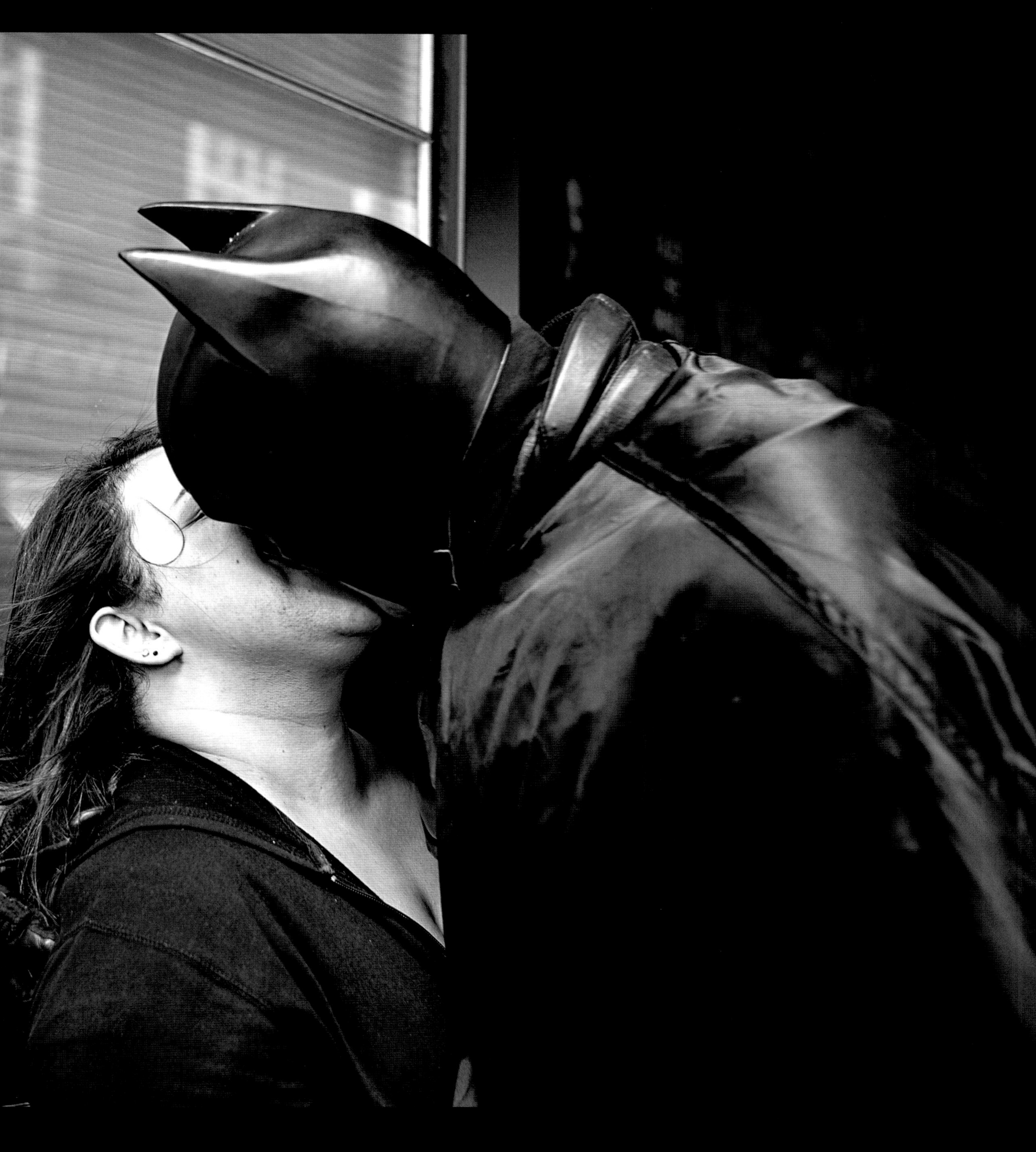

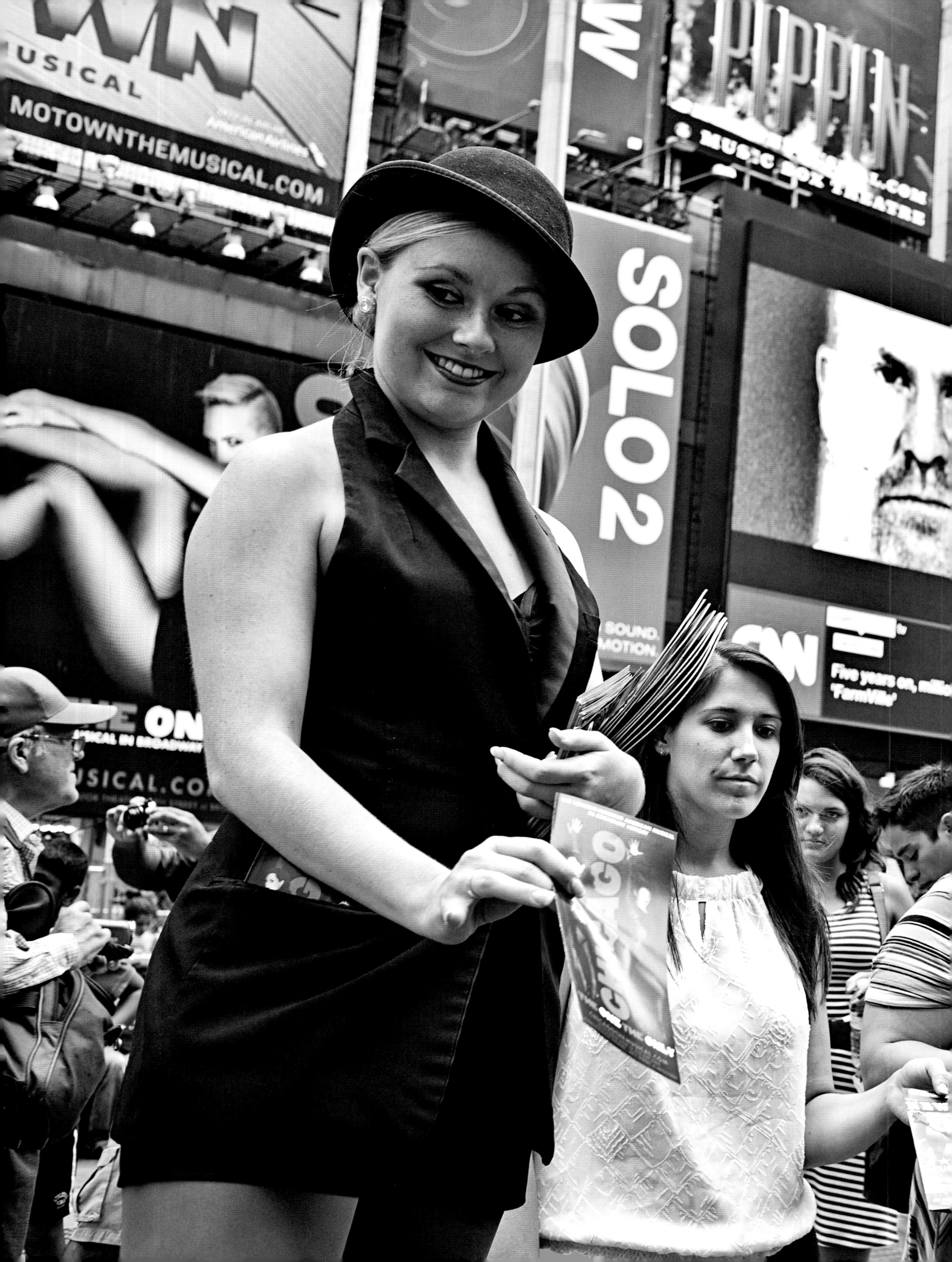
WN
MUSICAL
MOTOWNTHEMUSICAL.COM
W
PIPPIN
MUSIC BOX THEATRE
SOLO 2
SOUND.
MOTION.
CNN
Five years on, millio
'FarmVille'
ON
MUSICAL IN BROADWAY
MUSICAL.CO

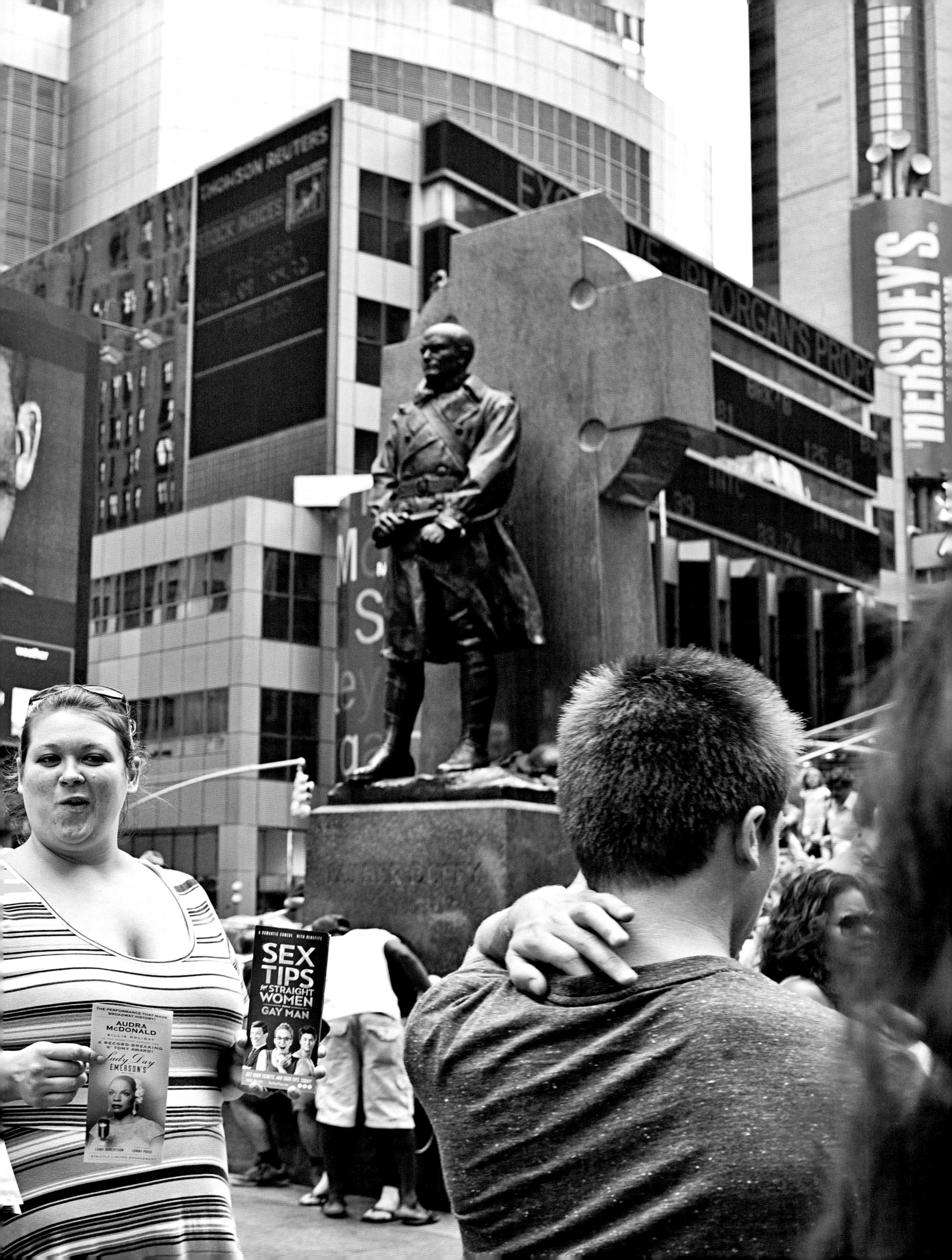

THOMSON REUTERS
MORGAN'S
HERSHEY'S
SEX
TIPS
for
STRAIGHT
WOMEN
from a
GAY MAN
THE PERFORMANCE THAT MADE
BROADWAY HISTORY
AUDRA
McDONALD
A RECORD-BREAKING
6th TONY AWARD!
Lady Day
EMERSON'S

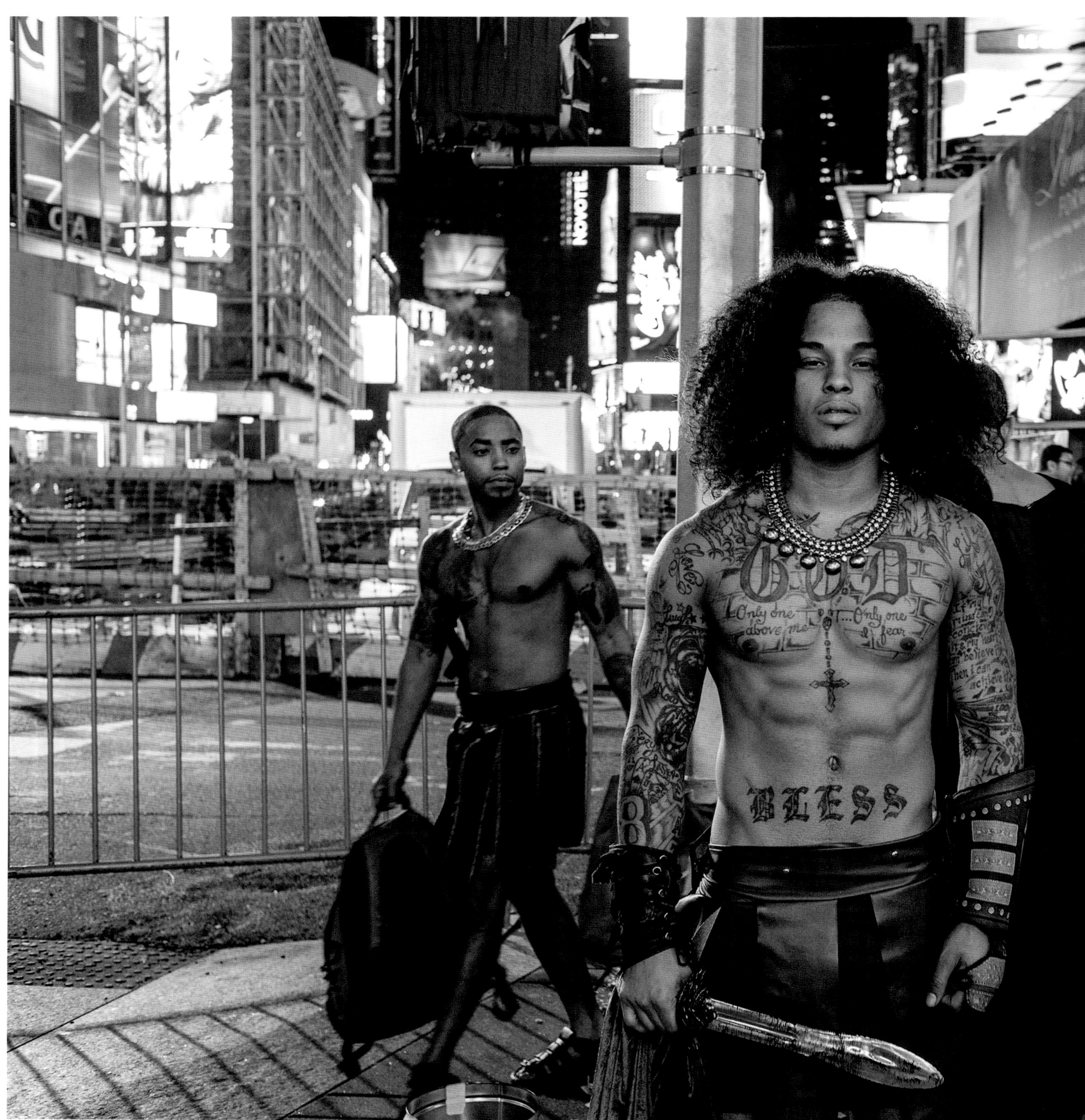

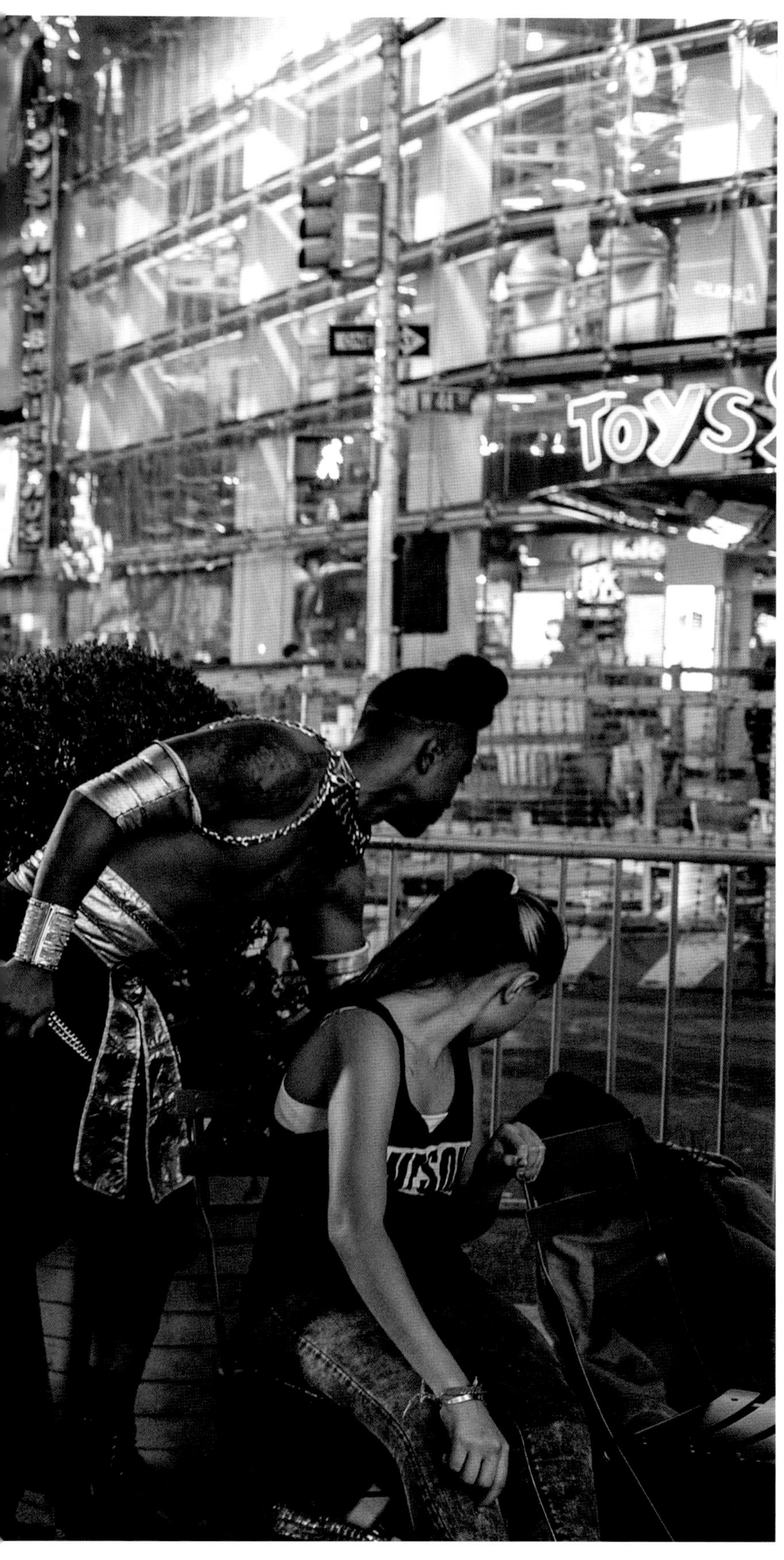

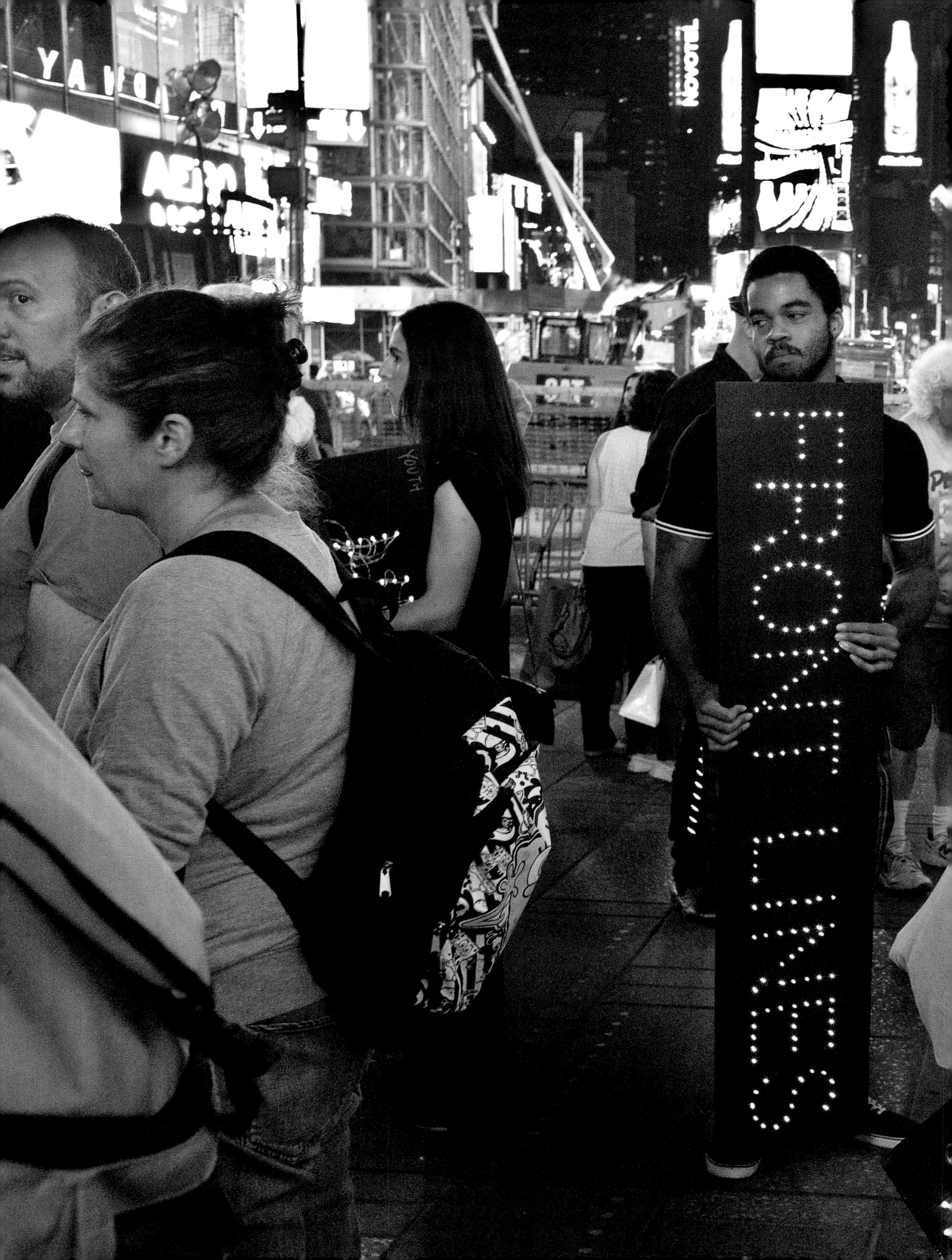

NOVOTEL
AERO
YOUTH

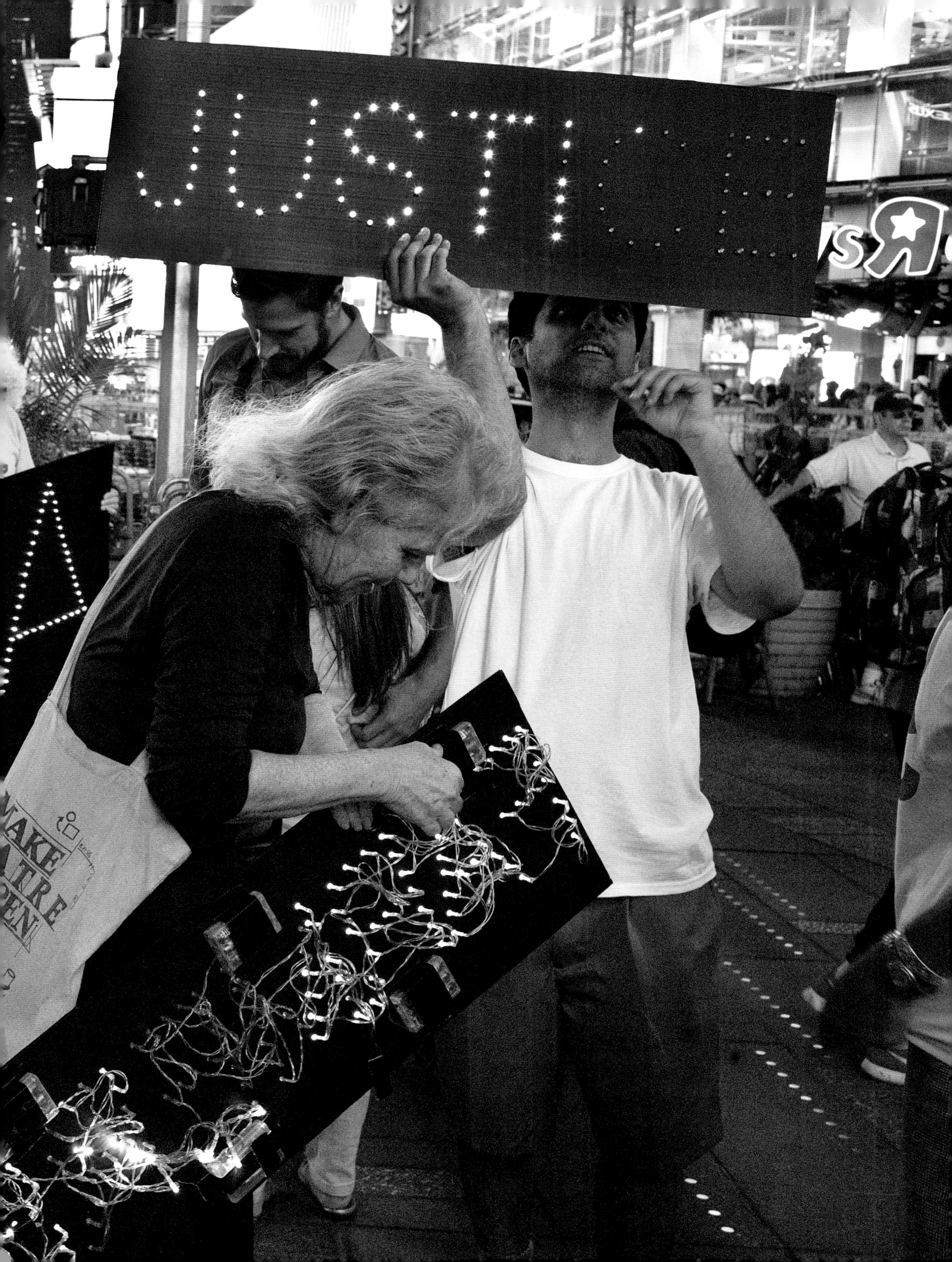

JUSTICE
MAKE
THEATRE
OPEN

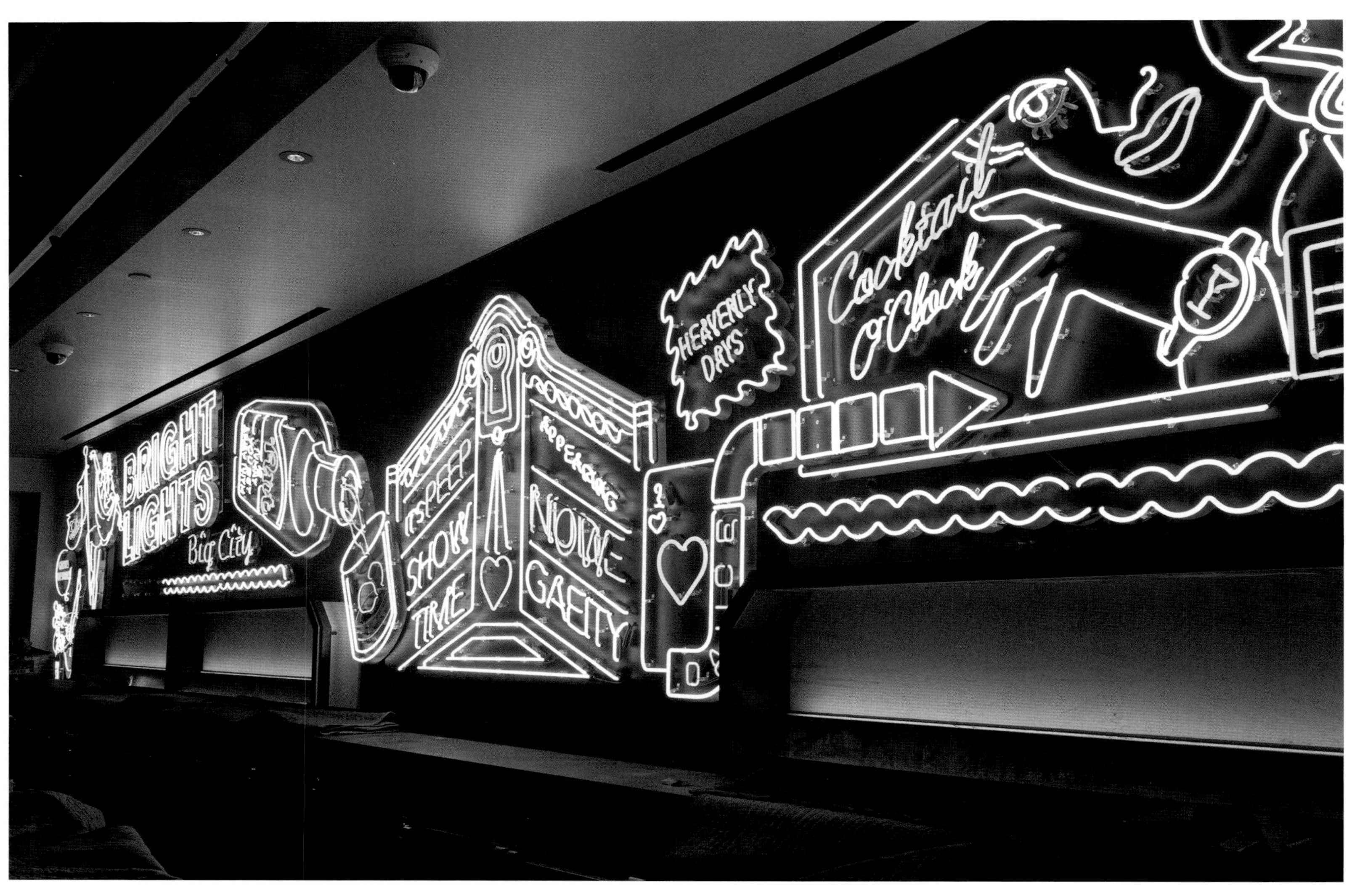

BRIGHT LIGHTS
Big City
SHOW TIME
GAEITY
NOISE
HEAVENLY DAYS
Cocktail o'Clock

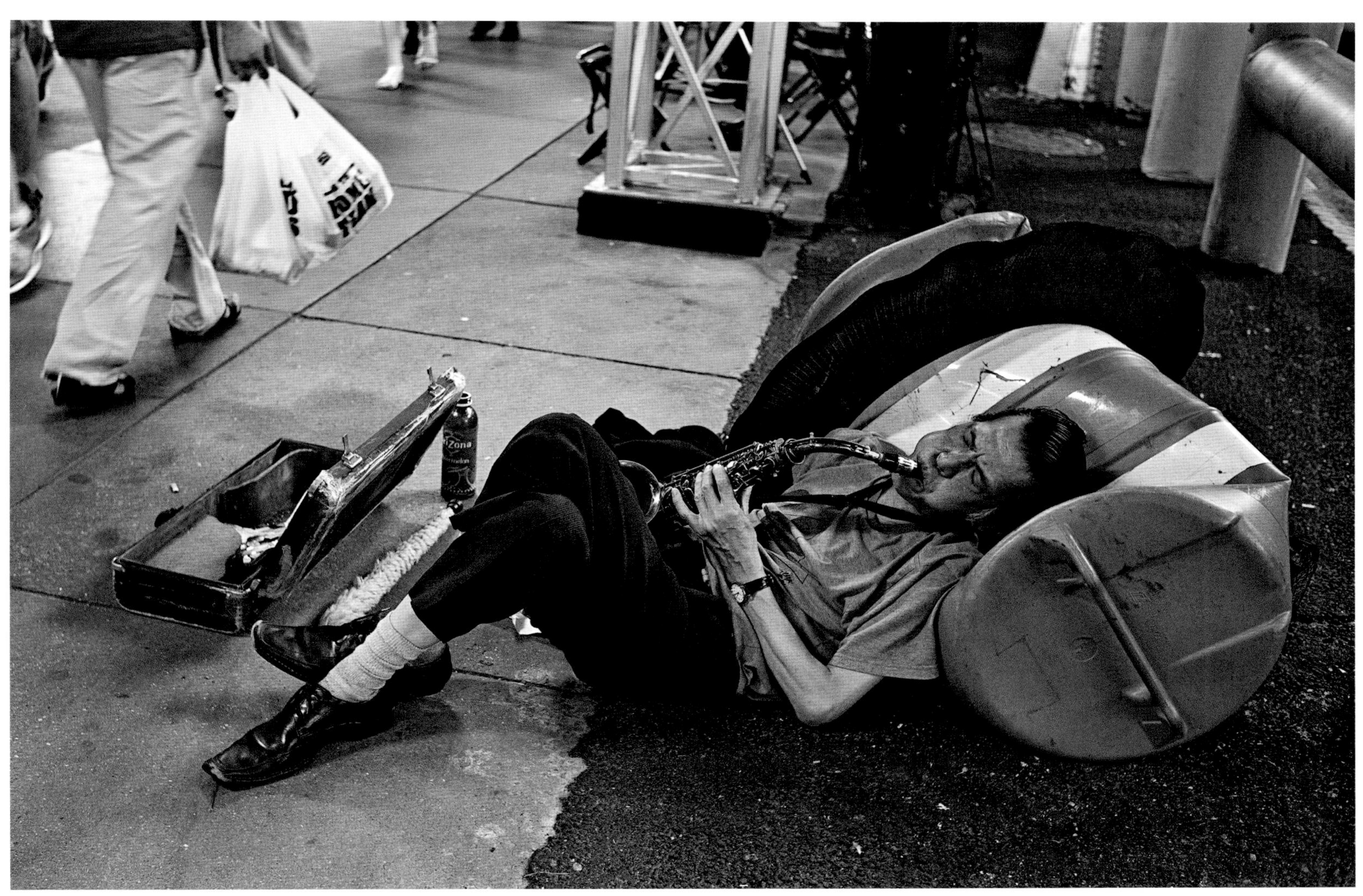

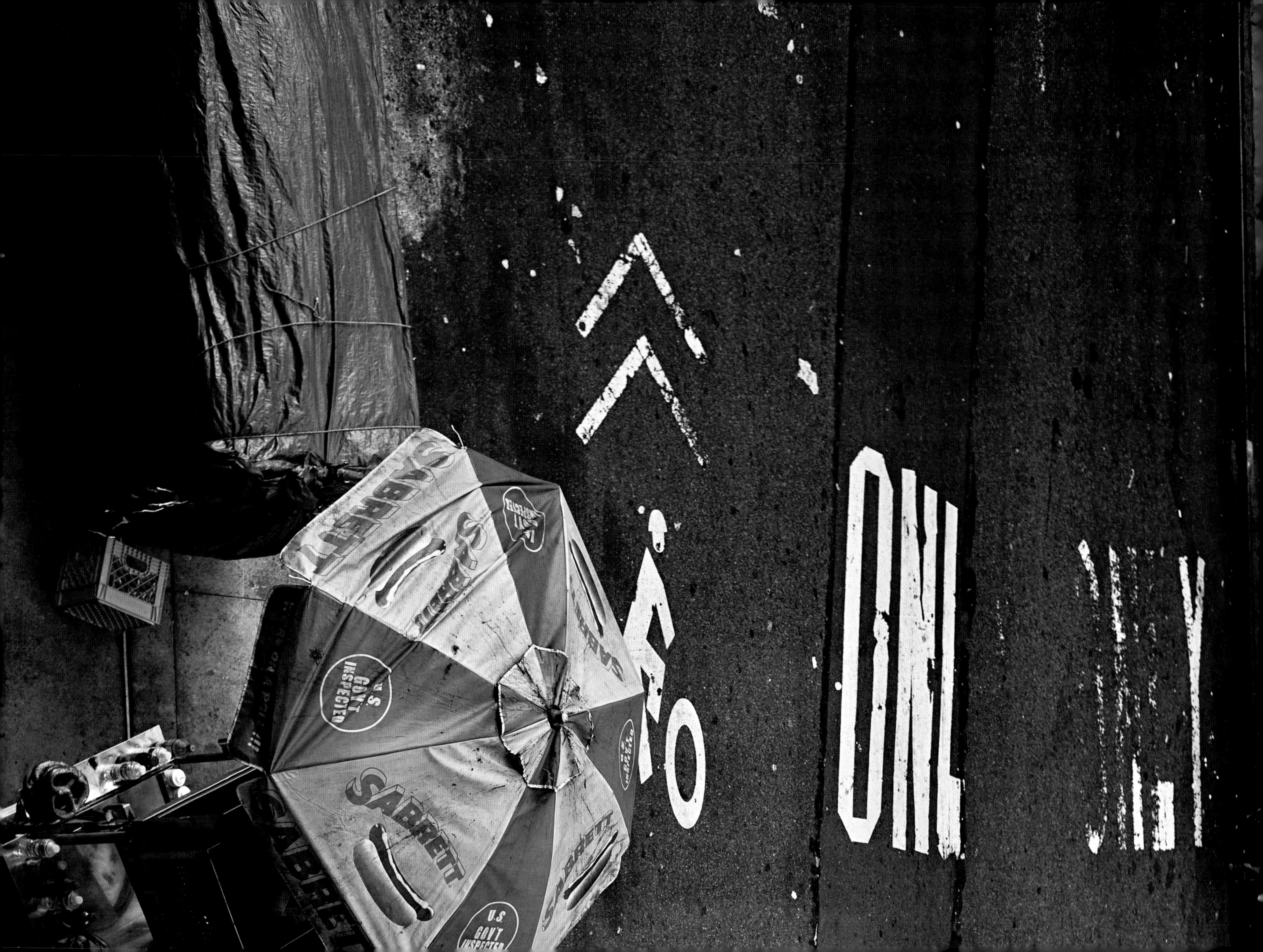
SABRETT
SABRETT
SABRETT
SABRETT
SABRETT
U.S. GOV'T INSPECTED
U.S. GOV'T INSPECTED
WE'RE ON A ROLL!!!
ONLY

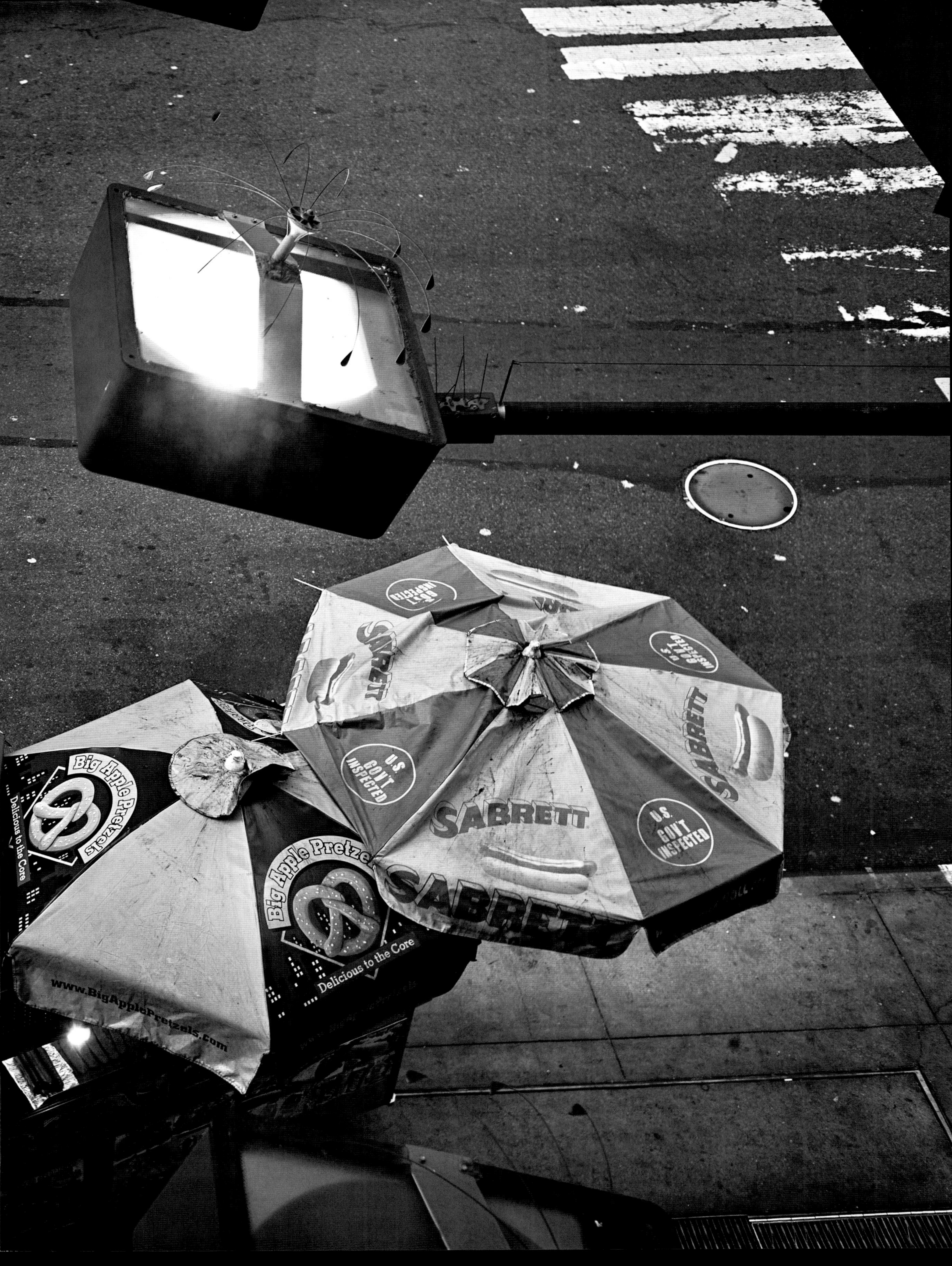

SABRETT
U.S. GOV'T INSPECTED
U.S. GOV'T INSPECTED
SABRETT
Big Apple Pretzels
Delicious to the Core
www.BigApplePretzels.com

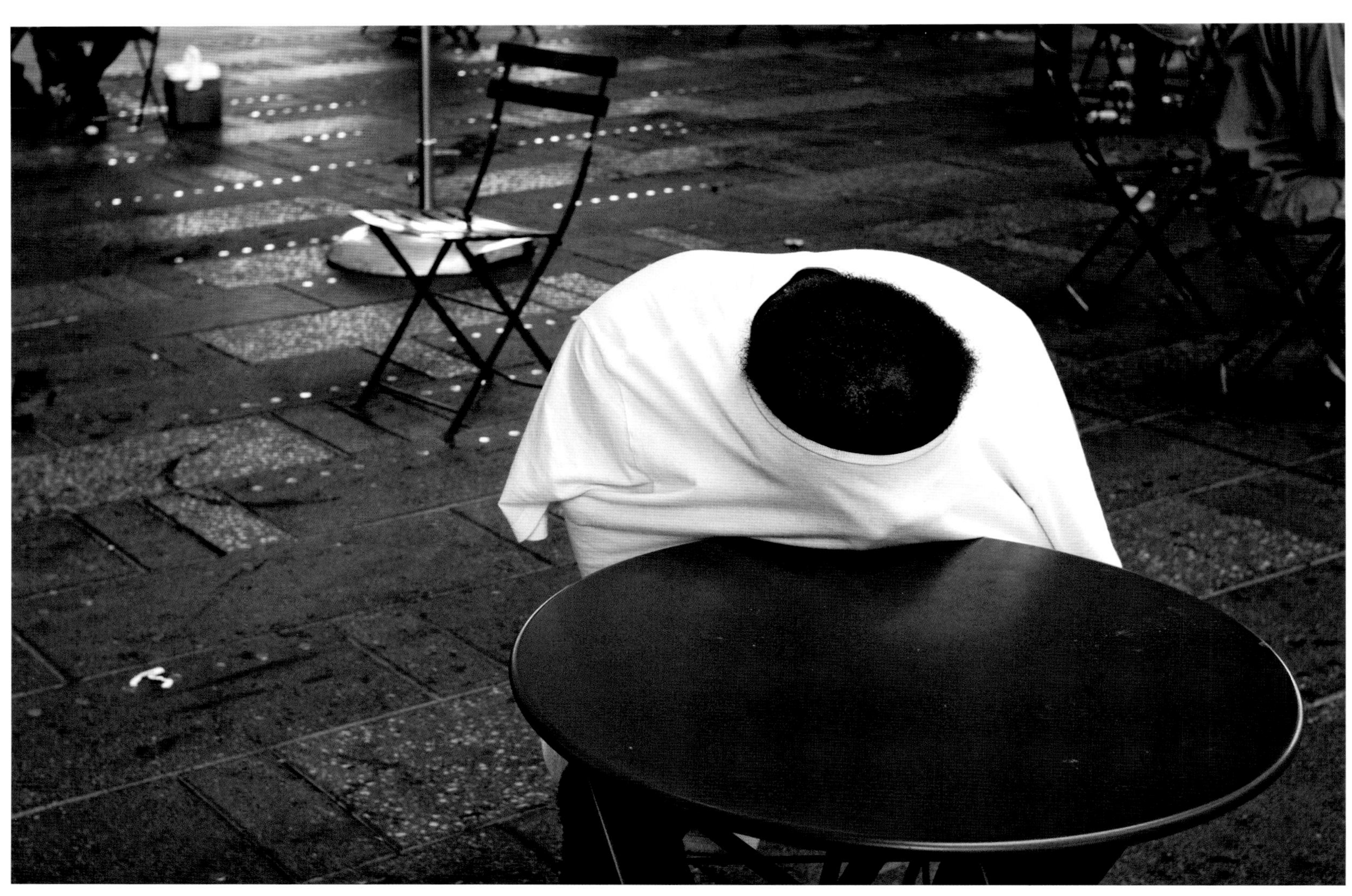

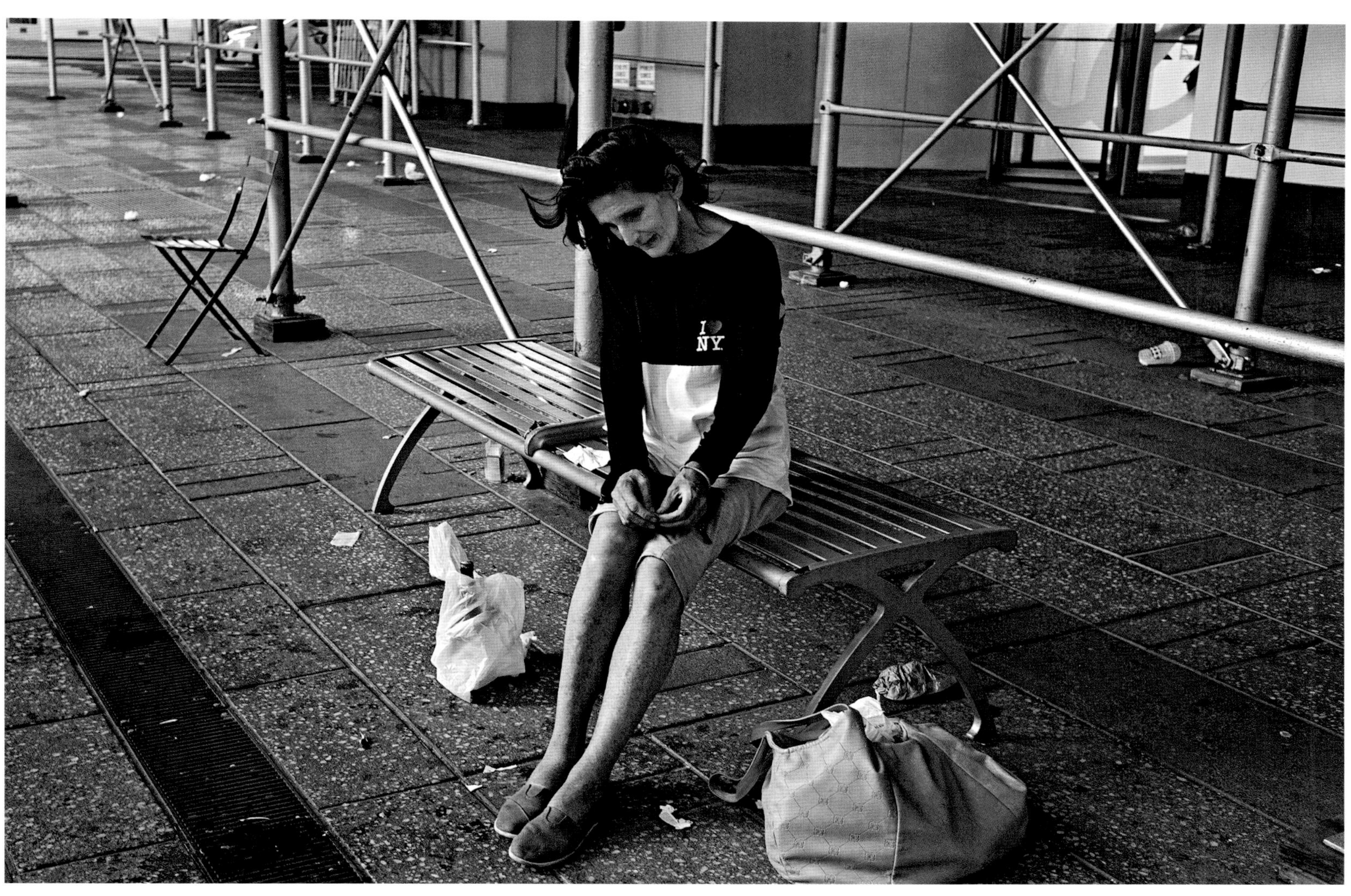

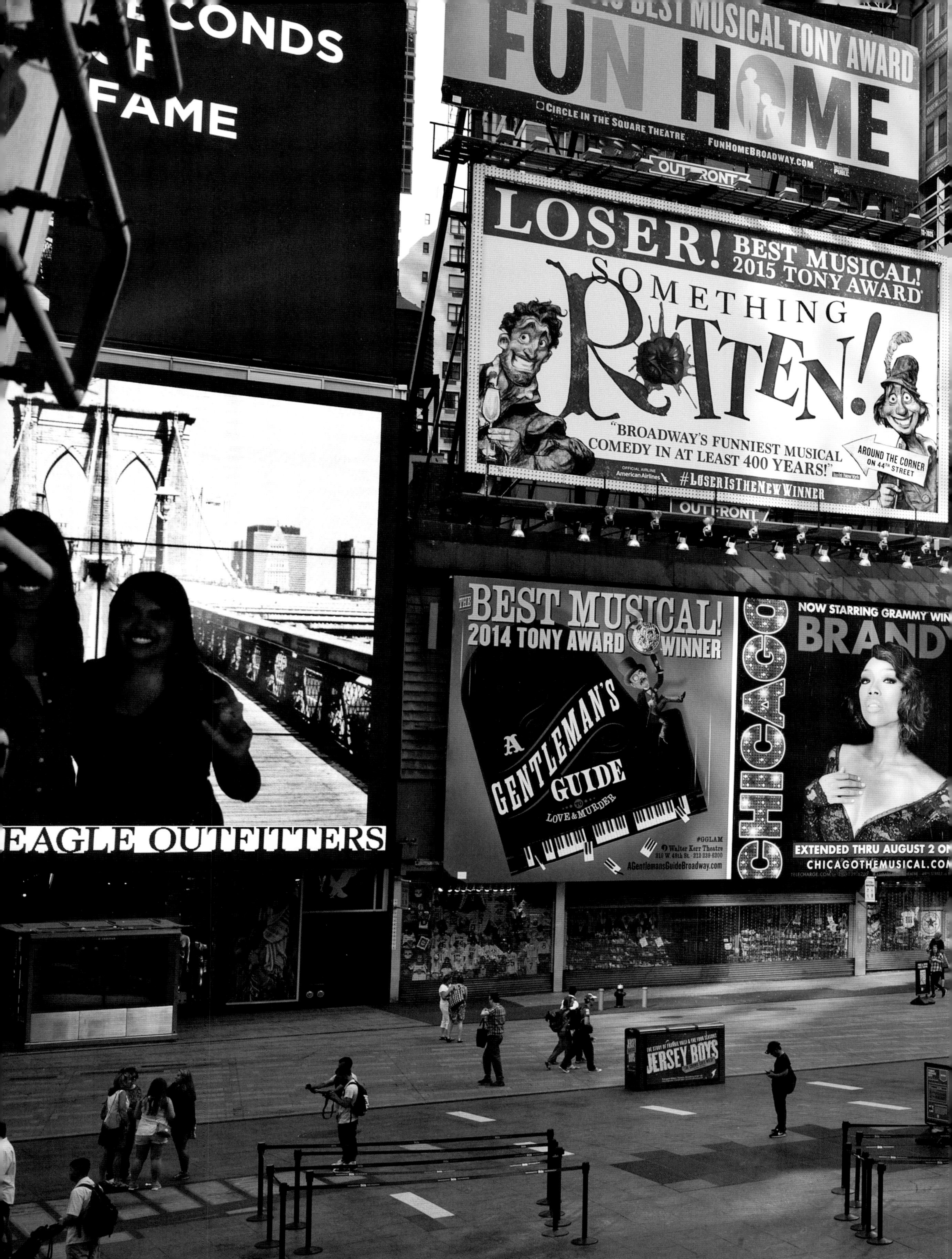
CONDS
FAME
FUN HOME
BEST MUSICAL TONY AWARD
CIRCLE IN THE SQUARE THEATRE
FUNHOMEBROADWAY.COM
OUTFRONT
LOSER! BEST MUSICAL!
2015 TONY AWARD
SOMETHING ROTTEN!
"BROADWAY'S FUNNIEST MUSICAL
COMEDY IN AT LEAST 400 YEARS!"
OFFICIAL AIRLINE
American Airlines
#LoserIsTheNewWinner
AROUND THE CORNER
ON 44TH STREET
OUTFRONT
THE BEST MUSICAL!
2014 TONY AWARD WINNER
A GENTLEMAN'S GUIDE
TO LOVE & MURDER
#GGLAM
Walter Kerr Theatre
219 W. 48th St. · 212-239-6200
AGentlemansGuideBroadway.com
NOW STARRING GRAMMY WIN
BRAND
CHICAGO
EXTENDED THRU AUGUST 2 ON
CHICAGOTHEMUSICAL.COM
EAGLE OUTFITTERS
THE STORY OF FRANKIE VALLI & THE FOUR SEASONS
JERSEY BOYS

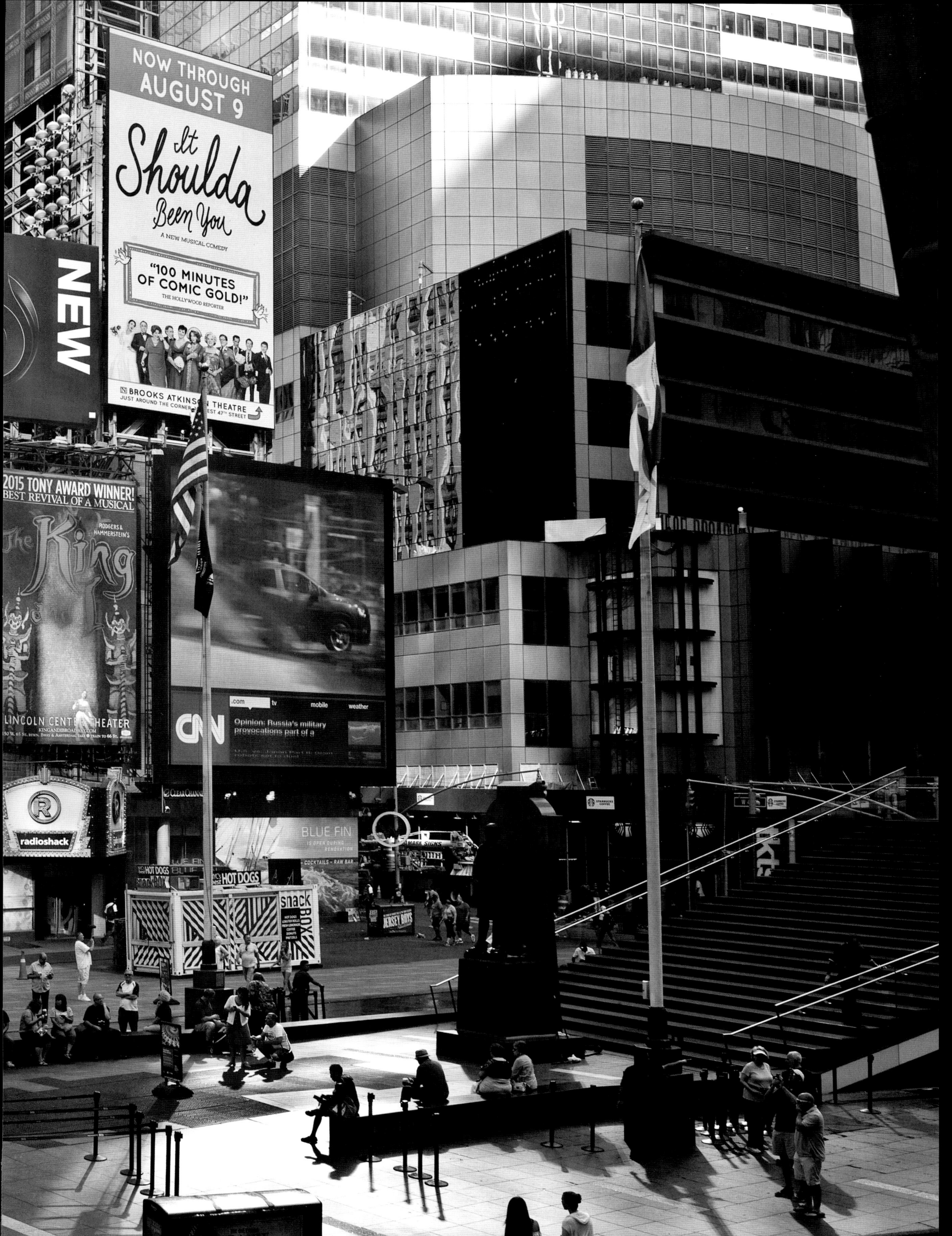
NOW THROUGH
AUGUST 9
It Shoulda Been You
A NEW MUSICAL COMEDY
"100 MINUTES
OF COMIC GOLD!"
THE HOLLYWOOD REPORTER
BROOKS ATKINSON THEATRE
JUST AROUND THE CORNER WEST 47TH STREET
NEW
2015 TONY AWARD WINNER!
BEST REVIVAL OF A MUSICAL
RODGERS & HAMMERSTEIN'S
The King
LINCOLN CENTER THEATER
KINGANDIBROADWAY.COM
150 W. 65 St. BTWN. BWAY & AMSTERDAM. TAKE 1 TRAIN TO 66 St.
R
radioshack
CNN
.com   tv   mobile   weather
Opinion: Russia's military
provocations part of a
BLUE FIN
IS OPEN DURING
RENOVATION
- COCKTAILS · RAW BAR
HOT DOGS
NYC's best HOT DOGS
snack
BOX
JERSEY BOYS
STARBUCKS COFFEE
tkts

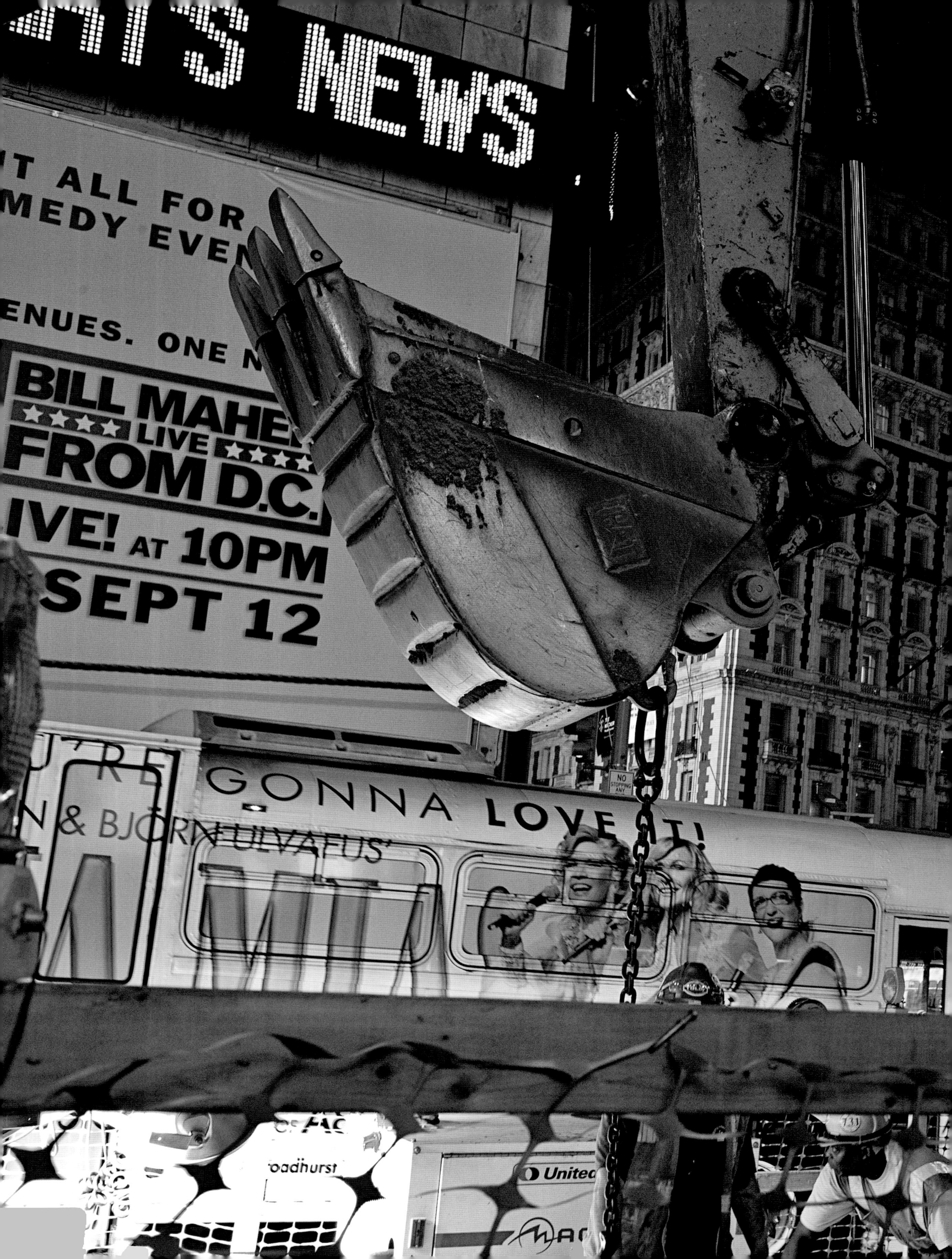
'S NEWS
IT ALL FOR
MEDY EVEN
ENUES. ONE N
BILL MAHER
LIVE
FROM D.C.
IVE! AT 10PM
SEPT 12
URE GONNA LOVE IT!
N & BJORN ULVAEUS'
NO STOPPING ANY
oadhurst
United

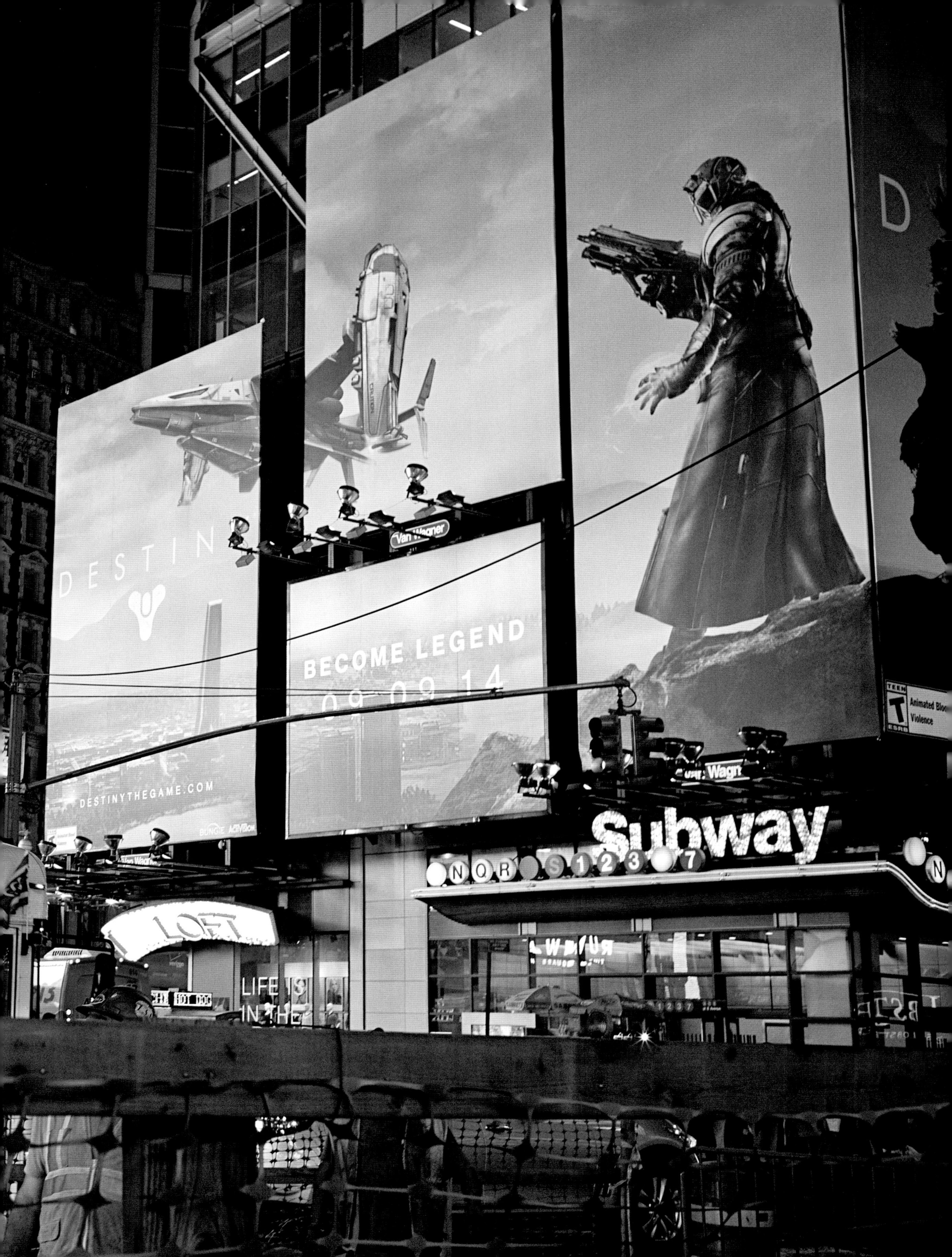
DESTINY
BECOME LEGEND
09 09 14
DESTINYTHEGAME.COM
BUNGIE ACTIVISION
Van Wagner
TEEN
T
ESRB
Animated Blood
Violence
Subway
N O R S 1 2 3 7 N
LOFT
LIFE IS
IN THE

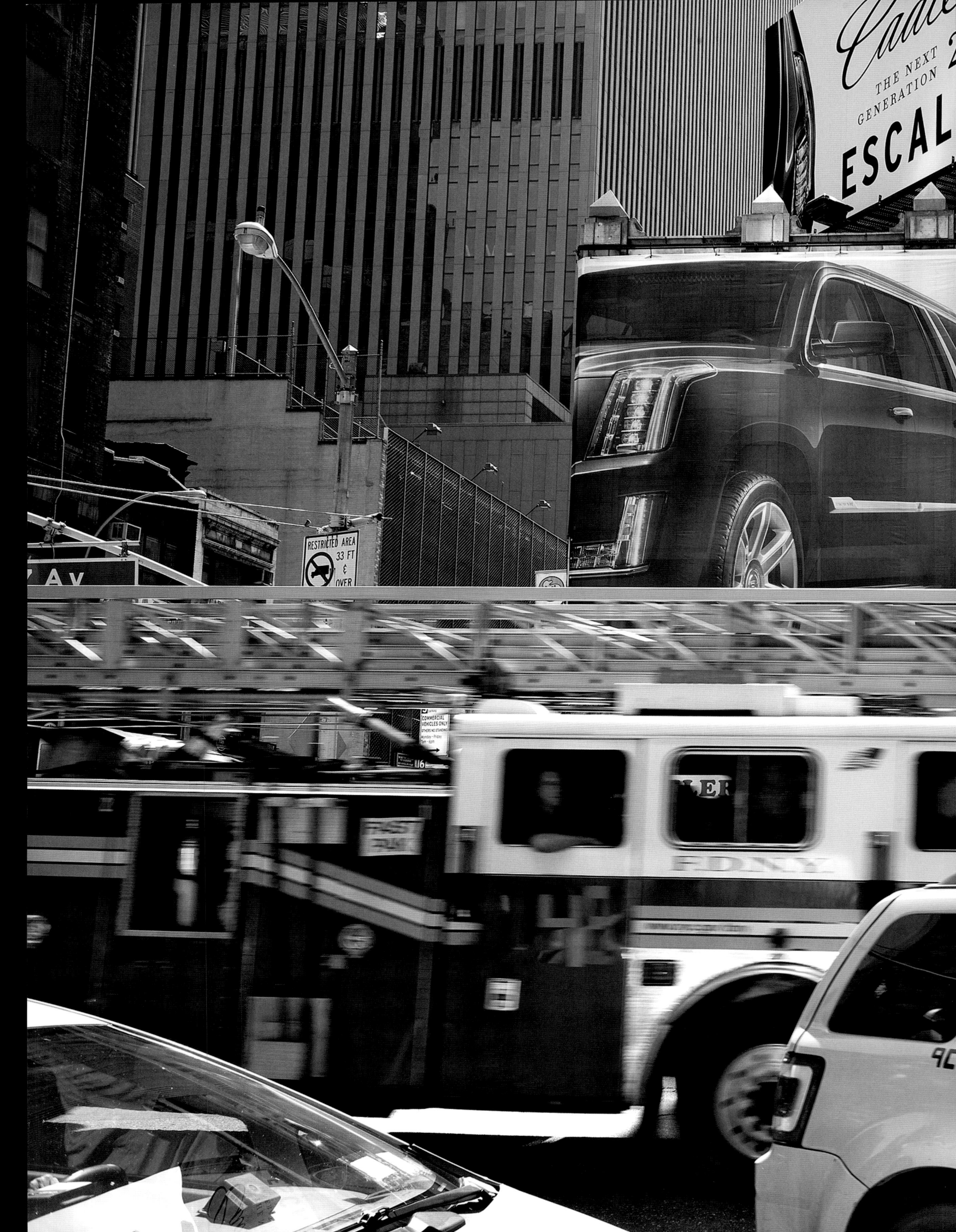
Cadillac
THE NEXT
GENERATION
ESCAL
7 Av
RESTRICTED AREA
33 FT
&
OVER
COMMERCIAL
VEHICLES ONLY
OTHERS NO STANDING
Monday - Friday
7am - 6pm
FDNY

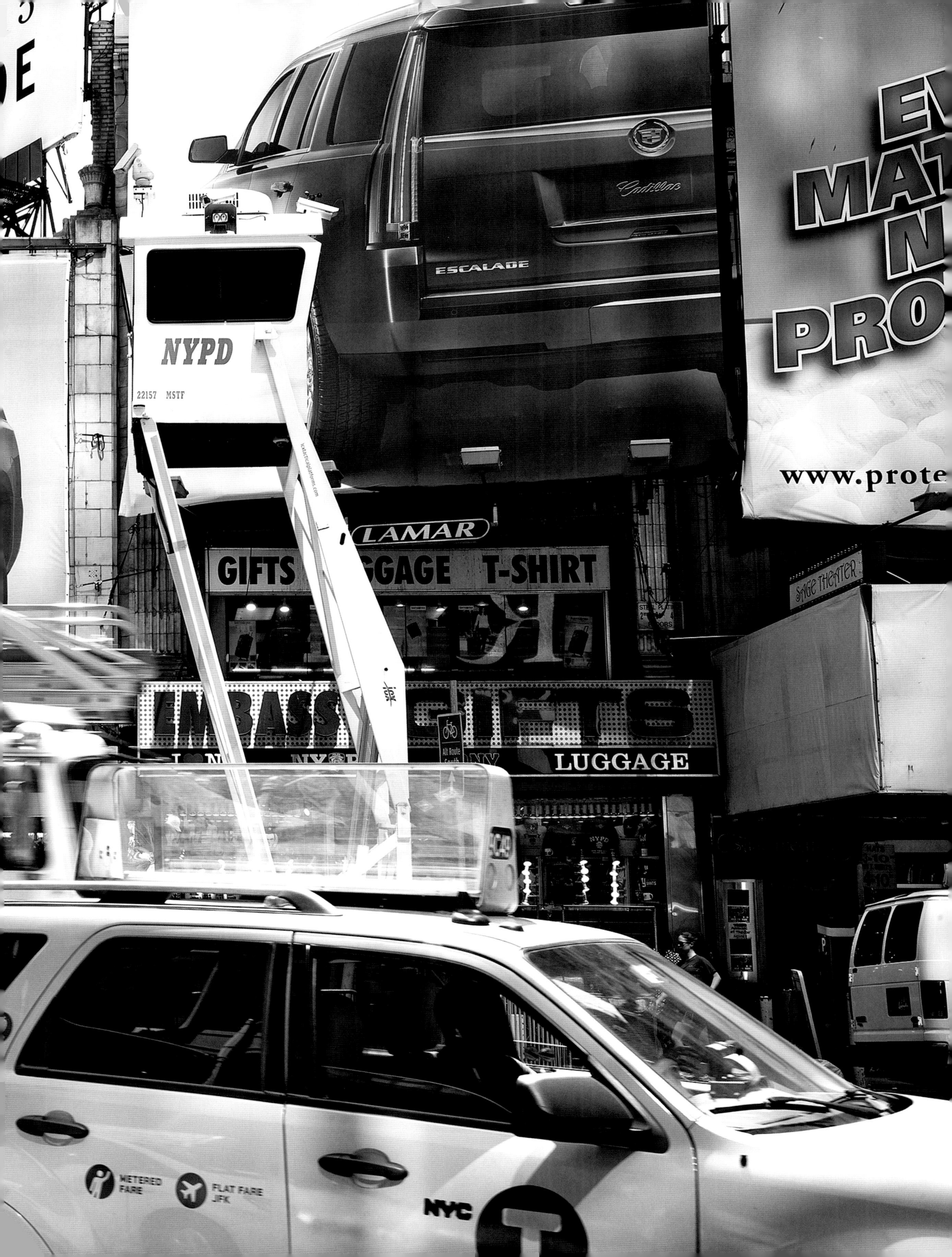
Cadillac
ESCALADE
NYPD
22157 MSTF
EV
MAT
N
PRO
www.prote
LAMAR
GIFTS LUGGAGE T-SHIRT
STAGE THEATER
EMBASSY GIFTS
LUGGAGE
NYPD
Alt Route
South
NY
METERED FARE
FLAT FARE JFK
NYC

The ruby red, translucent stairs that anchor the north end of Times Square at 47th Street, magical stairs that go nowhere, first drew me to this area. I had never explored the area on foot, and I wanted to survey Times Square from the top, a view that turned out to be flat-out spectacular. It was the eve of the summer solstice, 2014.

Immediately, I knew that I wanted to photograph here and, after wandering around for a few hours, I began to see this iconic landscape as a metaphor for urban America today. My premise is that, here in these five blocks from 42nd to 47th Streets, many of the major trends of our society—consumerism, hyper-sexualization, hucksterism, surveillance, narcissism, globalism—are condensed and amplified. Fantasy parades as reality. Tourists flock to Times Square to see and be seen. It is the "ground zero" of our post-fact world, where media and audience engage in a constantly shifting dance, unclear who is leading whom. Corporate interests claim almost every inch of public space. Change is constant.

And yet, beneath the incessant barrage of the football-field-sized billboards, there is something redemptive about this place. Those with political, religious, or social messages have seemingly unlimited freedom of expression. People from every background peacefully co-exist. In the wee hours of the morning the homeless find a safe place to sleep. And occasionally moments of tenderness and care cut through the electric static.

No matter how many times I return to Times Square, I am still filled with wonder and horror.

— BETSY KAREL

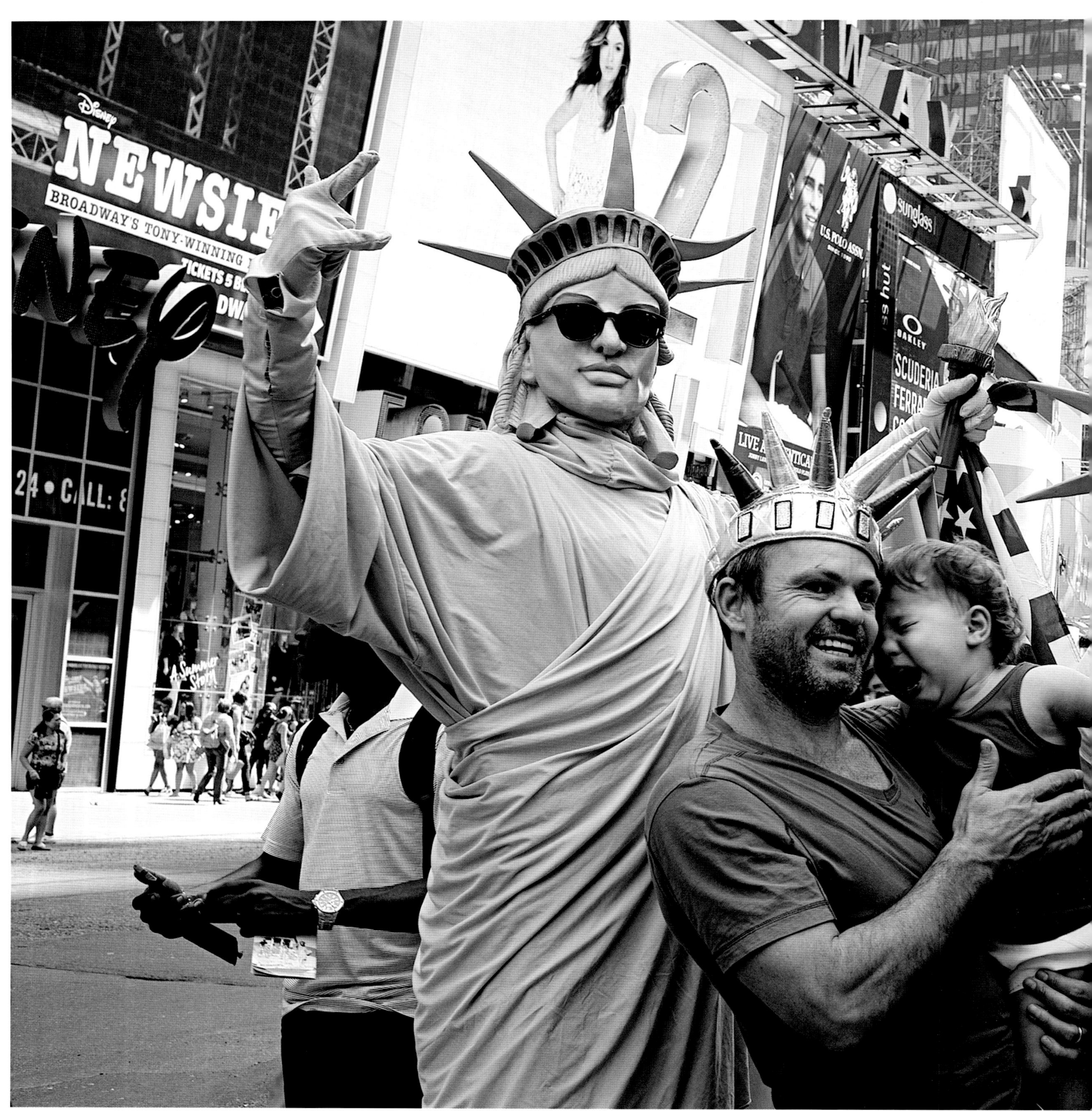

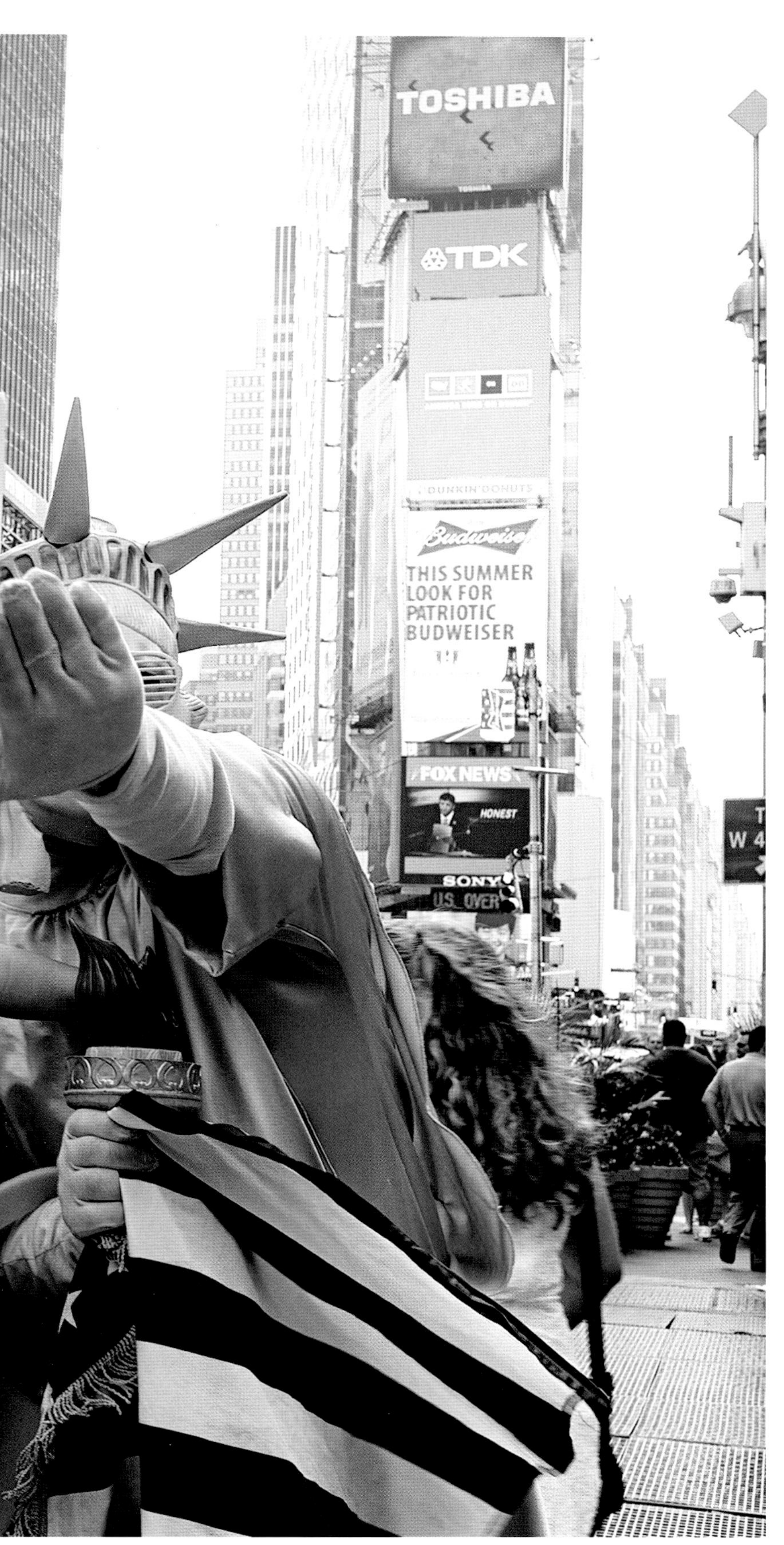

TOSHIBA
TDK
DUNKIN'DONUTS
Budweiser
THIS SUMMER
LOOK FOR
PATRIOTIC
BUDWEISER
FOX NEWS
HONEST
SONY
U.S. OVER
W 4

"It's like going into the sea and letting the waves break over you. You feel the power of the sea. On the street each successive wave brings a whole cast of characters. You take wave after wave, you bathe in it. There is something exciting about being in the crowd, in all that chance and change—it's tough out there—but if you can keep paying attention something will reveal itself—just a split second—and then there's a crazy cockeyed picture."
— JOEL MEYEROWITZ

Betsy Karel, the Washington DC based photographer, generally photographs on the streets and other places where the public gathers. She is a street photographer, in other words. In her latest body of work, she has taken to photographing in the Mecca of street photography—New York City—and focusing upon the heart of the city—Times Square.

Making photographs of strangers in public places, for that is the general modus operandi of the street photographer, requires not only a certain talent but courage and persistence. It is not easy. If one was to equate its practice and art to a sporting activity, an apt analogy, something like skydiving might fit the bill. Joel Meyerowitz talks about going into the sea, and that also seems pertinent. Street photography comes behind only combat or news reportage as the genre of the medium providing its protagonists with the biggest adrenalin rush. The skydiver has the tense, but also exhilarating interval before the parachute opens, followed by a sense of both triumph and relief. The street photographer has a similar mixture of emotions. Triumph at having secured the perfect image—for nothing less than perfect will do for the authentic street shooter—combined with relief at not being harangued—or worse—by the object of his attentions.

Street shooting is a high risk, high reward kind of photography. In general, it is candid photography, where the subject is largely unaware of the photographer's interest. This means that it is sneaky, or rather that a certain amount of subterfuge is called for on the photographer's part, either to keep the subject in blissful ignorance, or unselfconscious enough to present an aspect of candid revelation. Anything much beyond a minimal awareness of the photographer's game could lead to rigidity, aggression, or—heaven forbid—posing. This constitutes the street photographer's biggest bugbear, because he is generally searching for a pure, unconsciousness, revealing "slice of life."

Of course, there is another sporting analogy which is frequently used in relation to street photography, and that is hunting. The term "street shooter" has been deployed already, and the hunting metaphor can be extended to take in the photographer "stalking" his "target," "shooting" the pictures, and "capturing"

the ideal "shot." Furthermore, like hunting, the act of photographing on the street can become almost an end in itself, and therefore one of the most compulsive and obsessive genres of the medium.

But here the comparison to hunting ends, for the ultimate aim of street shooting is not to end life. Quite the opposite, for the best street photographs—and the best street photographers—confer a perhaps peculiar, but special kind of immortality upon their subjects. Any good street photograph, or any good photographic portrait for that matter, makes us care about another life—as we do sometimes when we are struck by someone on the street, whom we will never likely see again, and wonder about them. Who are they? What are their lives like?

But let us now bring Betsy Karel into our musings upon the street photographer's art, specifically through her pictures of Times Square. It may or may not have been noticed, but in earlier paragraphs I used the word "his"—his attentions, his target—in relation to street photography. This was quite deliberate, in order to make the point that the genre has been, or at least has been regarded, as an almost exclusively male preserve.

The whole notion of "stalking" one's subject on the streets would predicate a photographer who is not only male, but blessed—if that is the word—with plenty of testosterone aggression. An image which comes immediately to mind is that of Garry Winogrand, with two Leicas around his neck and wearing a hunting or a fishing jacket, with numerous pockets for holding spare rounds of ammunition, that is, rolls of film. The traditional method was to load the camera with film from the "unused" pocket, then transfer the "shot" film to a "used" pocket to avoid confusion. Quasi-military, masculine terminology everywhere.

However, Betsy Karel is a woman, which not only means she is taking the men on at their own game, but begs a question. Not why, because why not? The question is, rather, what does a woman street photographer potentially bring to the party?

Well, talent and a point of view are two things—the most important factors of all—but a cornerstone of feminist art theory has been that if the "male gaze" is typically aggressive and colonizing, can one talk about a "female gaze" embodying different, rather more useful characteristics in the scheme of things? Some young female photo-critics have been making an argument for a distinctive female gaze, but this seems a slightly speculative line of reasoning, rather on the lines of the old argument as to whether members of a community made a more authentic view of that community as opposed to outsiders. Well, it all depends—and perhaps seems a more entertaining than useful debate—tending to demand a simple answer to an extremely complex question.

What seems clear is that, for many reasons—some of them possibly practical as well as theoretical—more male photographers are drawn to classic street photography than female, so Betsy Karel is not your commonplace street photographer.

And what seems equally clear, whether or not one can detect a female gaze in operation, is that Betsy Karel's vision is a particularly personal one. She declares emphatically that it was not so much a case of her decision to photograph Times Square, but more a question of Times Square compelling her to make these photographs. The sheer facts about Times Square might serve to trump even Donald Trump. The location attracts an estimated 50 million visitors annually, with upwards of 330,000 pedestrians passing through every day. That represents quite a lot of potentially interesting street portraits, and an almost irresistible draw for a photographer. Although if something is photographically irresistible, the serious photographer should usually resist it.

However, as Karel indicated, it was a matter of intuition, a case of the heart rather than the head. That is an interesting point. It has become almost *de rigueur* to justify an artistic enterprise with a theoretical text, and many artists today, especially from an art college background, begin with their project outline, their theory signed, sealed, and delivered before they begin to make the work. Art made primarily with the intuition is regarded with a degree of suspicion in comparison to art made primarily with the intellect and accompanied by that irreplaceable theoretical crutch. It seems that theory forms an almost talismanic function, providing a surefire formula for good art. Art at the phenomenological end of the spectrum is considered to be lacking intellectual rigor.

But intuition is central to photography, surely more than most media, and of the various photographic genres, street photography is blatantly one of the most intuitive. Theory does not help you at 1/1000 of a second. In a recent, interesting essay on the value of photography, *Why Fhotography Matters*, Jerry Thompson, one-time assistant of Walker Evans, muses upon photography's characteristics, and rather relegates theory to the basement. Quoting his old boss, Thompson urges photographers to explore such qualities as "swift chance, disarray, wonder, and experiment." This edict by the twentieth century's most important thinker on photography applies to much of the medium, but—in that vital word "swift"—particularly to street photographers like Betsy Karel.

Of course, Evans omitted another vital quality, and that is intelligence. In looking for, and accepting the vagaries of swift chance and disarray while shooting, serendipity places a large part in the street photographer's life—but only while shooting. When dealing with the day's "catch," the intellect enters into it as much as it defines any art. Photography is a matter of intuition combined with intellect, in different proportions at different stages in the process.

Evans also stated that good photography should be about "structure and coherence," but also about "paradox and play and oxymoron." Betsy Karel's work embraces structure and coherence, like that of all good street photographers, but also paradox, play, and oxymoron—the camera being naturally drawn to incongruity—as well as metaphor and symbol. Many of these qualities come together in an early key image, the pictures that "kicked off" the project, as she put it.

In the kind of photography practiced by Karel, when one follows one's intuition, there are frequently a few key images—one, or maybe two or three—that both lift and define a project, providing a stimulus, a leap forward, and suggesting the future direction. This is a great moment, because what previously could be considered a rehearsal, suddenly turns into a performance The photographer is still faced with false starts, cul-de-sacs requiring a certain degree of retreat, but the key picture, or key pictures, not only give him or her a direction but a goal, setting a benchmark for the work.

In Karel's case, the image in question depicts a mass public yoga class, and shows a field of people lying upon their backs on yoga mats. It is a photograph which confirms her notion that Times Square is "America's Stage," a place where theatricality and a certain throwing off of conventional inhibition pertains. A bunch of people were doing outdoors and in public what normally would be done indoors and in private. But for her this image meant more. In the supine bodies stretched out as far as the eye could see, a couple of people bending over them as if anxious, even the star-spangled banner and an NYPD sign, this picture suggested to Karel the defining event in recent New York City history—9/11.

Karel's vision is by no means pessimistic, it is life affirming, and she is not broadcasting this 9/11 connection with a megaphone. It is simply a thought that occurred to her. This is my 9/11 picture. A private, almost passing thought, but an important one, because it somehow crystallized a larger idea in her mind, and confirmed the overriding metaphorical thrust of the work. Times Square, in its chaos and cacophony, in its commercialism and hedonism, in its expression of both narcissistic and heroic individualism—even in the fact that there is probably more surveillance there than in any other location in New York City—is a metaphor for present day America. Stick Trump Tower in there and it would be perfect, but it is pretty good as it is.

Betsy Karel, however, is no didactic artist. Her pictures are, to quote Jerry Thompson once more, a product of "observation and instinct rather than theory or analysis." The metaphorical idea equating Times Square with America pulses subtly through the imagery, which was made for pleasure rather than polemics. We never seem to talk much about the pleasure principle in art these days, but it is surely there somewhere in all but the most nakedly commercial art, and is certainly a motive for much street photography, tying in with the hunting notion and the sheer challenge of winkling a coherent image out of the incoherent flux of life that meets the eye in a busy city.

The "9/11" photograph is only one example here of the kind of picture where the street photographer gets maximum pleasure. That is to say, it is a formally complex image, incorporating four, five, six, or more people, not only geometrically perfect—capturing fully that "decisive moment"—but venturing beyond geometry in meaning, beyond both what photojournalism used to term "human interest" and formalism for its own sake.

Consider also, an image of a tour bus—THE TOUR it claims assertively in capital letters. In the bus window a crowd of people can be seen—some actually inside the coach, some behind it on the street. The picture is an oblique reference to Robert Frank's "bus" image from his book *The Americans*—used on the cover in some editions—that signals America is a multi-cultural society. Karel's reiteration of this fact, it hardly needs to be said, is especially timely at this particular moment in American and world history, with so many forces looking to divide rather than unite us. A nod towards photographic history is asking whether, on the larger stage, we ever learn as we ought to do from history. Her whole view of Times Square is as a place where Americans come together as one family, a chaotic family perhaps, but a family nevertheless.

Another message that also requires constant restatement refers to the American Constitution's First Amendment and the right to freedom of speech and expression. As we turn the pages featuring a number of highly complicated images—one signifying business freedom, another religious freedom—we are brought up short by a picture of naked men and women. Naked men and women? In Times Square? And not in a sex shop booth? No, this is a group of people parading naked in public and advertising the joys of body painting. Here, freedom of expression outweighs public decency, but maybe only because this is Times Square and not Fifth Avenue, or because the body paint can be regarded as a minimal costume.

These spectacular, formally complex photographs naturally draw the attention, but her single and double figure pictures also demonstrate that Betsy Karel is an accomplished portraitist, warm and sympathetic, yet with a fine sense of the idiosyncratic. A half-naked Homer Simpson character, or a fully naked female guitarist—the "Naked Cowgirl"—are cases in point. Some might argue that if you want idiosyncratic characters, Times Square is like shooting fish in a barrel, but Karel never laughs at her subjects. She photographs them for what they are, a not-so-easy thing to do, and a rarer trait—especially with street photographers—than one might imagine.

This is significant, because Betsy Karel is fashioning a portrait of Times Square, as both a physical space and as an idea. She is not simply making street pictures for their own sake, one of the genre's great temptations. She has assembled her cast of characters, to be sure, but is always aware of the *mise en scène,* the theatrical backdrop, which she depicts in a number of impressive general views of the square. Of course, as most people know, it is not a square in the strict sense of the term, but a bow-tie-shaped area formed by Broadway cutting diagonally across Seventh Avenue and interrupting Manhattan's regular midtown grid.

Times Square is one of the most photographed locations in the world, even by serious photographers, so one might query, do we need more photographs of the place? Yet anyone asking the question does not understand photography, at least not in the way that Betsy Karel understands it, and they certainly have little chance of appreciating her achievement. As Joel Meyerowitz has said, "as long as there's photography there'll always be people trying to make street pictures." Adding that these will be pictures "made out of your guts, out of your instinct."

Street photography is about picture-making of course. You cannot get away with sloppy picture-making on the streets, waving a cellphone about vaguely, as too many photography students seem to do nowadays. Karel used a digital version of the classic street photographer's weapon, the Leica.

Street photography is about making sharp (in a psychological sense), coherent photographs, but in a fundamental sense it is not about style, or fashion, and is therefore timeless—right at the existential heart of photography. It is timeless, and yet deals with time and the specifics of time at every turn. Betsy Karel has photographed the square at a particular moment, and others will do so at other moments. She has not only captured a mood with flair and intelligence, at a pivotal point in American history, but more importantly, in a perhaps small but vital way, she has shaped our understanding of both life and society from her personal experience.

— GERRY BADGER

Acknowledgments

I would like to thank a few of the many generous people who encouraged
and helped me during this time: Gerry Badger, Charles Simic, John Gossage,
Sarah Greenough, Peter MacGill, Lauren Panzo, Dan Halpern, David Adamson,
David Chickey, Amy Bonoff, Gerhard Steidl and his remarkable staff at
Steidlville, and all my family.

First edition published in 2017

Book design: David Chickey, Holger Feroudj, Gerhard Steidl
Tritone separations by Steidl
Production and printing: Steidl, Göttingen

Steidl
Düstere Str. 4 / 37073 Göttingen, Germany
Phone +49 551 49 60 60 / Fax +49 551 49 60 649
mail@steidl.de
steidl.de

ISBN 978-3-95829-272-7
Printed in Germany by Steidl